TOWARD A MORE
EFFECTIVE DEFENSE

TOWARD A MORE EFFECTIVE DEFENSE

REPORT OF THE DEFENSE ORGANIZATION PROJECT

Edited by
BARRY M. BLECHMAN and WILLIAM J. LYNN

BALLINGER PUBLISHING COMPANY
Cambridge, Massachusetts
A Subsidiary of Harper & Row, Publishers, Inc.

ABU 1902 - 3/1

International Standard Book Number: 0-88730-026-X

Library of Congress Catalog Card Number: 85-11214

Printed in the United States of America

Library of Congress Cataloging in Publication Data

Main entry under title:

Toward a more effective defense.

    Includes index.
    1. United States—Defenses—Addresses, essays, lectures. 2. United States—Armed Forces—Addresses, essays, lectures. 3. United States—Military policy—Addresses, essays, lectures. I. Blechman, Barry M. II. Lynn, William J. III. CSIS Defense Organization Project
UA23.T674   1985   355'.033073   85-11214
ISBN 0-88730-026-X

CONTENTS

List of Figures and Tables   vii

Foreword: The View from the Top   ix

Preface   xi

Chapter 1
Report of the Steering Committee
—*Philip A. Odeen* et al.   1

Chapter 2
Report of the Working Group on Military
Command Structure
—*Edward C. Meyer* et al.   41

Chapter 3
Report of the Working Group on Defense
Planning and Resource Allocation
—*John P. White* et al.   61

Chapter 4
Report of the Working Group on Weapons Acquisition
—Jacques S. Gansler et al.   87

Chapter 5
Report of the Working Group on the Congressional Defense Budget Process
—Alice M. Rivlin et al.   103

Chapter 6
Reorganizing Combat Forces
—Morton Halperin and *David Halperin*   113

Chapter 7
Congress and the Defense Budget: New Procedures and Old Realities
—Robert J. Art   125

Chapter 8
Potential New Patterns of Congressional Review of Defense Budget Requests
—John J. Hamre   169

Chapter 9
The Office of the Secretary of Defense with a Strengthened Joint Staff System
—John G. Kester   181

Chapter 10
Accounting and Budgeting Systems in the Department of Defense
—Robert C. Moot   199

Chapter 11
Joint Military Advice and the DoD Planning, Programming, and Budgeting System
—Russell Murray II   215

Index   233

List of Participants   239

About the Editors   249

LIST OF FIGURES
AND TABLES

FIGURES

1-1   The Organization of the Department of Defense   4

1-2   The Current Organization of the Office of the Secretary
       of Defense   15

1-3   Proposed Realignment of the Office of the Secretary
       of Defense   16

8-1   Hypothetical Matrix Authorization for a Weapon System   177

TABLES

7-1   Congressional Budget Timetable Established by the
       1974 Act   131

7-2   Growth in the Scope of Annual Authorization of the
       Defense Budget   133

7-3   Number of Pages in Appropriation Committees'
       DoD Reports   136

7-4   Number of Pages in Armed Services Committees' Reports:
       DoD Authorizations   137

7-5   Congressional Budget Timetable Recommended
by Beilenson Task Force   155

8-1   Principal Features of Alternative Biennial Budgeting
Proposals   171

FOREWORD: THE VIEW FROM THE TOP

The once strong consensus for sustained increases in U.S. defense spending has eroded; as they did in the early 1970s, a large majority of Americans again believe that too much is spent on defense. To some exent, this shift may reflect the Reagan administration's first-term expansion of the defense budget, as well as the size of prospective deficits. But the decline of the defense consensus also reflects widespread frustration with the management of available defense resources.

Is the public's concern well-placed? Are there serious problems in the way the United States goes about planning, acquiring, and operating its armed forces? Or, as some maintain, has the public been misled by an overzealous media that exploits managerial lapses of only marginal significance?

In our view, the public's concern is well-founded; there are serious deficiencies in the organization and managerial procedures of the U.S. defense establishment. Yet, although concern is well-placed, its focus is too narrow and idiosyncratic. As former secretaries of defense, we are in a special position to identify the real problems in defense management; we are also able to testify about the degree to which they weaken efforts to ensure U.S. security.

The Defense Organization Project of Georgetown University's Center for Strategic and International Studies has mounted an impressive effort to survey the organizational and procedural problems of the U.S. defense establishment. The members of the study group, including many with whom we have worked, can speak authoritatively of the problems they describe. Their recommendations collectively have the compelling merit of both comprehensiveness and the general sharing of pain. The study group is correct in noting that if reform is to be most effective, it should touch all elements of the defense establishment. The Congress, the Office of the Secretary of Defense, the military departments, the joint military structures, and the defense industry all contribute to today's procedural inadequacies. All will have to implement some changes if a more effective defense establishment is to be achieved.

We also agree with the study group's decision not to propose radical solutions but to opt instead for a package of moderate changes that build on past reform efforts. Their recommendations deserve the support of a broad-based political coalition, encompassing both political parties and all sides of the political spectrum.

The waning years of the twentieth century, and the early years of the next, will be difficult ones. Our adversaries will continue to test and probe our defenses. Increasingly, our friends are likely to look to us for leadership and support. U.S. interests around the world will demand constant vigilance and preparedness for action. We cannot afford to waste scarce defense resources, nor can we afford to allow organizational deficiencies to impair the effectiveness of our military forces. The stakes are too great.

While each of us may disagree with one or more of the many specific recommendations contained in the study group's report, we are united in support for the general thrust of its proposals. We agree specifically that it is desirable to strengthen joint military institutions in order to inject a more effective integrated military viewpoint into defense planning, resource allocation procedures, and the execution of military operations. By improving the quality of military advice, stronger joint military institutions should reinforce, not usurp, the ability of civilian leaders to manage the Department of Defense.

The package of reforms proposed by the CSIS Defense Organization Project in our judgment deserves careful consideration by both the Congress and the executive. We commend it to all citizens for their review and evaluation.

Harold Brown
Secretary of Defense (1977–1981)

Clark M. Clifford
Secretary of Defense (1968–1969)

Melvin R. Laird
Secretary of Defense (1969–1973)

Robert S. McNamara
Secretary of Defense (1961–1968)

Elliot L. Richardson
Secretary of Defense (1973)

James R. Schlesinger
Secretary of Defense (1973–1975)

PREFACE

The Defense Organization Project was initiated in mid-1983 on the premise that the national defense debate had maintained a myopic focus on the overall level of defense expenditures and a few major weapon systems, neglecting the more fundamental issues of how to give coherent direction to the complex military operations and large-scale scientific and industrial processes that have come to characterize the national defense effort. Without effective defense policy and management, no peacetime level of defense spending would be sufficient to meet the needs of our nation's security.

There have been sporadic pressures for defense organizational reform, but no major changes have been implemented since 1958. Soundings of defense experts, military officers, and legislators indicate that substantial support now exists for significant structural and procedural changes in the Department of Defense, and in congressional defense policy and budget processes. Clearly, these harbingers of support for constructive change indicate that the topic is ripe for reexamination.

With this goal in mind, the Center for Strategic and International Studies of Georgetown University (CSIS) has sponsored the Defense Organization Project. The project's central purpose has been to identify those measures that would, if implemented, help to build a more effective and responsive defense structure. Too often, past studies of this kind have operated in a political vacuum, offering proposals that have a sound internal logic, but which lie outside the bounds of political acceptability. Accordingly, in its proposals, the study group has sought not only to ensure intellectual rigor, but also to take into account existing bureaucratic and political realities.

This report was prepared by the project's steering committee, chaired by Philip A. Odeen, Andrew J. Goodpaster, and Melvin R. Laird. A complete listing of the members of the committee and of the project's working groups can be found in the chapters that follow. Each of the proposals reflects the consensus view of the members of the steering committee, though all members do not necessarily endorse every recommendation. In formulating its proposals, the steering committee relied heavily on the analyses and recommendations of four working groups: Military Command Structure, chaired by Edward C. Meyer; Defense Planning and Resource Allocation, chaired by John P. White; Weapons Acquisition, chaired by Jacques S. Gansler; and Congressional Defense Budget Process, chaired by Alice M. Rivlin. The steering committee also drew upon individual papers prepared for the project by Robert J. Art, Morton and David Halperin, John J. Hamre, John G. Kester, Robert C. Moot, and Russell Murray. The full text of both the working group reports and the commissioned papers, edited by Barry M. Blechman and William J. Lynn, are included here. Dr. Blechman coordinated the Defense Organization Project for CSIS and Mr. Lynn served as its executive director.

In view of the special importance of this project, I convened an ad hoc group of former senior defense officials to review the report in draft. The group consisted of the Honorable James R. Schlesinger, formerly secretary of defense; General Brent Scowcroft, formerly national security adviser to President Gerald Ford; and Admiral Thomas H. Moorer, formerly chairman of the Joint Chiefs of Staff. After reviewing their reactions, I am persuaded that this high quality, but likely controversial, study is best served by summarizing their views.

As suggested by his endorsement in the foreword to this study, James Schlesinger is sympathetic to the thrust of the study and to many of its recommendations. Dr. Schlesinger generally supports those portions of the report dealing with the organization and procedures of the Joint Chiefs of Staff, terming the study group's recommendations potentially useful steps toward a more effective defense posture. He also supports the proposals for shifting to a biennial budget cycle and reform of the resource allocation system. Although he does not disagree with the proposals for improving the weapons acquisition process, Dr. Schlesinger does not believe that they go far enough to rectify existing problems. Finally, Dr. Schlesinger is skeptical of the proposals for reorganizing the Office of the Secretary of Defense along mission lines; there are advantages to the current functional orientation, he notes, which should not be dispensed with lightly.

General Scowcroft is enthusiastic in his praise for the study, terming it the best report on issues of U.S. defense organization and procedures he has seen. On specific issues, he is especially supportive of the analysis and recommendations relating to JCS organization and procedures. He is dubious that the proposed budget reforms are sufficient to deal adequately with problems in that area and he would proceed cautiously with organizational reform of OSD. On the whole, however, while not necessarily endorsing each specific recommendation, General

Scowcroft shares the study group's belief that it is essential to build stronger joint military structures, to improve the utility of military advice in defense planning and resource allocation, and to impart greater stability to the force programming and budgeting process.

Admiral Moorer's reaction to the report was very different than the reactions of General Scowcroft and Dr. Schlesinger. Based on his personal experience as chief of naval operations and chairman of the Joint Chiefs of Staff, Admiral Moorer believes that "assignment of good people, both civilian and military, and a clear-cut designation of authority, responsibility, and accountability will ensure the best performance" rather than periodic reorganizations. In particular, he disagrees with the proposals to strengthen joint military structures. He also disagrees strongly with the proposals to strengthen the unified and specified commanders.

Acknowledgments

The project's chairmen wish to express their gratitude to the many specialists who gave generously of their time and expertise and to those individuals who drafted papers and reports, served on the steering committee, or were members of one of the working groups. Many others, including Archie D. Barrett, John G. Kester, James Locher, and Bruce Porter provided insightful reviews of drafts and other advice. The chairmen are especially grateful to Lenda Walker, secretary to the project, for her energy and endurance in this endeavor.

The Defense Organization Project has been funded jointly by the Ford and Rockefeller Foundations. Initial support for the project came from the Roosevelt Center for American Policy Studies, then under the direction of Douglas Bennet. On behalf of these institutions and the Center, I would like to express our gratitude to the three chairmen—Philip Odeen, Andrew Goodpaster, and Melvin Laird—for their tremendous investment of time and expertise, and to congratulate them on the success of the project.

CSIS is a research institution founded in 1962 to foster scholarship and public awareness of emerging international issues on a broad, interdisciplinary basis. It is bipartisan and nonprofit. Its areas of research are selected in consultation with its governing bodies; and its work is entirely unclassified.

Amos A. Jordan, Jr.
President
Center for Strategic and International Studies
Georgetown University
February 1985

1 REPORT OF THE STEERING COMMITTEE

Chair: Philip A. Odeen

Vice Chairmen: Andrew J. Goodpaster
                        Melvin R. Laird

Members: Les Aspin   Edward C. Meyer
                        Norman R. Augustine   Sam Nunn
                        Barry M. Blechman   William J. Perry
                        William K. Brehm   Donald B. Rice
                        William S. Cohen   Alice M. Rivlin
                        Edwin A. Deagle   Thomas B. Ross
                        Robert F. Ellsworth   William Y. Smith
                        Jacques S. Gansler   Samuel S. Stratton
                        Newt Gingrich   Harry S. Train
                        Samuel P. Huntington   Togo D. West, Jr.
                        David C. Jones   John P. White
                        Nancy L. Kassebaum   R. James Woolsey

Executive Director: William J. Lynn

1

In 1958 President Dwight D. Eisenhower, a man uniquely qualified by experience and temperament to address the organization and management of the nation's military establishment, proposed major changes in the structure of the Department of Defense. He had three objectives.

First, he proposed to clarify and strengthen the authority of the secretary of defense relative to the individual military departments—army, navy, and air force—in order to grant the secretary full authority over all defense activities. This objective has been largely achieved.

Second, President Eisenhower sought to improve the quality of the military advice given to civilian leaders by granting more authority to the chairman of the Joint Chiefs of Staff and giving him full control over the Joint Staff. The Congress amended Eisenhower's proposals, limiting the chairman's authority to managing the Joint Staff on behalf of the four members of the Joint Chiefs of Staff, who are also the heads of the four military services.

Third, he sought to ensure the unity of operational command of U.S. armed forces in the field by separating the military services from the unified and specified combatant commands. In effect, he sought to clarify the division of labor between the services and the commands. The services, organized along traditional lines of air, land, and sea warfare, would perform the maintaining functions of recruiting, organizing, training, and equipping the armed forces. The unified and specified commanders-in-chief (CinCs), organized along geographic and functional lines, would operate and lead the forces in combat theaters. This division of labor was incorporated in law; nine unified and specified commands are now in existence. The commanders in chief, however, have never been provided with adequate authority in peacetime. As a consequence, their ability to perform their missions has been compromised.

In our view, this failure to complete the Department of Defense reforms that President Eisenhower proposed in 1958 is among the root causes of current problems in the U.S. defense establishment. Despite the good will, competence, and effort of the individuals who have in the past and are now leading the Department of Defense, we continue to face a broad range of problems in the management of our national security activities. It has become increasingly clear that these problems are inherent in the organizational structure and procedures within which these activities are conducted. Specifically, current weaknesses include the following:

- The current system fails to provide timely, cross-service military advice to the president, the Congress, and the secretary of defense for the planning and allocation of defense resources.
- The force development process emphasizes inputs (budget dollars, manpower, etc.) rather than programmatic outputs (capabilities to perform specific missions), and delivers service-oriented programs that are inadequately balanced by mission and theater perspectives.

- Defense management processes are overly cumbersome and repetitive, forcing all participants—military and civilian, executive and congressional—to spend an inordinate amount of time on the details of programs at the expense of policy issues and oversight considerations.

Most of us have spent a major part, if not all, of our careers in the defense establishment or Congress. We have studied and debated these issues as a group for eighteen months and have concluded that three sets of improvements would help resolve these problems. Each set of recommendations includes specific proposals for organizational and procedural reforms. We are convinced that these improvements are feasible on both substantive and political grounds.

The first set of improvements is intended to achieve more effective planning on the part of senior military and civilian managers of the Department of Defense. It would enhance particularly the utility of military advice presented to civilian leaders during the planning process. Our proposals include an expansion of the charter of the under secretary of defense for policy and greater responsibilities for the chairman of the Joint Chiefs of Staff.

Second, extensive improvements can be made in the way the Department of Defense and the Congress allocate resources, as well as the way the two branches interact during this process. These recommendations include shifting to a biennial budget cycle, merging the programming and budgeting portions of the resource allocation system, expanding the role of the unified and specified commanders in the programming/budgeting process, and creating a third under secretary of defense charged with the integration and oversight of the programs necessary to ensure that the armed forces are prepared to undertake and sustain combat operations.

Third, we propose a number of changes that are designed to improve the execution of the defense program. Our most extensive recommendations have to do with the weapon system acquisition process and include increased competition, more accurate cost projections, and the development of a long-range investment plan. In addition, we would enhance the role of evaluation in the Planning, Programming, and Budgeting System (PPBS) and make major changes in the accounting and reporting systems within the Department of Defense. We also propose simultaneous reductions in the size of the Office of the Secretary of Defense, the civilian and military staffs of the military departments, and the relevant congressional committees and agencies. We not only believe less staff would be warranted under the proposed new structure, but that smaller staffs would be less likely to indulge in detailed management and more likely to focus on the more important functions of oversight and policy formulation.

We believe that if these recommendations were implemented, they would have a salutary effect on the conduct of our national security affairs. In particular, we think that they would

Figure 1-1. The Organization of the Department of Defense.

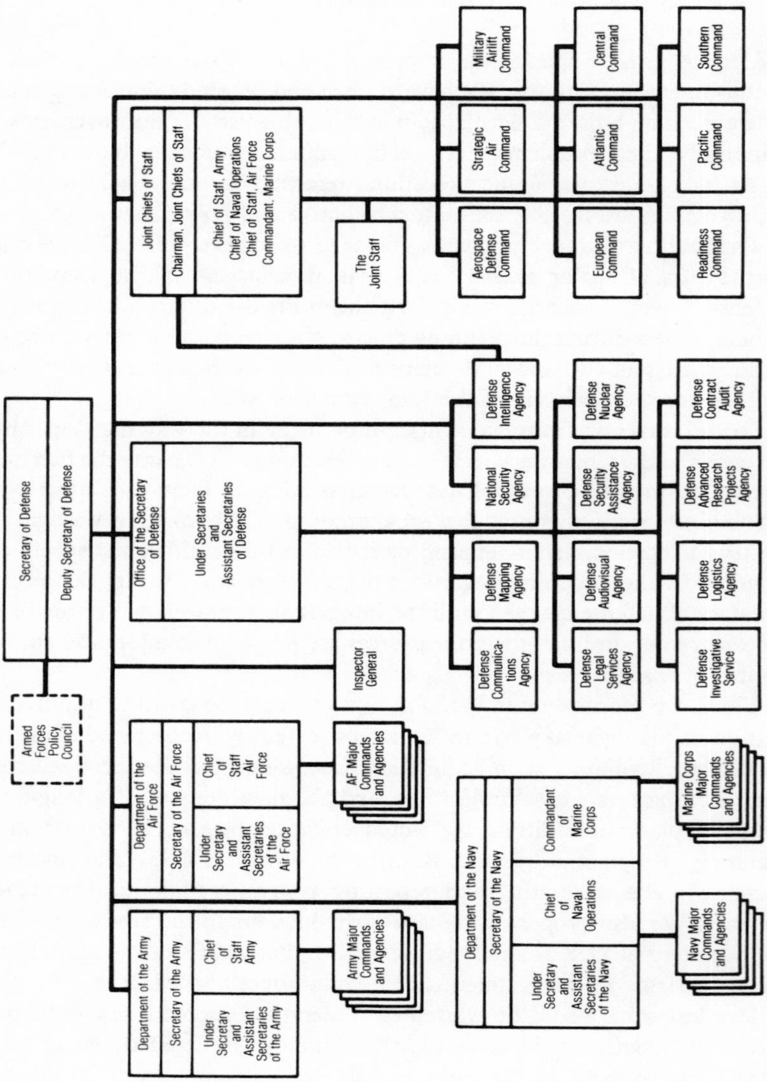

- Promote a reorientation of the civilian leadership of the executive branch toward greater concentration on plans and priorities, the management of major programs, and the continual evaluation of current and past activities to ensure more productive performance in the future.
- Provide a more effective and broader role for military leaders in planning, programmatic, and budgetary decisions.
- Enhance the policy formulation and oversight roles of the Congress.

Because of the enormous breadth of the subject, we have organized the report in four parts, three focused on organizational changes—joint military structures, OSD, and the Congress—and a final section directed at procedural arrangements—PPBS and the weapons acquisition system. We conclude with some brief remarks concerning the current politics of defense reform.

Before looking at the details of our proposals, a brief comment on the human aspect of defense management is in order. Although better organizational structures and procedures would improve the management of the defense establishment, the most critical factor will always be the competence and experience of the people involved. Even the best-structured organization cannot work effectively with unqualified people. But the converse is also true: outdated or cumbersome organizations and procedures will handicap even the most outstanding and dedicated individuals. Thus, in the interest of a more effective defense, we support steps to facilitate the recruitment and retention of exceptional individuals for key management positions in the defense establishment. But we also believe it essential to strengthen defense structures in the ways described below, in order to allow these people to perform to the full extent of their capabilities. Indeed, by making their roles more productive and rewarding, these reforms would reinforce efforts to attract and retain the best minds in the defense establishment.

JOINT MILITARY STRUCTURES

In our view, there are compelling reasons to develop stronger joint military organizations capable of acting from a cross-service perspective to integrate the special requirements of air, land, sea, and space operations. This strengthened joint military structure would have three primary functions: (1) to provide cross-service military advice to civilian leaders, (2) to develop strategic plans that link military capabilities to national objectives, and (3) to plan and conduct combined-arms military operations. Current joint structures do not lend themselves to the effective execution of any of these crucial functions.

Advisory Functions

Professional military advice that rises above individual service interests to provide a broader cross-service perspective is an essential ingredient for the effective direction and management of the defense establishment. In all defense activities, from the formulation of overall national security strategy to decisions on the use of armed force, civilian leaders need sound and timely military advice. Today, that advice comes primarily from the services, reflecting their traditions and interests, as well as their expertise. What is lacking is an independent, cross-service perspective. As now organized, the Joint Chiefs of Staff (JCS) are too frequently unable to provide effective, cross-service advice on issues that affect important service interests or prerogatives. These issues include the most important on the JCS agenda: the formulation of national military strategy, the allocation of service roles and missions, revision of the Unified Command Plan, and particularly the allocation of scarce defense resources among competing needs.

Even on questions that do not involve sharp interservice differences, the JCS system has been slow to develop formal positions. Moreover, when joint advice is finally rendered, all too often it is diluted through cumbersome staffing procedures that accommodate the interests of all relevant parties at multiple levels. Although civilian leaders consistently praise the advice they receive from the individual chiefs of the services, they almost uniformly criticize the institutional products of the JCS as ponderous in presentation, predictably wedded to the status quo, and reactive rather than innovative. As a consequence, civilians have filled this void, serving as the major source of advice to the secretary on matters for which concise, independent military inputs would have been preferred.

These shortcomings are neither new nor the product of a single administration. Instead, they reflect weaknesses in the structure of the joint military system itself. Each member of the JCS, except the chairman, faces an inherent conflict between his joint role on the one hand and his responsibility to represent the interests of his service on the other. As the senior military planning and advisory body, the JCS are charged with providing military advice that transcends individual service concerns. At the same time, each chief is the military leader of his service and its primary spokesman to the civilian leadership. Although the National Security Act mandates that a service chief's joint role should take precedence over his duties as leader of a service, this does not occur in practice—and for good reason. If a chief did not defend service positions in the joint forum, he would lose the support and loyalty of his service, thus destroying his effectiveness.

Because of this fundamental reality, the JCS have constructed an array of Joint Staff procedures for drafting and coordinating documents that ensure that all services pass on every item at several levels. In effect, each service has a veto over every joint recommendation, forcing joint advice toward the level of common assent.

Further, the officers who serve on the Joint Staff have strong incentives to protect the interests of their services in the joint arena. Joint Staff officers usually serve only a single tour there and must look to their parent service for promotions and future assignments. Their performance is judged in large part by how effectively they have represented service interests.

Recommendation. The National Security Act should be amended to designate the chairman as the principal military adviser to the president, the secretary of defense, and the National Security Council, replacing the corporate JCS in that role. The chairman must also be given the staff support necessary to carry out that role effectively. Service chiefs should continue to provide advice to the chairman and service secretaries on all issues, and to the secretary of defense and the president on issues of crucial importance, but the chairman should have a unique position as the individual who presents the integrated professional military perspective on all questions.

Four specific changes are required to implement this recommendation.

Principal Military Adviser. As the only member of the JCS without a service portfolio, the chairman is uniquely situated to provide independent military advice and planning that cuts across service boundaries. Accordingly, the National Security Act should be amended to make the chairman the principal military adviser to the president, the secretary of defense, and the National Security Council, a role now filled by the JCS as a corporate body. (At least one member of the study group believes that those steps strengthening the role of the chairman that have not already occurred can and should be undertaken by the secretary of defense through regulation, rather than through statutory change.)

Our purpose in proposing a more significant role for the chairman is not to deny civilian leaders military advice from multiple sources, but rather to ensure that they have an additional military perspective not tied directly to the individual services. As the principal military adviser, the chairman would have the authority to provide professional military recommendations to the secretary without obtaining unanimous service approval. The current single-service veto over joint positions would be abolished and responsibility for formulating joint positions would rest with the chairman supported by the Joint Staff and the unified and specified commanders.

Service Advice. Designating the chairman the principal military adviser is not intended to reduce the diversity of military views available to political decisionmakers. Rather, the objective is to supplement the service-based military advice available under the current system with advice from a cross-service perspective provided by the chairman with the support of the Joint Staff. We recognize, however, that there is a danger that the changes we recommend may submerge service views. Accordingly, we propose two safeguards to ensure that individual service viewpoints continue to be well represented throughout the decision process.

First, in formulating joint positions, the chairman should be required to consult fully with the other members of the JCS. This would ensure that the chairman's advice benefited from the expertise of all the service chiefs and guarantee that the chiefs were informed of the content of the chairman's recommendations. The service chiefs also would retain their right of dissent. A service chief could forward dissenting views directly to the secretary of defense or, if deemed sufficiently important, to the president through the secretary. In addition, service chiefs would continue to have opportunities to present service views via the secretaries of the military departments. Finally, none of the reforms proposed above would limit the freedom the chiefs currently enjoy to testify before Congress.

Second, on issues of crucial national importance, such as arms control treaties or proposed uses of military force, the chairman should be required to provide civilian leaders with the individual positions of all the chiefs to the extent that they differed from the chairman's recommendation. It is likely that only a handful of issues would merit such consideration each year. Although it would be the chairman's responsibility with the concurrence of the secretary to designate such issues, the chiefs could influence this designation through the chairman's requirement to consult them on all issues. Moreover, the president or the secretary of defense could request full JCS advice on any issue either deemed appropriate.

Joint Staff.   To provide the chairman with the support essential to perform his new roles, the National Security Act should be further amended to provide for the Joint Staff to report directly to the chairman, rather than to the corporate JCS. The chairman should also be assigned authority to manage the Joint Staff independent of the JCS. Legislation passed in 1984 has already given the chairman the authority to select officers for Joint Staff duty from lists submitted by the services.

Giving the chairman greater authority over the Joint Staff would only improve cross-service military advice if the military personnel system were also modified so that officers were attracted to, trained for, and rewarded for service in joint positions. Toward this end, we recommend that each service establish a "joint specialty" that selected officers could enter in addition to their normal service specialties. These officers would be trained at existing joint schools and could spend up to half of their subsequent assignments in joint positions—the staffs of the unified and specified commanders, OSD offices and other civilian agencies, as well as the Joint Staff. In this context, it would be necessary to remove the remaining statutory restrictions on Joint Staff tenure and reassignments.

It is not contemplated that all joint positions would be filled by officers with a joint specialty. Instead, we believe that there should be a mix of officers with varied backgrounds and specialties in joint positions to ensure that these staffs do not become isolated or in any sense a general staff. To ensure that officers with joint specialties have adequate promotion opportunities, an officer with a joint specialty should be included on service promotion boards for colonels/captains and flag and general officers. (A more detailed description of how a joint career specialty would operate is contained in *The Organization and Functions of the JCS,* a report for the chairman of the Joint Chiefs of Staff prepared by the Chairman's Special Study Group in April 1982.)

Deputy Chairman. To assist the chairman further, the National Security Act also should be amended to designate the director of the Joint Staff as the deputy chairman of the JCS. The deputy, who would be a four-star officer chosen from a different service than the chairman, would act for the chairman when the latter was unavailable.

Currently, the chairman is the only senior executive—civilian or military—in the Department of Defense without a deputy. Designating the director of the Joint Staff to be deputy chairman would improve continuity in the direction of the joint military apparatus, both in its day-to-day activities and its management of crisis situations. A deputy would also free the chairman to interact more fully with the unified and specified commands in line with his recently legislated role to act as their spokesman on operational requirements and the even greater expansion of the role proposed in this report.

Strategic Planning

Strategic planning, the process linking ends (national objectives established by political authorities) and means (the military forces, weapons, and capabilities developed by the service departments) would also benefit from a stronger and more independent joint military voice. The chairman is the only member of the JCS who is unconstrained by current service responsibilities. But he lacks both the staff and the statutory mandate to make consistently meaningful strategic planning recommendations on the broad range of subjects required. The recent addition of the Strategic Planning and Resource Analysis Agency (SPRAA) to the Joint Staff increased the chairman's capabilities for strategic planning. But SPRAA, like the rest of the Joint Staff, reports to the JCS as a whole, rather than to the chairman as an individual, and thus lacks the ability to bring an independent cross-service perspective to bear on these issues.

With regard to the service chiefs, the inherent conflict between their joint and service responsibilities has precluded their effective participation in resource planning. As the 1978 Department of Defense Report on the National Military Command Structure (the Steadman Report) pointed out, a chief's responsibility to manage and lead his service virtually precludes his agreement to joint force planning recommendations that are inconsistent with programs supported by his service. For example, a chief cannot be expected to argue for additional aircraft carriers, army divisions, or air force wings when constructing a service budget and then agree in the joint forum that such programs should be dropped in favor of another service's programs. As a result, the JCS are unable to help civilian leaders set cross-service priorities and make the necessary tradeoffs to construct the defense program and budget. Instead, JCS recommendations are generally limited to endorsing the full program proposed by each military department with little regard to resource constraints.

This practice is reflected in the development of the Joint Strategic Planning Document (JSPD), which is the primary JCS input to the Department of Defense planning process. The JSPD initiates the department's annual planning cycle by defining the scope of the military threat posed to identified national interests and recommending a force to meet that threat. The force structure recommended in the JSPD, however, is designed with only limited regard to cost. As a result, it is a much larger and more expensive force than the United States has been willing to sustain in peacetime. The JSPD is an important document nonetheless, serving as a benchmark to assess the risks inherent in alternative force structures. But it is of only limited help to the secretary in the actual allocation of defense resources, since it makes no recommendations as to priorities and does not take positions on the tradeoffs necessary to construct a force structure within the bounds of available financial resources. The secretary must make those force structure decisions without benefit of cross-service military advice. Instead, he must rely heavily on his civilian staff to ensure that service programs are balanced and consistent with national strategic priorities. In short, budgetary priorities tend to be established in separate dialogues between the individual services and the Office of the Secretary of Defense, with only minimal joint military participation.

Recommendation.   The chairman, with the assistance of the Joint Staff, should prepare force planning recommendations constrained by realistic projections of future resources, based on policy and fiscal guidance issued by the secretary of defense.

Military planning must be constrained by realistic estimates of future resources if it is to be helpful in the programming and budgeting processes. The responsibility for developing cross-service military recommendations concerning a resource-constrained force structure should be assigned to the chairman. His ability to carry out this function, however, is dependent on adoption of the reforms recommended earlier that would give him greater independent authority and staff support. Specifically, with the assistance of the Joint Staff, the chairman should prepare an additional version of the JSPD that recommends the optimal combination of forces, modernization programs, and readiness levels that could be supported within the secretary's fiscal guidance. This would provide civilian decisionmakers with professional military advice on the tradeoffs required by limits on defense resources. This constrained JSPD would supplement, not replace, the comprehensive, unconstrained assessments of U.S. defense requirements that are already prepared by the JCS. The fiscally unconstrained planning recommendation should be retained because of its value as a baseline for judging the military risks of the smaller force structures made necessary by resource limitations.

Planning and Conducting Military Operations

The joint military organizations are responsible for planning and conducting military operations. Joint direction of operations is crucial because modern warfare increasingly requires combined-arms operations in which land, sea, and air forces are integrated effectively under a single command. As previously noted, President Eisenhower established in 1958 a clear division of labor between the military services and the unified and specified commands in order to ensure unified command of operations. But the distinction between maintaining and operating function has never been achieved in practice. The unified and specified commanders (CinCs) lack adequate peacetime authority over the allocation of resources to their forces and the conduct of operations to carry out their missions effectively.

The National Security Act grants the CinCs "full operational command" over all forces assigned to them, but in peacetime this authority is significantly limited because of the influence retained by the individual services. Within each unified command, there is a component command corresponding to each military department from which forces have been drawn. The unified commander normally exercises operational control only through these component commands, greatly limiting his flexibility and authority. Equally important, on such vital matters as logistical support, training, and maintenance, the component commanders report directly to their respective military departments, leaving the CinCs with only limited and indirect influence.

Several developments over the past several years have enhanced the role of the CinCs in the resource allocation process. They now appear before the Defense Resources Board (DRB) twice during each annual budget cycle—once to articulate their requirements and once to comment on the services' programs. The CinCs also submit to the military departments a list of their most important requirements, prioritized within reasonable fiscal constraints across service and functional lines. And in recent legislation, the Congress has designated the chairman to act as the CinCs' spokesman for operational requirements.

These developments are constructive steps toward granting the operational commanders needed influence over the makeup and readiness of the forces under their command. Nevertheless, the CinCs still have too limited an institutional role in the resource allocation process. The Program Objective Memoranda (POMs), which the individual military departments prepare, remain the key building blocks of the defense program. The primary inputs to each service's POM regarding the needs of the operational forces continue to come from the service components in each command. The CinCs exercise only a limited review of their components' submissions, and this review occurs very late in the process. Moreover, budgetary requests for readiness and sustainability funds from the commands must compete with requests to develop new weapons and to expand the force structure at the service level. Given that the primary responsibilities of the military departments are for maintaining, not operating, the forces, it is not surprising that requests for operational needs tend to receive a lower priority.

Recommendation.   The unified and specified commanders should be given a stronger institutional role in the resource allocation process and greater authority over their component commands. Toward this end, we recommend three specific measures:

1. A separate program and budget should be established to cover the in-theater operational costs of the unified and specified commands.
2. The chairman should replace the corporate JCS as the transmitter of orders from civilian authorities to the CinCs.
3. The CinCs should be given greater operational authority over their component commands.

Readiness Budgets. The military division of labor between force-maintaining and force-operating structures should be reflected in the programming and budgeting processes. Specifically, we propose that a separate program and budget be established for the operational forces that would be prepared and executed by the unified and specified commanders under the supervision of the chairman of the JCS. Under this proposal, each service would continue to produce its program and budget for procurement, research and development, training, and associated operational and personnel costs. But, many of the in-theater operating costs of the service components of the unified and specified commands would be shifted to a new joint account. This separate "readiness program" and budget would include such items as operating and maintenance expenses, in-theater training and exercise costs, certain military construction costs (ammunition storage, for example), and some family housing costs. The specific items that would be included in the new account would be determined on the basis of a line-by-line review of current department accounts.

The development and review of this readiness program and budget would parallel that of the military departments' programs and budgets. The role of the Joint Staff would similarly parallel the role of the service staffs in elaborating the program and budget guidance of the secretary of defense and in reviewing and coordinating the CinCs' submissions. The chairman would represent the interests of the CinCs on the Defense Resources Board and later before the Congress. To perform this role, the chairman should be given statutory authority under the National Security Act to supervise the unified and specified commands on behalf of the secretary of defense, in addition to his recently granted authority to act as their spokesman on operational requirements.

We recognize that establishing a separate readiness program and budget would cause, at least initially, some dislocations in the department as the new procedures were established. It is likely that it would also require some shifts in staff from the military departments to the Joint Staff and from the component commands to the unified commands. Nevertheless, we believe that these short-term costs would be substantially outweighed by two long-term benefits.

First, a readiness program and budget would enfranchise in the planning and allocation processes the major institutional constituency for readiness and sustainability—the unified and specified commanders. This fundamental change would add needed balance to the flow of military recommendations to the civilian leadership. Instead of having all such recommendations manifested in the programs and budgets of the military departments, there would be recommendations on two sets of issues: one grounded in concerns about readiness and sustainability, the other in concerns about force structure modernization and expansion. In each case, the recommendations would reflect the responsibilities and perspectives of the officers involved. In this way, civilian leaders would be able to make better informed judgments regarding the proper balance in the defense budget between short-term considerations of readiness and sustainability and long-term considerations of force structure modernization and expansion.

Second, by assigning the CinCs a greater role in determining the readiness and sustainability of their forces, the operations program and budget would help smooth the transition between the current peacetime dominance of the individual services and the expected wartime dominance of the operational commanders. Specifically, the readiness program and budget would allow resources to flow down the same channels as operational authority and responsibility without depriving the services of their primary role as the maintaining arm of the forces.

Chain of Command. The chairman should replace the corporate JCS as the transmitter of orders from the civilian national command authorities to the unified and specified commanders. In addition to clarifying the operational chain of command by replacing a committee with an individual, this proposal would confirm the authority of the chairman as the representative of the operational commanders in Washington. To ensure civilian control, this change in the chain of command should not be made by statute but simply by revising the 1958 secretary of defense directive that placed the JCS in the chain of command in support of the secretary.

Authority of the CinCs over Component Commands. Although the National Security Act grants the unified and specified commanders full operational command of the forces assigned to the combatant commands, it leaves the definition of that phrase to the JCS. In our view, the JCS have defined full operational command too narrowly. Specifically, the JCS guidelines that require a CinC to exercise operational command only through the component commands and those that allow the component commander to select subordinate units to perform tasks assigned by the unified commander should be relaxed. Subject to approval by the secretary of defense, the CinC should have the authority to establish the operational chain of command in his theater and to select the units he believes necessary for a given military operation. The component commanders should not be service representatives with independent authority. Instead, the relationship between a unified commander and his service component commanders should be that of a commander and his deputies for air, land, and sea operations.

14   TOWARD A MORE EFFECTIVE DEFENSE

Civilian Control of the Military

The proposals outlined above are intended to strengthen the influence and authority of the joint military structure in order to ensure that timely cross-service military advice and planning is presented to civilian leaders and to improve the responsiveness and operational effectiveness of U.S. armed forces. Nothing in these measures would undermine civilian control of the military. To the contrary, better professional advice and planning from military leaders would give civilian officials a sounder grasp of the implications and likely outcomes of the employment of military forces, thereby enhancing their practical control as a complement to their existing statutory authority. Likewise, more effective control of deployed forces by the joint military structure would increase the likelihood of responsive implementation of civilian policies. In short, better cross-service advice and improved capabilities to implement civilian decisions can only strengthen civilian control of the military establishment.

THE OFFICE OF THE SECRETARY OF DEFENSE

It is likely that the beneficial effects of strengthening joint military institutions would be wasted unless these improvements were matched with changes in the structure and role of the Office of the Secretary of Defense (OSD). In our view, weaknesses in OSD's organization and procedures affect its performance in three ways:

* OSD's internal structure does not conform to the department's strategic purposes, thereby weakening its ability to provide clear, consistent policy direction.
* There is inadequate institutional voice for such operational concerns as readiness and sustainability.
* The OSD staff is too heavily involved in the details of program management and is too large.

By correcting these deficiencies, we believe that OSD will be in a better position to help the secretary carry out his most important functions—providing overall policy direction and program guidance and making major resource allocation choices—without excessive involvement in those specifics of program management that are best left to the military departments and operational commands.

In proposing the following changes in the structure of the OSD, we are not suggesting that the Congress should legislate such a reorganization unilaterally. We believe strongly that each secretary of defense should be given considerable leeway in organizing his staff. In our view, the Congress should at most specify the overall size of the staff and the number of key officials (deputy, under, and

Figure 1-2. The Organization of the Office of the Secretary of Defense.

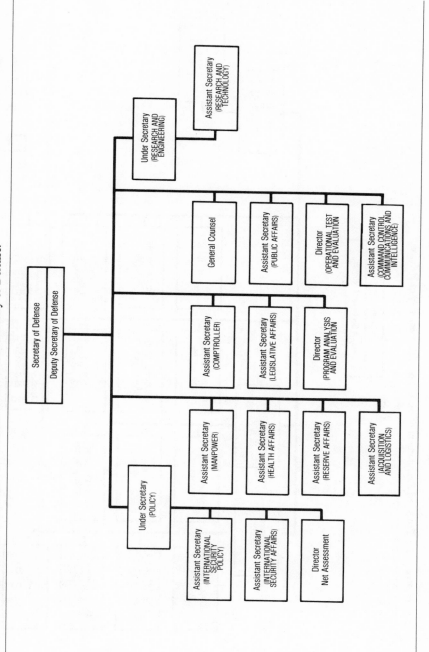

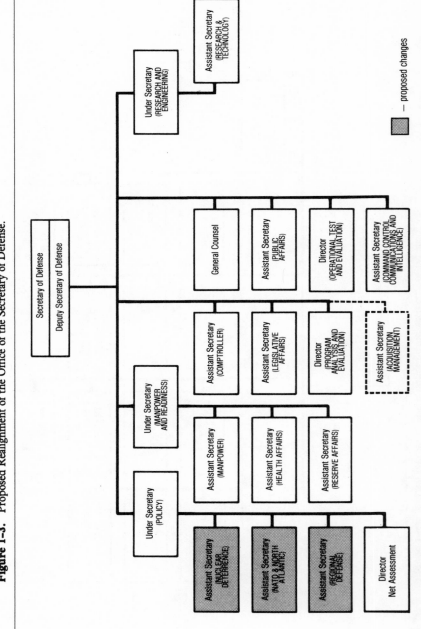

Figure 1-3. Proposed Realignment of the Office of the Secretary of Defense.

assistant secretaries), leaving it to the secretary to organize their responsibilities to suit his management style. Based on our experience and this study, however, we believe that the following recommendations would substantially improve the current organization of OSD.

Mission Orientation

The secretary of defense is the president's principal assistant responsible for national security matters. In this role, he must provide strategic direction to the Department of Defense to ensure that the separate programs of the military departments are integrated and adequate to support the president's national security goals. Unfortunately, OSD is not well structured to support the secretary in these efforts. OSD's primary components are structured along functional or input lines (e.g., manpower, research and engineering, health affairs), rather than in terms that conform to the department's output, the provision of capabilities to perform military missions. As a result, OSD is ill-equipped to translate mission-oriented planning and programming guidance into force requirements and weapon programs. For example, OSD has an office with responsibility for the manpower function and consequently can oversee manpower plans and programs on a department-wide basis. But OSD has only limited capability to help the secretary ensure that the services' manpower, logistics, procurement, and construction programs are integrated to meet the requirements of the European theater.

At the broadest level, U.S. military forces have three major missions: to deter nuclear attacks on the United States and its allies, to deter and, if necessary, defend against an attack on Western Europe, and to project U.S. military power where necessary to defend vital interests and support U.S. foreign policy in other parts of the globe.

The single most striking deficiency in the organization of OSD today is the absence of a senior official with exclusive responsibility for any one of these three strategic missions. Various functional offices are responsible for parts of each mission, but except for a small program analysis and evaluation staff (PA&E), no one is responsible for pulling them together. The under secretary of defense for policy has a general responsibility for all three missions but lacks the wherewithal to ensure that the services' programs are consistent with the department's priorities. This gap leaves the secretary of defense without adequate support to ensure that policy priorities are translated into programming and budgeting decisions. More precisely, OSD's limited capability to integrate the overall defense effort along mission lines means that functional priorities and service interests, rather than strategic needs, tend to drive program decisions and budget allocations. This sometimes leads to imbalances in military capabilities, since the services tend to assign lower priority to support functions such as airlift, sealift, and close air support. Although these functions are not associated closely with the service's traditional core missions, they are crucial to the NATO and regional defense missions. Moreover, without senior civilian officials responsible for oversight by major mission, opportunities for improving overall military effectiveness in ways that cut across traditional service roles and missions are seldom identified or exploited systematically.

OSD's emphasis on functional rather than mission organization also contributes to its excessive involvement in the details of service programs. By immersing itself in too many functional and program management issues that would be better left to the individual services, OSD has neglected its primary role of establishing clear policy guidelines and monitoring their implementation. In other words, OSD's functional orientation leads it to focus too much on routine programmatic decisions while providing too little direction on central policy matters.

▪ **Recommendation.**   To improve policy formulation and strengthen the link between national defense priorities and allocation decisions, the role of the under secretary of defense for policy should be expanded to include responsibility for program integration on a mission basis. This would constitute a logical extension of the under secretary's current responsibilities, which include the integration of Department of Defense plans and policies with overall national security objectives. Under our proposal, he would retain responsibility for drafting the Defense Guidance but would broaden his involvement in the program and budget review phases of the force development process. To support him in this expanded role, the under secretary's office should include an assistant secretary for each of the three major mission categories: nuclear deterrence, North Atlantic and European defense, and regional defense.

The principal objective of this realignment would be to link mission-oriented planning to the force development and acquisition process. Each of the mission-oriented assistant secretaries would coordinate department activities related to that specific strategic purpose. Such activities would include long-range planning, strategy formulation, force development, and operational planning.

The specific division of labor between the three assistant secretaries might be defined in a variety of ways. We envision that the assistant secretary for nuclear deterrence would have cognizance over all strategic offensive and defensive forces and capabilities, as well as missions in space. The assistant secretary for North Atlantic and European defense would be responsible for issues related to NATO, including both U.S. conventional forces allocated to that purpose and tactical nuclear forces. The assistant secretary for regional defense would be responsible for issues related to planning and programming forces for military contingencies in the Pacific, the Middle East and Persian Gulf, Latin America, and other Third World areas, including coordinating military assistance and counterinsurgency programs—and special operations—for those regions.

To carry out their functions, the mission-oriented assistant secretaries would need to be strengthened, especially with staff able to oversee the translation of policy into force requirements, programs, and budgets. The goal would be to enable the policy office to ensure that the secretary's goals and priorities were incorporated in the services' programs and that budgets were consistent with overall policy and priorities. This augmentation would not undercut the basic responsibility of the under secretary for research and engineering to oversee the development of weapons and equipment. Nor would it reduce the need for an effective PA&E staff to oversee the department's analytic and programming efforts on behalf of the secretary.

We considered proposals that would restructure OSD further, aligning all its functions under three mission-oriented under secretaries. Such a proposal might make it difficult for the secretary of defense to deal effectively with other government agencies and lead to duplicated efforts within the department. More important, we see a continued need for strong functional leadership in such areas as manpower and research. Accordingly, we concluded that a hybrid OSD structure was best, with the under secretary for policy oriented along mission lines and the rest of OSD focusing on specific functional areas.

Oversight of Readiness and Sustainability

The changes just described would allow OSD to establish a strong linkage between overall national security strategies and priorities on the one hand and specific Defense Department programs and budgets on the other. But we believe that further measures are needed to bolster OSD's policy oversight of the broad range of functions that support military operations. These functions include manpower, installations, and logistics as well as reserve affairs and health affairs.

In 1977, the offices of the assistant secretary for manpower and reserve affairs and the assistant secretary for installations and logistics were combined under a single assistant secretary. The purpose was to locate responsibility for policy matters concerning the provisioning, supply, and support functions of the department under one official. The combined office meant that a large number of related policies could be integrated without requiring the attention of the secretary of defense. The secretary would not be faced with making the many detailed tradeoffs and rationalizations necessary in this area, a time-consuming task that he simply cannot perform effectively in view of the many other demands on his time.

This objective was never fully achieved, however. Congress insisted that the assistant secretary for health affairs continue to report directly to the secretary of defense rather than through the new assistant secretary for manpower, reserve affairs, and logistics. Subsequently, Congress created another special interest office with the establishment of a separate assistant secretary for reserve affairs. Finally, the department recently established a separate assistant secretary for acquisition and logistics. The result of these developments has been that OSD oversight of these functions has been broken up among several assistant secretaries, with their integration—a crucial function—too often forced up to the level of the secretary of defense. Moreover, creation of these additional assistant secretaries led to an even larger OSD staff, created new coordination problems, and further stretched the secretary of defense's already too broad span of control.

Given the natural institutional bias of the military departments toward their long-term programmatic needs at the expense of near-term readiness and sustainability, the lack of an OSD official below the secretary empowered to integrate these functions is crippling. A strong OSD oversight role in this area is needed to ensure balanced tradeoffs between the requirements of readiness and sustainability and considerations of force structure expansion and modernization.

Recommendation. A third under secretary of defense should be established with broad policy oversight responsibilities for functions related to the readiness and sustainability of the operational forces.

This new office would oversee the various functions concerning the provisioning, supply, and support of operational forces. In organizational terms, we recommend the retention of the assistant secretary for manpower, with the proviso that he report through the new under secretary. If the assistant secretaries for health affairs and reserve affairs are retained (which we do not recommend), they should also report through the new under secretary to the secretary of defense. Finally, with regard to the new assistant secretary for acquisition management, we take no position on the desirability of separating procurement from research and engineering. However, we do believe that responsibility for installations and logistics should be shifted from the acquisition office to the new under secretary for manpower and readiness.

We believe that establishment of this third under secretary would complement our earlier proposal for an increased role for the CinCs in the programming and budgeting processes. The upgraded office would have greater capability to review the expanded inputs from the CinCs for the secretary and ensure that, if approved, their recommendations are reflected in the department's programs and budgets.

Finally, as will be discussed in a later section, we recommend that program evaluation receive far greater emphasis than it currently does. Pulling together the various OSD offices that focus on operational support functions would provide an institutional sponsor for many of these expanded evaluation capabilities.

Size of OSD Staff

The number of people necessary to support the secretary of defense has long been a source of controversy. While the official size of the secretary's staff has not changed substantially in many years, there has been considerable growth in the number of people working for the secretary. A wholly new organization, Washington Headquarters Services, has been created to carry out many of the administrative functions previously performed by members of OSD. We share the view that the size of OSD contributes to its tendency to micromanage by delving too deeply into the details of service programs.

Recommendation.   In the context of the realignment described previously, we believe that the secretary of defense should review the staffing needs of OSD and Washington Headquarters Services with a view to making substantial reductions in its size.

Admittedly, a blanket staff reduction is a blunt tool, but we believe that cutbacks in the size of OSD would inhibit it from becoming involved in detailed program management. With a smaller staff and some staff shifts from functional offices to the under secretary for policy, OSD would be forced to focus most of its efforts on the broader and more appropriate areas of defense policy and oversight.

Cuts in OSD staff, however, must be made in conjunction with reductions in congressional staffs. The dramatic increase in the size of all congressional staffs—personal, committee, and related agencies—has been a major factor in the growth of micromanagement of defense issues by the Congress. Because the Pentagon must respond to the flood of inquiries, directives, and studies emanating from congressional committees and individual members, the growth in congressional staffs has also contributed to expansion of OSD.

Finally, cuts should also be made in the individual services' military and departmental staffs. At least 15,000 civilians and military officers are assigned to OSD and service staffs, and even larger numbers of personnel are assigned to supporting headquarters such as the services' systems commands. Unless cuts are made in all components, it will be difficult to make them in any.

CONGRESSIONAL DEFENSE OVERSIGHT

No legislature in the world devotes as much time, energy, and talent to decision-making on the defense budget as does the U.S. Congress. Nevertheless, almost everyone involved in the process, both in the Congress itself and in the executive branch, has expressed dissatisfaction not only with the outcome of this effort but with the process itself. Congressional procedures for review of the defense budget reflect and reinforce many of the obstacles to effective policymaking and management in the Department of Defense. In particular, the Congress contributes to turbulence in the defense program and budget by focusing excessively on the details of program management. By using its time to review virtually every line item in the budget, the Congress forgoes opportunities to address the more fundamental issues of defense policy: the establishment of national strategic

◦ priorities and the broad allocation of defense resources toward those priorities. Changing the way that Congress reviews the budget would not only improve legislative oversight of defense policy but would also encourage and reinforce reforms in the Pentagon.

There are three primary problems in congressional procedures for defense oversight: work overload, redundant review procedures, and excessive attention to short-term issues.

Work Overload.   The members of Congress have too much to do. There are too many issues to debate and too little time to review each thoroughly. To a degree, this excessive workload results from the complexity of contemporary public policy issues and the character of national politics in recent years. But the members of Congress also contribute to the overload by broadening the scope of their overview process while continually deepening the level of detail sought on each issue. One or the other, scope or detail, must be sacrificed if there is to be sufficient time and energy for careful and responsible oversight.

Redundant Reviews.   Redundancy in the congressional review process seriously aggravates the problem. Each chamber reviews the defense budget at least three times annually. In each chamber, a separate committee controls each of the three annual reviews. At the same time, the differentiation among functions, which once clearly distinguished the committees, has become blurred. The armed services committees in both chambers have expanded their authorization functions to encompass nearly the entire defense budget. At the same time, the appropriating committees increasingly apportion funds without regard to authorizations. Moreover, the question of how budgeting committees can rationally establish overall budgetary levels without delving into the detailed questions traditionally considered by authorizing, and even appropriating, committees has never been answered satisfactorily.

Redundancies in the congressional process have reinforced the natural reluctance of politicians to make final decisions. It is always tempting to suggest that another court of appeal exists for difficult and controversial decisions; and, indeed, the reality is that no decision ever seems final. Defense contractors, military departments, and other claimants who lose in one phase of the process can appeal the decision in the next or, at worst, in the opening phase of the next annual cycle, a few months later.

Short-term Focus.   Congressional budgetary decisionmaking, like that of the executive branch, is oriented primarily toward the upcoming year's budget. Although the Congress insists that the Department of Defense produce long-term plans, it takes seriously—and reviews in detail—only the plan for the next year. This short-term focus has a number of adverse implications. It crowds out policy review and program evaluation by concentrating congressional attention on functional categories in a single budget—a practice that is mirrored in OSD. It also undermines any rigorous review of the long-term fiscal implications of new program starts, allowing more programs to be initiated than can actually be supported at efficient production levels. The result is far too many claimants for the limited weapon acquisition funds that are available. Because programs are rarely terminated once they have reached full-scale development, excessive program starts force repeated decisions to stretch out the production and development schedules of existing programs, raising unit costs and delaying the introduction of new technologies to the field.

The overwhelming workload, the redundancies in the process, and the focus on program details all inhibit serious congressional attention to the broader issues of the overall direction and content of U.S. security policy. The Congress is so immersed in the fine points of the defense program that it lacks the time, the resources, and the fundamental orientation to engage in a substantive dialogue with the executive branch on the nation's strategic objectives and policies. It is lost in the trees of program management, unable to see—far less to influence—the policy forest. The executive branch reinforces this tendency by avoiding discussion of basic defense issues with the Congress while simultaneously bemoaning congressional micromanagement.

These problems are not the result of deliberate decisions; they are a by-product of the political dynamics that have characterized executive-legislative relations for many years. Congress is an institution in which no one can guarantee the outcome of an issue but almost everyone can influence its ultimate resolution. Repetitive procedures, overlapping committee responsibilities, and attention to programmatic details all reflect the quest of individual legislators to maximize their ability to serve their constituents and increase their own influence on government policy. Any serious reform of the congressional process is difficult to achieve because in the end it means that members of Congress will have to yield some of their ability to serve individual constituents' interests to the common interest of the nation's security.

Removing redundant steps in the process sounds simple in theory but in fact it is not. Different committees control those duplicative procedures. Deciding which of the three committees should give up or even circumscribe its prerogatives and influence would be difficult. Similarly, moving the entire system from an annual process to a multi-year one would be difficult, since annual reviews are a critical lever of legislative influence. Moreover, as gridlock has developed in so many aspects of legislative activity in recent years, the annual defense bill, which for a variety of reasons is unlikely to be vetoed, has become a primary means of advancing legislative proposals that would otherwise perish.

For all these reasons, reform in the congressional process might best be accomplished in conjunction with reforms in the organization and procedures of the Department of Defense. If the two branches could begin a dialogue on these issues and mutually develop a comprehensive and cooperative approach, existing institutions might be persuaded that the sacrifices demanded of them were being matched by the sacrifices of others—all in the national interest.

Recommendation.   To streamline the congressional review process and refocus legislative attention on the broader issues of national strategic priorities and the allocation of defense resources to support them, we recommend two measures:

1. Shifting the defense budget from an annual to a biennial cycle.
2. Reestablishing the division of labor between the defense-authorizing and defense-appropriating committees.

Multi-year Budgets.   We believe that shifting to a multi-year budget is crucial for an effective legislative role in defense policy. Certainly, the Congress should review the details of budgets and weapon programs, but it need not undertake such a time-consuming task every year for every weapon—much less three times per year. Ideally, budgeting would be accomplished on a multi-year basis and weapons would be reviewed only in conjunction with the three or four major decision milestones in their acquisition cycle. Once it were decided to procure a major system, authorization for purchases over several years should be the normal practice rather than the exception.

As a first step toward this long-range objective of a multi-year budget process, we recommend that the Congress immediately adopt a biennial budget cycle for defense. Under this proposal, the administration would submit and the Congress would debate, amend, and eventually approve a two-year authorization and appropriation in the first year of each new Congress. In the second year, relevant committees would direct their attention to the review, evaluation, and oversight of existing programs.

Although we believe there are likely to be substantial benefits in shifting the entire federal budget to a biennial cycle, such a proposal extends beyond the mandate and expertise of this committee. For the defense budget, however, we can say with confidence that a shift to a biennial cycle—whether in conjunction with the rest of the federal budget or alone—would have a number of significant benefits. It would foster greater stability in the defense planning process and ease the burden now imposed by the annual budget process on the members of Congress. By reducing the time spent on budget review, a biennial cycle would allow greater efforts to be directed at broad questions of policy oversight. And it would permit more attention to be paid to those long-term issues of purpose and strategy that are of the greatest importance to the nation's security.

At the same time, a biennial defense budget would have a salutary effect on internal Department of Defense resource allocation procedures. It would impart greater stability into the planning process. It would also reduce the amount of time the department spends on budget issues, allowing greater attention to be paid to broader issues of defense strategy and priorities, as well as the evaluation of past decisions.

We recognize that there are some risks in adopting a two-year defense budget. In particular, the economic assumptions and the assessment of the threat that underpin the budget are more likely to require adjustments over the course of a longer cycle. In our opinion, however, these potential adjustments can be accommodated within a biennial cycle by allowing a supplemental appropriation in the off year and granting the Department of Defense wider authority for reprogramming funds. In short, we believe that the gains in terms of budget and program stability far outweigh the risks of sudden, unforeseen shifts in the assumptions underlying the defense program.

Committee Functions.   The separation of authorizing and appropriating functions may have outlived its usefulness. Consolidating the current authorizing and appropriating authorities into a single defense program committee would substantially improve both the efficiency and the effectiveness of congressional defense oversight. This new committee would first debate longer range issues of national military strategy and allocation priorities and then translate its decisions into multi-year budgets. In between budget years, the defense committee would review and evaluate the ongoing defense program, as well as oversee manpower and procurement policies. In other words, it would have the time, the resources, and the mandate to exercise serious policy oversight of the defense establishment.

Despite the attractiveness of such a committee consolidation, we judge that under current circumstances the political obstacles to its implementation are insurmountable. Accordingly, we recommend that the roles of the authorizing and appropriating committees be differentiated more clearly. The armed services committees should review the department's long-range plan, insist that it be based on realistic outyear forecasts of resources, and debate the underlying issues of overall defense policy that the plan reflects. The appropriating committees should focus their attention on the decisions necessary to translate the defense program approved by the armed services committees into a two-year budget.

FORCE DEVELOPMENT AND ACQUISITION

The Department of Defense has developed two major processes to aid the secretary of defense in integrating the plans, programs, and budgets of the individual military departments: the Planning, Programming, and Budgeting System (PPBS) and the major system acquisition process. Both processes need to be adjusted in line with the organizational changes recommended in the previous three sections to ensure that the secretary can carry out his integrative roles effectively.

PLANNING, PROGRAMMING, AND BUDGETING

PPBS is the department's formal process for planning and allocating resources.
• Its central purpose is to design a military strategy and force posture that can
achieve the nation's strategic objectives at the least cost. The system consists of
three phases. Planning translates the overall defense priorities established by the
president and his senior advisers into guidance for force development. Programming develops and evaluates specific multi-year force structure alternatives on a
mission-oriented basis. The product of this second phase is the Five-Year
Defense Program (FYDP). Budgeting determines the cost of the first year of the
FYDP and produces the administration's budget submission to Congress.

PPBS has not fulfilled the promise of a multi-year process that would proceed deductively from the establishment of national defense priorities through
the development of specific defense programs to the formulation of each year's
budget request. The model of PPBS as a series of interlocking functions, the
output of one forming the input of the next, has not been realized. To meet
these objectives, we believe that all three phases of PPBS need to be overhauled
and mechanisms for evaluation must be improved.

Planning

• There is broad agreement that, in the words of the 1979 Defense Resource Management Study, "the first P in PPBS is silent." More precisely, the planning that
takes place in the Department of Defense is not linked adequately to subsequent
programming and budgeting decisions. This shortcoming has two organizational
sources.

• First, OSD does not adequately translate national strategic objectives into a
policy framework and set of priorities to guide program development. This is not
to say that OSD's strategic and policy thinking does not influence allocation
decisions; it does. But rather than making an integrated contribution to the planning phase, OSD relies on detailed involvement in individual program and
budget decisions to produce, inferentially, an overall military plan.

• Second, joint military planning is not constrained by realistic projections of
future defense budgets. Consequently, the primary JCS planning documents are
fiscally unrealistic and therefore largely ignored in the programming and
budgeting process. Instead, national military force planning results from loosely
coordinated, parallel dialogues between OSD and each of the individual service
departments. This often results in disparate plans that do not optimize the
potential contribution of each military service to national strategic objectives.

Recommendation. Two measures would make the planning phase more
meaningful:

1. The responsibilities of the under secretary of defense for policy should be ex-
    panded to ensure that program and resource decisions reflect mission-
    oriented planning.
2. The chairman of the JCS, with the assistance of the Joint Staff, should be
    charged with preparing force planning recommendations constrained by
    realistic estimates of available resources.

The detailed content and implications of these recommendations have already
been discussed. These organizational reforms of OSD and the JCS would have
substantial benefits in enhancing the quality and the relevance of defense planning, as well as in improving and expanding the contribution of cross-service
military advice.

Programming and Budgeting

The rationale for the division of the resource allocation process into three identifiable phases rests in large part on the concept that the programming process
should serve to translate security plans and priorities into specific budget requests. In practice, however, programming and budgeting have evolved into
competing, rather than complementary, processes. As originally intended, the
programming phase was to be the forum in which senior decisionmakers would
evaluate alternative programs and approve a rolling FYDP. The subsequent
budgeting phase would then be limited to the mechanical process of costing out
the first year of the approved program in detail. Instead, the budgeting phase has
developed into a separate decisionmaking process, in which many of the issues
ostensibly decided in the programming phase are reconsidered. On issues where
the secretary of defense has been heavily involved in the programming phase,
major decisions usually survive the subsequent budget review. For less visible
issues, however, decisions made during the programming phase are often over-
turned or changed significantly at budget time—even when the underlying conditions supporting the original decisions remain unchanged. This pattern of
revisiting program decisions undermines the programming process and wastes
much effort by senior civilian and military officials.

The problem is compounded by the fact that the Department of Defense programs funds on a different basis than it budgets them. Moreover, the link between these two processes is inadequate. Programs are developed in terms that
emphasize outputs or missions such as strategic nuclear forces, tactical aircraft,
or airlift. In contrast, budgets are formulated in terms of resource inputs such as
military personnel, operations and maintenance, and procurement. The FYDP,
which arrays each of the major mission programs in terms of dollars and forces,
provides a crosswalk between the programming and budgeting data, but it is not
sufficiently flexible or responsive to translate readily between programs and

budgets. As a result, it is difficult for decisionmakers to evaluate the longer term program implications of the budget cuts that inevitably take place toward the end of the process.

The limited ability to translate between programming and budgeting processes is exacerbated by the gaps that occur between the overall fiscal levels used to guide the preparation of defense programs and the actual size of the budgets the president proposes and the Congress eventually approves. The problem begins with the often wide differences between the fiscal guidance assumed by the Department of Defense at the beginning of the annual program cycle in the spring and the actual budget level eventually approved by the president late in the fall. Having put together a program using optimistic fiscal assumptions, the department is faced with the need to make program cuts to meet the president's final budget decision at the end of the cycle. Given the difficulty of moving between programming and budgeting, the department finds it difficult to map out the programmatic consequences of these budgetary adjustments.

Recommendation.   The programming and budgeting phases of PPBS should be merged into a single process that retains a program and mission orientation but simultaneously establishes relevant budget inputs.

We recommend the integration of the programming and budgeting processes in order to promote the matching of resource inputs to program outputs and the linking of both to defense objectives and missions. Under this proposal, the programming and budgeting functions would be merged at each stage of the process:

- The issuance of policy and fiscal guidance by the secretary of defense.
- The preparation of program and budget requests by the military departments and the operational commands.
- The review of those requests by OSD.

The mechanical adjustments needed to unify programming and budgeting would have to be worked out in detail. A number of approaches are possible. For example, an OSD committee in the late 1970s proposed a single cycle, in which program and budget decisions would be established in parallel review processes. Whatever review process is instituted, the merger of programming and budgeting would also require restructuring the budget into program or mission terms, as well as developing improved means of translating program categories into traditional appropriation categories for presentation to Congress.

Merging the two phases would make the system more efficient by minimizing the need to revisit decisions. It would also provide greater constancy to program decisions. Moreover, merging programming and budgeting should help to alleviate the problems caused by large gaps between the budget mark used to design the program and the eventual budget submitted to Congress. A variety of factors makes it inevitable that presidents delay final decisions on the size of the defense budget until shortly before submitting the budget to Congress; consolidating programming and budgeting would accommodate this requirement. With budget inputs integrated into program categories, defense decisionmakers would be better able to evaluate the ramifications of late adjustments in the defense budget total. This, in turn, would reduce the likelihood that these budgetary changes would unbalance the program.

Merging the two phases would not be risk free. There is some possibility that programming would be submerged if the urgency of making short-term budget decisions came to dominate the entire process. In fact, to a degree the present system already suffers from this problem. We believe, however, that the proposed merger of programming and budgeting would help balance the short-term focus of the current process by ensuring that decisionmakers have a better understanding of the program implications of their budget decisions.

If a biennial budget cycle is adopted, the PPBS process should be revamped to take advantage of the additional time made available in the nonbudget year. During that year, the department's focus could be directed at long-range planning and programming (years three through fifteen). As is discussed in the section on weapons acquisition below, the centerpiece would be a long-term resource plan.

Evaluation

Evaluation is the orphan function in the current resource allocation process. Insufficient attention has been devoted to program evaluation and to the review and feedback procedures necessary for such evaluations. In theory, PPBS should be a circular process with financial and performance data from one year's cycle serving as the planning base for the early phases of the next year's process. In practice, however, PPBS essentially starts fresh each year. Little systematic attention is given to the evaluation of past program decisions. Major weapon programs that have high congressional visibility are sometimes an exception to this generalization, because their cost and performance data tend to be monitored more closely. But PPBS has never included an explicit and comprehensive system for measuring and reporting progress in implementing approved programs.

Further, the department's accounting base is inadequate to support effective evaluation. Department of Defense financial reports provide a mass of data, but the financial information in these reports is often inconsistent, incomplete, and untimely. The source of many of these shortcomings is the department's reliance on accounting systems that operate almost exclusively on an obligational basis. Under this system, an economic event is measured when the resources are "obligated"—that is, when contracts are awarded or orders placed. This emphasis on obligation-based data is understandable in terms of the department's fiduciary responsibilities, but it inhibits the evaluation of program effectiveness and management performance by focusing attention on the time of the commitment, with little monitoring of the actual delivery or the effective use of the resources acquired. For example, the entire cost of a navy ship may be obligated in one year, but the ship may not be completed for as many as seven years. An obligation-based accounting system records the bulk of the cost in that first year and does not monitor how those resources are expended over the seven-year building cycle.

The absence of sophisticated management information systems also impedes effective program evaluation. There are some areas, such as personnel recruiting and retention, in which the department has developed effective management information systems, but there are numerous others in which such systems are either incomplete or do not exist. The lack of integrated performance data is particularly severe with respect to combat readiness, as the 1978 Steadman Report pointed out. Although there are many detailed reports on the operational readiness and warfighting capabilities of U.S. combat forces, these reports focus on unit, rather than theater or command-wide, capabilities. Not only are these reports conducted and routed through service channels, but the services use differing standards to measure unit readiness. Accordingly, both operational commanders and senior policymakers lack comprehensive measures of the readiness of the forces upon which they would rely in time of war.

Recommendation. The Department of Defense should implement an explicit evaluation process that systematically reviews progress made in implementing programs and cycles that information into subsequent planning, programming, and budgeting phases. In effect, this evaluation system would constitute a fourth phase of PPBS, completing the allocation cycle by linking objectives to performance standards. Specifically, we recommend three measures:

1. Conducting programming, budgeting, and execution processes within a unified accounting structure.
2. Supplementing the current obligation-based accounting system with reporting on an accrual basis.
3. Improving management information systems to enable decisionmakers to evaluate progress toward identified objectives.

Unified Accounting Structure. The value of merging programming and budgeting would be enhanced by parallel improvements in the accounting system. The new system should record the use of resources in the same manner as they are planned, programmed, and budgeted. In this way, the reported status of current programs would provide valuable performance and cost information for decisions in the planning cycle for future years.

Accrual Accounting. The Department of Defense should also update and improve its accounting system to provide complete, accurate, and timely cost information to decisionmakers. The accounting system should record the use of resources on an accrual, as well as an obligational, basis. Accounting on an accrual basis (recording resources as they are expended) is a key factor in improving the evaluation system, in that it would provide the basis for judging the impact of spending on a program in terms of its output.

Management Information Systems.   Finally, the Department of Defense should adopt more comprehensive management information systems in order to assess performance in crucial areas such as equipment maintenance and combat readiness. Since these systems would have to be tailored individually to specific program needs, the details of their operation and implementation are beyond the scope of this report.

The comptroller-general has prepared a comprehensive and thoughtful program to enhance financial management in the government covering all three areas discussed above. We believe that it deserves sympathetic review by both the executive and legislative branches.

WEAPONS ACQUISITION

Problems in the weapon acquisition process have received more critical attention over the past few years than any other defense issue. Delays in deliveries of new weapons, cost overruns, and questions about the performance of new systems have given rise to congressional investigations, banner headlines, and much soul-searching in recent administrations. We have attempted to look beyond the recent debates over such issues as warranties and operational testing to illuminate the underlying causes that so often lead to rising costs, schedule delays, and disappointing performance. We have identified three basic determinants of problems in the weapon acquisition process:

1. An inadequate planning and selection process.
2. Instability in programs and budgets.
3. The lack of natural market incentives throughout the acquisition process.

Planning and Selection Process

To ensure that the United States develops the proper mix of weapon systems to support its defense priorities, OSD must define the links between national strategy and specific acquisition decisions. OSD's attraction to managing the details of individual weapon programs, however, has diverted its attention from establishing this crucial linkage. With the exception of such high profile areas as strategic nuclear forces, OSD has failed to provide an overall framework and set of guidelines within which service acquisition decisions can be supervised and coordinated. The military services thus develop weapons independently, each according to its own sense of national priorities. As a consequence, many weapons are procured without a defined relationship to overall national strategic objectives and priorities. While weapons of questionable value that fulfill service priorities sometimes assume a life of their own, often surviving despite strong evidence of inadequate performance or excessive costs, weapons needed for national purposes that do not fit a service's core function tend to be developed slowly, if at all.

The Department of Defense has been often unable to procure planned numbers and types of weapon systems within planned budgets. Some of this cost growth can be attributed to the uncertainties inherent in building weapons that are on the frontiers of modern technology, and some is the result of the instabilities in programs and budgets described below. A substantial portion, however, is attributable to specific deficiencies within the acquisition process itself.

Estimating the cost of high technology systems involves enormous uncertainty. An entire range of estimates is possible depending on the desired confidence level. The current process, however, is structured in such a way that defense contractors, the military departments, and the Congress all have incentives to keep initial cost estimates at the low end of the possible range. Defense contractors have an incentive to submit optimistically low bids in order to secure weapon development and production contracts. If costs have in fact been underestimated, they can then usually rely on later changes in engineering and design specifications to negotiate the final price upward. The Pentagon's reliance on sole-source contracts for most major systems provides a hospitable environment for this practice of "buying in" to new programs. Contractors typically compete with each other only in the initial phases of the acquisition cycle. Once a development contract has been awarded, there is generally no further competition throughout the life of the program. As the only producer of what may be a crucial weapon system, the contractor then has substantial leverage in negotiating the ultimate price and other terms of the new system.

Nor is it usually in the short-term interest of the military services to question low bids. The services themselves are competing for scarce defense dollars and wish to minimize their apparent demands. When a service is seeking initial funding for a new weapon system, the lower the estimated cost of that system, the more receptive the secretary of defense, the Office of Management and Budget, the president, and the Congress are likely to be. By the time these initial cost estimates have been proven to be too low, the weapon is likely to have acquired its own constituency—including the administration, which has an interest in demonstrating the validity of its decision, and those legislators in whose districts the weapon and its various components are to be built. Accordingly, although cost growth frequently results in the stretch out of development and production schedules, the cancellation of a program after a decision to enter full-scale development is unusual, regardless of cost growth.

Recommendation. The Department of Defense should develop an overall, •
long-range capital investment plan to provide a sound basis for force development and acquisition. In this context, the department will require more accurate cost projections for major weapon systems.

Long-Range Investment Plan. To coordinate the acquisition strategies of the individual military services, we recommend that the Department of Defense prepare an integrated, long-range investment plan that allocates resources in broad •
categories to mission areas. Because major system development takes eight to twelve years, this plan should be based on a fifteen-year assessment of the nature and scope of the military threat. To be useful, it should be constrained by a •
realistic estimate of the resources likely to be available for defense. Under our proposal, the under secretary of defense for policy and the director of program analyses and evaluation would prepare this plan for review and approval by the secretary of defense. Once the initial plan had been prepared, the primary task would be to prepare an annual update that would take into account shifts in the assessment of threats posed to the nation, new technological opportunities, and altered judgments of fiscal constraints on future defense budgets.

The long-range investment plan would not be an extension of the FYDP. It •
would be less detailed and would be used by defense decisionmakers as a planning guide, not a definitive decision document. The value of the capital investment plan would be twofold. First, it would integrate long-range service acquisi- •
tion plans, providing a road map in each major mission area that linked national strategic objectives with major acquisition programs. Second, it would serve to highlight the aggregate demand on the overall resources that the Department of Defense is likely to have available over the next fifteen years, forcing early assessments of the tradeoffs that competing commitments to major weapon systems make necessary. In this manner, the plan would help focus greater attention on the costs of burdening the budget with too many major program starts.

All three military departments have experimented with such long-term re- •
source plans, with the army using the approach most extensively. Reportedly, these experiments have been most useful in shaping planning priorities. Their integration into a department-wide planning tool is a logical and necessary next step.

Accurate Cost Projections. To be useful as a planning tool, however, the long-range investment plan must be based on accurate projections of the costs of major weapon systems. Accordingly, we recommend that in preparing the plan the under secretary for policy rely on independent cost estimates, rather than the projections of the services and defense contractors. In addition, given the inherent uncertainty in cost estimating, each major program should be provided with adequate management reserves. There is a danger that providing such reserves at the start of a program may actually encourage cost growth. We believe, however, that there is legitimate uncertainty in projecting the costs of major weapons and that it is short-sighted not to make allowances for cost growth. More specifically, we believe that the provision of budgetary reserves for increases in the cost of new weapons, or "planning wedges" as they are sometimes called, could help to control excessive program starts and, thus, minimize costly stretch-outs.

Program and Budget Stability

The acquisition process suffers greatly from what one observer has called its "ubiquitous turbulence": shifting funding levels, lengthening production schedules, frequent personnel transfers, and rapidly changing design specifications. Continual revisions in a program divert management attention from the task at hand, encourage inefficiency, discourage capital investment by contractors, and undermine employee motivation and morale. Three major factors are at the source of much of the turbulence.

First, congressional procedures that result in the detailed review of every program every year, together with the legislators' attention to the concerns of particular constituents, have produced strong incentives and multiple opportunities for micromanagement by the legislature. Annual congressional alteration of hundreds of procurement and research and development line items produce year-to-year uncertainties for program managers and defense contractors. The inevitable result is less efficient management, higher unit costs, and longer production schedules. Congressional preoccupation with the details of programs has also served to short circuit its constitutional responsibility to help formulate overall national strategies and purposes, and to conduct effective oversight of the execution of national security policy by the executive branch.

Second, there is the problem of too many new program starts. As explained above, the Department of Defense systematically underestimates the costs of new weapon programs. At the same time, the department's five-year defense plan is consistently optimistic regarding the aggregate spending levels that Congress will approve in the outyears. Congress contributes to this problem by focusing primarily on the upcoming budget year, largely ignoring longer range issues. Congress insists that the Department of Defense establish viable long-term plans, but then undermines their effectiveness by reviewing the budget in detail only for the immediate fiscal year. As a consequence, more weapon programs enter development than budgets in future years will be able to sustain. Moreover, since new programs are terminated only rarely, even weapons of marginal promise limp from one budget year to the next. In short, too many competitors for too few dollars produce continual stretch-outs in the development and production schedules of ongoing programs. Combined with stretch-outs brought on by cost growth within individual programs, the result is a slower than desirable pace of modernization and constantly escalating program and unit costs.

Third, the bureaus and officials that oversee research and development in • both OSD and the military departments too frequently revise the technical requirements that drive weapon programs either to incorporate new advances in technology or to account for altered assessments of potential adversaries' capabilities. This so-called "requirements creep" is a natural outgrowth of laudable efforts to deploy the most modern and capable weapon systems. Nevertheless, the unsystematic nature of this process results in constant design revisions that contribute to higher unit costs and slowed development and production schedules, as well as reduced reliability and operability.

Recommendation. In addition to the long-range investment plan described above, we recommend two supporting measures to increase the stability of programs. First and most important, Congress should review the defense budget request on a biennial basis. Second, the military services should be required to establish internal contracts that set cost, performance, and schedule baselines for their weapon programs. The cost baseline should include reserves that are commensurate with the uncertainties entailed.

Biennial Budgeting. The details of our proposal for a biennial budget process were discussed in the section on congressional reform. A biennial budget cycle would have several benefits in the weapon acquisition process. It would introduce greater stability to weapon programs by reducing the year-to-year uncertainty about budget levels. Biennial budgets would also allow contractors to establish more efficient production rates with correspondingly lower unit costs. Finally, biennial budgets would permit both the Department of Defense and the Congress to devote more time to the long-term implications of weapon development and procurement decisions.

Baselining. To obtain greater stability, it is also essential that the services restrain themselves from readjusting the parameters and specifications of their weapon programs too frequently. Toward that end, we recommend that all services adopt the baselining technique the air force developed for the B-1B program and has used successfully for other major weapons. Under this system, each service would establish an internal "contract" for each major weapon program, specifying the desired performance parameters as well as the annual funding levels, quantities, and production schedule. Once established, these contracts could not be altered, except as a result of an explicit review and approval by the service secretary. In this way, both the service itself and OSD's research and engineering office would be discouraged from encumbering the program with frequent design changes. The improved performance expected from a desired design change would have to be significant enough to merit raising the issue with the service secretary. In more marginal cases, it is likely that proposed changes would be clustered together and incorporated into the program only as a new version of the system was developed.

Creation of Natural Market Incentives

In spite of the fact that defense is not normally considered a regulated industry, it is important to recognize the very high degree of regulation present. Moreover, this regulation is unique in that the regulator is also the dominant buyer. With so much involvement on the part of the buyer in the operation of the supplier, it is difficult for the free market to operate. Nevertheless, there is a strong tendency within the department, the Congress, and the defense industry to act as if free market conditions exist and rely on the invisible hand of the market to produce economic efficiency.

Perhaps the dominant characteristic of the weapon acquisition process is the lack of competition for most of the dollars involved. When the Department of Defense initiates competitive bidding for the development of a new generation of a weapon system, there is usually fierce rivalry among several large firms. But once the selection for initial development is complete, the rest of the program— product development, testing, and eventual production—is normally conducted in a sole-source environment. Thus, unlike the commercial marketplace, the buyer—the government—has no alternative sellers or competing products to meet its need. Essentially, the contractor has achieved a monopoly position. The Department of Defense is dependent on that producer for crucial equipment and thus lacks leverage in setting the terms of subsequent contracts. This distinction between competition for an initial award and the lack of competition during the execution of a program is the primary difference between the defense market and the commerical world.

Besides this lack of a continuous alternative, the normal profit incentive for cost reduction is minimized in defense contracting. Under the current system, the department typically negotiates annual production contracts based upon the previous year's costs plus a profit margin that remains relatively constant. Accordingly, the contractor is often rewarded when costs rise, since the profit of the follow-on contract is computed on a larger cost base. With such incentives, there is little pressure to hold down future labor and material costs because the contractor can usually pass on these costs directly to the department.

The lack of natural market incentives on the industry's side is matched by similar disincentives within the Department of Defense. The military services have little incentive to reduce unit costs. Because the number of systems to be procured is usually fixed, any savings from reductions in unit costs usually end up as budget cuts in the next fiscal cycle. Moreover, the military personnel system does not provide adequate incentives for officers to seek assignments in acquisition management. Most military officers recognize that there are limited opportunities for enhancing their careers in the acquisition world. Accordingly, many seek to avoid such duty and those who do serve in acquisition management positions seldom seek further assignments. The result is that the overall experience levels and training of uniformed personnel in acquisition is inadequate.

Finally, unlike the practice in the commercial sector, cost is rarely a primary criterion in the design of weapons; it is derived instead from performance criteria. The normal Department of Defense procedure is to optimize weapon designs for maximum performance with limited attention to unit cost. The department then seeks industry bids on those specifications, awarding the contract to the lowest responsible bidder. This practice discourages employing advanced technology to lower costs. It also makes it difficult to determine systematically the marginal costs of specific improvements in performance, thus complicating assessments of the tradeoffs between fewer highly capable weapons and a greater number of somewhat less capable weapons.

Recommendations. The Department of Defense should seek to create market incentives to reduce costs in the defense acquisition process. Specifically, we recommend:

1. Promoting competition among defense contractors throughout the life of a weapon program.
2. Allowing contractors to increase profit margins when costs fall.
3. Encouraging the services to reinvest cost savings toward increased quantities or improved performance of the same weapon system.
4. Enhancing career opportunities and training for acquisition managers.
5. Establishing unit cost as a primary criterion in the initial design of weapons.

Continuous Competition. In the commercial world, the maintenance of some form of alternative—either between two suppliers for the same product or between two products for the same mission—is the norm. The Department of Defense should seek to institute a similar incentive structure for defense contractors by promoting, where possible, competition throughout all phases of a program's development and production. Competition throughout the development and production phases of a weapon program would provide incentives for lower costs and greater performance. It would also reduce the opportunities for contractors to "buy in" to a sole-source contract with an optimistically low bid.

Profit Incentives. The Department of Defense should adjust the future profit margins of defense contractors to reward cost underruns and punish cost overruns. We propose that the negotiated profit margin be adjusted up or down based upon the contractor's prior-year performance in meeting the planned unit costs for its product. If costs exceed those specified in the contract, the profit margin on the next contract would be reduced. Conversely, if costs fall below those in the planned budget, the profit margin would be increased. In this way, both the government and the supplier would benefit from lower costs.

Service Incentives.   The incentives for the military services to achieve lower unit costs could be improved by a practice of allowing them to buy greater quantities or improve the performance of a particular system if its unit costs fell below planned funding levels. In other words, a portion of any cost savings would be returned to the services for the acquisition of greater military capabilities.

Career Incentives.   In order to attract and retain high quality officers in acquisition management, the military services should improve the possibilities for career advancement in the acquisition area. At the same time, the amount and level of training for acquisition managers should be enhanced. Perhaps most important, managing weapon programs well should be rewarded with promotions, including promotion to flag rank.

Design to Cost.   In order to ensure that the department and defense contractors take advantage of technological advances to reduce cost as well as maximize performance, unit cost should be made a primary design criterion of each weapon system. Contractors would be required to meet these cost limitations, just as they are expected to meet specified performance parameters. Indeed, the inclusion of cost as a primary design parameter would promote explicit tradeoffs between improved performance and lower unit costs with larger numbers deployed.

PROSPECTS FOR REFORM

We are not the first study group to recommend substantial changes in the organization and procedures of the U.S. defense establishment; we are unlikely to be the last. Yet, writing in the early days of 1985, it appears that the chances for defense reform may be significantly greater than at any time since President Eisenhower's 1958 reorganization. There is a growing consensus in the Congress, in the community of defense officials and specialists, and among the American people supporting the need for substantial efforts to revitalize and reform the defense establishment.

The program that we have set out in this document represents a pragmatic and politically feasible agenda for strengthening the organizations and procedures through which the nation establishes and executes its defense policies. Our objective has not been to reach for organizational perfection, which is an elusive goal at best. Rather, we have sought to assemble a set of proposals that can, if taken together, deal effectively with the most pressing problems and that can, because of their moderation and comprehensiveness, gain a critical mass of political, military, bureaucratic, and public support.

It is already evident that defense organizational reform legislation will be introduced in the 99th Congress. We urge all members to reexamine thoroughly the existing structures and procedures of the Department of Defense and the methods used by the Congress in considering defense issues. We urge the administration to work closely with the Congress in this effort to ensure that this review results in a more effective defense establishment. And we urge all citizens to consider these issues and to communicate their views to their representatives in Washington.

2 REPORT OF THE WORKING GROUP ON MILITARY COMMAND STRUCTURE

Chair: Edward C. Meyer

Members: Les Aspin   David C. Jones
                 John M. Collins   Jan M. Lodal
                 Vincent Davis   Edward N. Luttwak
                 Edwin A. Deagle   John S. Pustay
                 Paul Y. Hammond   W.Y. Smith
                 Thor Hanson   Lewis R. Sorley
                 Samuel P. Huntington   Edward L. Warner III

Rapporteur: Barry R. Posen

In 1958, President Dwight D. Eisenhower proposed amendments to the National Security Act seeking to improve the performance of the three components of the joint military establishment: (1) to enable the Joint Chiefs of Staff (JCS), led by its chairman, to provide cross-service military advice for strategic planning, resource allocation decisions, and military operations; (2) to establish the Joint Staff as a unified military staff; and (3) to ensure unified and integrated command of military operations under the commanders-in-chief of the unified and specified commands (CinCs).

The working group concludes that none of these three objectives has been fully achieved. The JCS remain incapable institutionally of providing meaningful advice on issues involving important service interests or prerogatives. The Joint Staff continues to act as an executive secretariat to coordinate service views rather than as an independent, unified military staff. The CinCs lack peacetime authority commensurate with their wartime responsibilities. Although the CinCs have full operational authority over their forces, they have little influence over such matters vital to operational effectiveness as weapon requirements, logistics, training, and maintenance. In short, none of the three components of the joint military establishment is able to perform its role effectively.

The effects of these disabilities are pervasive, undercutting the efficiency and effectiveness of U.S. armed forces in the formulation of defense strategy, programs, and budgets, as well as in the actual employment of forces in combat. Moreover, the problems are systemic; they are not the result of weaknesses in any one administration or the failures of any particular incumbent. There is an urgent need for measures to eliminate these weaknesses in the joint command and staff apparatus to enable them to provide better cross-service military advice and to execute the integrative functions for which they were conceived. It is to the accomplishment of such reforms that this working group has addressed itself.

BACKGROUND

The current joint military structure consists of three components: the Joint Chiefs of Staff, the Joint Staff, and the unified and specified commanders. All three trace their origins to World War II when pressing needs for cooperation among the sovereign members of the wartime alliance and coordination between the separate military services required the creation of new military organizational arrangements. These new organizations were established, however, without detailed study as to what would be the most effective form of military organization for war. Indeed, the joint structure was not the result of a single decision, but rather evolved over the course of World War II.

At the outbreak of the war, President Franklin D. Roosevelt established the first element of that structure, the Joint Chiefs of Staff, in order to facilitate U.S.-British military cooperation and coordination. The JCS expanded their authority as the war progressed, eventually assuming primary responsibility for setting military strategy and directing military operations.

The second element of the joint military structure, a supporting staff organization for the Joint Chiefs of Staff, came into existence piece by piece beginning in 1942. This forerunner of the Joint Staff was not an independent, multi-service staff responsible directly to the JCS, but rather an interlocking series of more than a dozen joint committees, boards, and agencies, each consisting of service representatives temporarily detailed from service staffs.

Unified operational commands, the final element of the joint structure, were established in each theater during the war. Although intended to facilitate combined-arms operations and planning, the unified commands were arranged such that a single service dominated each. The army controlled the European theater, while the Pacific was divided into two commands—one under army leadership, the other under navy leadership. Moreover, toward the end of the war, the heavy bomber forces in Europe and in the Pacific were constituted as separate operational commands independent of their respective theater commanders. The World War II command arrangements thus resulted in a system in which each of the commands was in effect an operating arm of one of the services.

At the end of the war, several military study groups recommended assigning greater authority to the joint military structure and establishing a single armed forces chief of staff who would preside over the JCS. Despite the support of President Harry S Truman for these recommendations, Congress instead codified the wartime joint military structure with passage of the National Security Act of 1947. The Act established a Joint Chiefs of Staff, consisting of the chiefs of staff of the army and air force, the chief of naval operations, and the chief of staff to the commander-in-chief, to serve as the principal military advisers to the president, the secretary of defense, and the National Security Council. The JCS were granted specific statutory authority to prepare joint strategic and logistical plans, to establish unified commands in strategic areas, and to formulate policies for joint training and education. To assist the JCS in carrying out these responsibilities, Congress authorized the establishment of a Joint Staff of 100 officers. Thus, under the original National Security Act, the JCS continued to operate on the World War II model as a committee of service representatives, without a chairman and with only a small, service-dominated Joint Staff. The JCS also continued to administer and direct the unified operational commands through a system in which one service acted as the executive agent for each command.

The 1947 Act did not end debate over the desirable character and structure of the joint military apparatus. Service dominance of the Joint Chiefs of Staff quickly attracted severe criticism. Most notably, then Secretary of Defense James V. Forrestal, who earlier had opposed creation of a more independent JCS, condemned the inability of the JCS as it existed in 1948 to offer integrated advice on any matter involving important service interests, particularly defense budget issues. To improve the performance of the JCS, Forrestal joined the 1948 Hoover Commission on Organization of the Executive Branch of Government in recommending establishment of the position of chairman of the Joint Chiefs of Staff. Acting to implement this recommendation, President Truman proposed to amend the 1947 Act to establish a JCS chairman, who would replace the corporate JCS as the principal military adviser to the president and secretary of defense. In 1949, Congress agreed to eliminate the post of chief of staff to the commander-in-chief and to establish instead a chairman of the JCS. But Congress did not grant the chairman the authority that Truman had requested. Instead, the corporate JCS remained the principal military advisers and the chairman's authority was limited to presiding over the JCS as a nonvoting member. Accordingly, the creation of the office of the chairman did little to alter the fundamental character of the joint military structure. The structure remained incapable of producing military planning and advice that rose above individual service interests.

President Dwight D. Eisenhower also was intent on reforming the joint military structure, having criticized its performance during the 1952 presidential campaign. Like Truman, Eisenhower sought to reduce service influence by strengthening all three joint actors—the chairman, the Joint Staff, and the CinCs. Eisenhower, however, proposed even more comprehensive reforms than had the Truman administration. In the 1953 Defense Reorganization Plan and the 1958 Defense Reorganization Act, Eisenhower attempted to address the four characteristics of the joint structure that inhibited its performance as an effective integrating force: (1) the chairman's lack of independent authority, (2) the dual and often conflicting functions of the service chiefs as both members of the JCS and military leaders of their services, (3) the dominance of the individual services over the Joint Staff, and (4) the institutional weakness of the unified and specified commanders.

The initial focus of Eisenhower's proposals was to strengthen the authority of the chairman. Toward that end, the 1953 Defense Reorganization Plan granted the chairman authority to manage the Joint Staff and to approve the selection of Joint Staff officers by the JCS. In 1958, Eisenhower sought two additional measures to increase the stature and authority of the chairman. First, he proposed to repeal the provision of the National Security Act that denied the chairman a vote in JCS proceedings. Second, he sought to place the Joint Staff directly under the chairman's control. Eisenhower proposed that the chairman, not the corporate JCS be responsible for assigning the Joint Staff duties and for selecting its director. In enacting these proposals, however, Congress substantially weakened Eisenhower's concept. Specifically, although the Congress repealed the provision denying the chairman a vote on the JCS, it carefully circumscribed his authority over the Joint Staff. Instead of shifting the authority to assign duties to the Joint Staff from the JCS to the chairman, as Eisenhower requested, Congress granted this authority simultaneously to both the chairman and the JCS. Similarly, the chairman was given authority to select the Joint Staff director, but only in consultation with the JCS. Moreover, the chairman's previously unencumbered authority to manage the Joint Staff was qualified with the phrase "on behalf of the Joint Chiefs of Staff."

The chairman thus emerged from the 1958 Defense Reorganization Act with somewhat greater managerial responsibilities, but still lacking the independent authority necessary to ensure that the joint structure produced military planning and advice from a cross-service perspective. As before, the chairman's primary source of authority remained personal, not institutional, deriving largely from the closeness of his relationship with civilian leaders and the force of his personality, not from the powers invested in his office.

Eisenhower also tried to resolve the inherent conflict between the dual roles of the service chiefs as members of the JCS and as military leaders of the separate services. While he rejected proposals to separate the two roles, the president recommended that the workloads of the chiefs as service heads be reduced to allow them to focus on their primary role of providing joint military planning and advice. Accordingly, he requested and Congress granted the service chiefs authority to delegate many of their service duties to their vice chiefs.

Eisenhower's vision of a non-parochial Joint Chiefs of Staff that acted as a unified, multi-service staff to the civilian leadership was never realized, however. The measures that allowed the chiefs greater authority to delegate service functions did not address the central cause of the chiefs' inability to put joint interests over service interests. It was not that a service chief lacked authority to divest himself of service duties, but rather that to do so would threaten his principal source of authority within the service and undermine his stature and power outside of it.

A chief's authority over his service derives substantially from how effectively he represents its interests in external forums, such as the JCS. At the same time, the chief's power and stature within the joint arena comes primarily from the resources and personnel he controls as the military leader of his service. Moreover, in formulating his JCS positions, a chief tends to rely on the staff that works exclusively and directly for him—the service staff, which itself has strong incentives to ensure that important service interests are not sacrificed in joint forums.

Given these organizational dynamics and the fact that a chief has spent most of his military career in service rather than joint assignments, it is difficult for even the most well-intentioned chief to abandon service positions in JCS deliberations. He would not only be inconsistent in opposing a position he was involved in developing, but would also risk losing the loyalty and support of his service as well. Since the 1958 reforms did nothing to alter these organizational incentives, they had little effect on the character or content of JCS decisionmaking.

The third focus of President Eisenhower's defense reforms was the structure and procedures of the Joint Staff. In particular, Eisenhower called for elimination of the Joint Staff committee system, in which representatives of the three military departments reviewed and approved all Joint Staff papers. But compliance with this Eisenhower directive came more in form than in substance. Although the committee system itself was largely eliminated, it was replaced by elaborate staffing procedures that continued to circulate joint papers to the military departments for approval at each level of preparation.

Further, Eisenhower's reforms failed to address the issues created by service control of the selection and advancement of Joint Staff officers. The Joint Staff consisted of officers who were selected by their services, who usually served only a single three-year tour, who had little joint training or experience, who looked to their services for promotions and future assignments, and who were judged largely on how effectively they represented their service's interests. Given this personnel structure, Joint Staff officers have little opportunity or incentive to give priority to cross-service interests. Thus, although the 1958 reforms altered the procedures of the Joint Staff, they did not change its basic character. It continued to serve as an executive secretariat to broker service views, rather than as a unified military staff to offer independent, cross-service judgments.

Eisenhower's reform efforts also addressed the unified operational command structure. The president sought to reduce the uniformed services' grip on the combatant commands by establishing an independent operational command structure that would promote integrated operations. Toward that end, he proposed to establish greater clarity in the division of labor between the military services and the operational commands. Under the reforms adopted in 1958, the military services, organized along traditional distinctions among land, sea, and air warfare, would be responsible for the maintaining functions: recruiting, organizing, training, and equipping the forces. The unified commands, organized geographically, and the specified commands, organized functionally, would command and operate the forces in the field. To underscore this division of labor between maintaining and operating functions, Congress repealed the service chiefs' statutory authority to command operational forces and assigned the unified and specified commanders full operational control of all deployed forces. At the same time, a 1958 directive from the secretary of defense established two command lines: one for operations, the other for administration and support activities. By statute, the operational chain of command runs from the president to the secretary of defense to the unified and specified commanders. The 1958 directive inserted the corporate JCS into the operational chain to advise the secretary and transmit his orders to the commands. The administrative chain of command, on the other hand, runs from the president and secretary of defense to the military service departments and finally to the service components of each of the operational commands.

This statutory division of labor between operating and maintaining functions has never been fulfilled in practice. Despite Eisenhower's reforms, the services have continued to dominate the operating functions in three ways. First, as members of the JCS, the service chiefs are in the operational chain of command—albeit only to advise the secretary and transmit orders to the commands. As the military interface between the secretary of defense and the unified and specified commands, the service chiefs (together with the chairman) have the dominant influence in operational planning and direction.

Second, the services have dominated the commands through their control of the administrative chain of command to the component commands. Although each CinC is invested with full operational authority over the forces under his command, he can exercise that authority only through the service component commands. Moreover, on matters other than operations, such as training, logistics, procurement, and maintenance, the component commanders report directly to their respective service departments, bypassing the CinC altogether. As a result, the individual services effectively determine the composition, structure, and readiness of the forces that the CinCs will lead in military operations.

Third, although the 1958 reforms abolished the system in which each unified and specified command had a service department that acted formally as its executive agent, they did not eliminate the association of each command with an individual service. The three specified commands—the Aerospace Defense Command, the Military Airlift Command, and the Strategic Air Command—are made up solely of air force units. As for the unified commands, the navy effectively controls the Atlantic Command and the Pacific Command, and the army exerts the dominant influence over the European Command, the Southern Command, and the Readiness Command. The newest unified command, the Central Command, originated as the marine-led Rapid Deployment Force, but is now also under army command.

In sum, the 1953 and 1958 reforms of the joint military structure fell far short of President Eisenhower's objective of strengthening joint military institutions sufficiently to provide independent, cross-service military advice, planning, and operational direction. Although the chairman gained more managerial authority, he continued to lack the mandate and tools to act as a strong force for integrating service positions. In particular, the failure of the 1958 reforms to establish the Joint Staff as an independent military staff severely weakened the chairman's effectiveness. Similarly, although the creation of separate chains of command for operations and administration enhanced the influence of the unified and specified commanders, the services still retained the dominant voice in operational decisions. Moreover, Eisenhower's reforms culminated the postwar development of the joint military establishment. The structure that emerged in 1958, with only minor changes, is the one in effect today.

CURRENT PROBLEMS

The working group's fundamental conclusion is that the objectives of President Eisenhower's reforms remain largely unachieved. The United States still lacks joint military institutions that are capable of acting from a broad, cross-service perspective to integrate the special requirements of air, land, sea, and space operations. A strengthened joint military establishment is necessary to perform three essential functions: (1) to provide cross-service military advice to civilian leaders, (2) to develop strategic plans that link military capabilities to national objectives, and (3) to plan and conduct combined-arms military operations. Weaknesses in current joint structures inhibit the effective execution of each of these crucial functions. These weaknesses are of such magnitude that failure to deal with them risks much more than continued waste and inefficiency. We in fact risk military failures that could cost lives and undercut important American interests. The evidence of these risks is so abundant that reform can no longer prudently be postponed.

Advisory Functions

Professional military advice that rises above individual service interests to provide a broader cross-service perspective is an essential ingredient for the effective direction and management of the defense establishment. In all defense activities, from the formulation of overall national security strategy to decisions on the use of armed force, civilian leaders need sound and timely military advice. Today, that advice comes primarily from the services, reflecting their traditions and interests, as well as their expertise. As now organized, the JCS too frequently are unable to provide effective, cross-service advice on issues that affect important
• service interests or prerogatives. These issues include the most important on the JCS agenda: the formulation of national military strategy, the allocation of service roles and missions, revision of the Unified Command Plan, and particularly the allocation of scarce defense resources among competing needs.

Even on questions that do not involve sharp interservice differences, the JCS system has been slow to develop formal positions. Moreover, when joint advice is finally rendered, all too often it is diluted through cumbersome staffing procedures that are designed to accommodate the interests of all four services, rather than seek the best cross-service solutions. Although civilian leaders consistently praise the advice they receive from the individual chiefs of the services, they almost uniformly criticize the institutional products of the JCS as ponderous in presentation, predictably wedded to the status quo, and reactive rather than in-
• novative. As a consequence, civilians have had to fill this void, serving as the major source of advice to the secretary on matters for which concise, independent military inputs would have been preferred.

These shortcomings are neither new nor the product of a single administration. Instead, they reflect weaknesses in the structure of the joint military system itself. Each member of the JCS, except the chairman, faces an inherent conflict between his joint role on the one hand and his responsibility to represent the interests of his service on the other. As the senior military planning and advisory body, the JCS are charged with providing military advice that transcends individual service concerns. At the same time, each chief is the military leader of his service and its primary spokesman to civilian leaders. Although the 1947 National Security

Act mandates that a service chief's joint role should take precedence over his duties as leader of a service, this does not occur in practice—and for good reason. If a chief did not defend service positions in the joint forum, he would lose the support and loyalty of his service, thus destroying his effectiveness.

Because of this fundamental reality, the JCS have constructed an array of Joint Staff procedures for drafting and coordinating documents which ensure that all services pass on every item at several levels. In effect, each service has a veto over every joint recommendation, forcing joint advice toward the level of common assent.

Further, the officers who serve on the Joint Staff have strong incentives to protect the interests of their services in the joint arena. As discussed earlier, Joint Staff officers usually serve only a single tour there, have little previous joint training or experience, and must look to their parent service for promotions and future assignments. Moreover, their performance is judged in large part by how effectively they have represented service interests.

Strategic Planning

Strategic planning, the process linking ends (national objectives established by political authorities) and means (the military forces, weapons, and capabilities developed by the service departments) would also benefit from a stronger and more independent joint military voice. To provide a stable framework for the development of a sound defense program, the military establishment should recommend cross-service priorities on the allocation of scarce defense resources to the civilian leadership.

The inherent conflict between their joint and service responsibilities has precluded the service chiefs from participating effectively in resource planning. As the 1978 Department of Defense Report on the National Military Command Structure (the "Steadman Report") pointed out, a chief's responsibility to manage and lead his service virtually precludes his agreement to joint force planning recommendations that are inconsistent with programs supported by his service. For example, a chief cannot be expected to argue for additional aircraft carriers, army divisions, or air force wings when constructing a service budget and then agree in the joint forum that such programs should be dropped in favor of another service's programs. As a result, the JCS are unable to help civilian leaders set cross-service priorities and make the necessary tradeoffs to construct the defense program and budget. Instead, JCS recommendations are generally limited to endorsing the full program proposed by each military department with little regard to resource constraints.

The chairman is the only member of the JCS who is unconstrained by current service responsibilities. But he lacks both the staff and the statutory mandate to make meaningful strategic planning recommendations on the broad range of subjects required. The recent addition of the Strategic Planning and Resource Analysis Agency (SPRAA) to the Joint Staff increased the chairman's capabilities for strategic planning. But SPRAA, like the rest of the Joint Staff, reports to the JCS as a whole, rather than to the chairman as an individual, and thus lacks an ability to bring an independent cross-service perspective to bear on these issues.

• The absence of an effective joint military voice in the planning and budgeting process has had significant costs. Whenever the capabilities required for effective joint military operations fail to coincide with the core missions of the services involved, significant deficiencies seem inevitable. For example, providing airlift for army forces diverts resources from the core air force missions of strategic bombing and air superiority, just as providing sealift is peripheral to the navy's core mission of controlling the seas. Thus, resources devoted to strategic air and sealift have for many years been inadequate to deploy and sustain combatant forces in accordance with existing contingency plans. The critical realm of command, control, and communications is a further example of the difficulty under present arrangements of gaining adequate priority for joint needs. The individual services are not only reluctant to commit sufficient resources to this essential function, they are unwilling to coordinate their peacetime efforts in a way that would facilitate wartime cooperation. As a result we continue to have major problems of interservice communications which could prove disastrous in conflict. Such military deficiencies are unlikely to be resolved until we have a more effective cross-service perspective in the programming and budgeting processes.

The highly publicized 1984 Army-Air Force agreement on complementary roles and missions is itself an example of the need for changes in the joint system. The necessity for two service chiefs to enter into a voluntary ad hoc agreement on such crucial operational matters is evidence of the ineffectiveness of the joint system in developing such arrangements and bringing about needed revisions in service roles and missions.

Planning and Conducting Military Operations

Finally, the joint military organizations are responsible for planning and conducting military operations. Joint direction of operations is crucial because modern warfare increasingly requires combined-arms operations in which land, sea, and air forces are integrated effectively under a single command. As previously noted, President Eisenhower established in 1958 a division of labor between the military services on the one hand and the unified and specified commands on the other, in order to ensure unified command of operations. But the distinction between maintaining and operating functions has never been achieved in practice. The unified and specified commanders continue to lack adequate peacetime authority over the allocation of resources to their forces and the conduct of operations to carry out their missions effectively.

The National Security Act grants the CinCs "full operational command" over all forces assigned to them, but in peacetime this authority is significantly limited because of the influence retained by the individual services. Within each unified command, there is a component command corresponding to each military department from which forces have been drawn. The unified commander normally exercises operational control only through these component commands, greatly limiting his flexibility and authority. Equally important, on such vital matters as logistical support, training, and maintenance, the component commanders report directly to their respective military departments, leaving the CinCs with only limited and indirect influence.

Several problems derive from the institutional weaknesses of the unified and specified commands. First, the CinCs' lack of influence in the resource allocation process has skewed budget priorities toward the modernization and expansion of the forces at the expense of both our current readiness for war and our ability to sustain high intensity conflict for more than a few weeks. As the operational commanders of all deployed forces, the CinCs are the most committed advocates for allocating resources to readiness and sustainability needs. Nevertheless, although they have some opportunities to articulate their requirements to the JCS and before the Defense Resources Board, they lack a permanent institutional role in the resource allocation process.

Second, the ability of the U.S. military to plan joint operations, from small political-military actions to theater-level campaigns, is inadequate for the kinds of contingencies the nation must expect to face in the future. Insufficient attention has been paid to the development of joint doctrine, the conduct of joint training, the practice of joint planning, and the development of meaningful measures of joint readiness in the combat forces. Moreover, the military educational system, as well as the respective services' career development practices, do little to create and nurture specialists in joint military operations. All of the technological trends of the last half-century have pointed toward a requirement for increased cooperation among forces of different types. Yet the U.S. military establishment remains overly constrained by the artificial divisions among these forces and the shortcomings of the current joint command arrangements.

The failure of the 1979 Iranian hostage rescue operation is a clear example. Forces from the several services were pulled together on an ad hoc basis, operated in unfamiliar configurations under ambiguous command and control arrangements, and organized with insufficient redundancy to handle unexpected attrition. There is widespread recognition among experienced professionals that the moment of incipient hostilities is exactly the wrong time to improvise or adjust to new modes of operations. Yet, inadequacies in the joint planning capabilities of the U.S. Armed Forces—from the Joint Staff down to the level of the joint task force—as well as inadequacies in the joint operational capabilities of the forces themselves, result time after time in lashed-together improvisations that increase the risk of failure.

Third, the operational chain of command suffers from major weaknesses. The individual services are working to implant a military command structure capable of reacting quickly at operational and tactical levels. The rapid pace of global change and the need for competent advice on short notice argue even more demandingly for a comparable capability at the strategic level. It is the judgment of the working group that the United States currently lacks such a capability. In many parts of the world, the operational chain of command is long and unwieldy. This makes for slow and erratic communications up and down the chain. This problem is particularly prevalent in such far-flung unified commands as the European and Pacific commands, each of which contains several sub-unified commands and/or component commands. As a consequence, the lines of military authority and responsibility are often unclear. This inhibits close command supervision by those higher in the chain and obscures the source of trouble when something goes wrong.

Recent events in Lebanon offer a sad but instructive example of flaws in the chain of command, flaws detailed by the Long Commission in its report on what went wrong and why. Effective employment of military forces in combat situations is critically dependent upon rapid responses to orders, clear-cut determinations of responsibility, rapid transmittal of intelligence and operational information from the field, and reliable communications up and down the chain of command. Under present arrangements these essential attributes are difficult or impossible to achieve. As in the case of Lebanon, the chain of command is too lengthy, cumbersome, and clogged by inappropriate interfaces to be able to react quickly and professionally to operational necessities. As a result, responsibilities become blurred, perception of key changes in the situation or in missions and guidance is made more difficult, and the ability of the chain of command to convey important political and military information between the field and the national military and political leadership is degraded. In Lebanon, this meant that although the mission assigned to the marine corps by civilian leaders evolved substantially during the period of the marines' presence ashore, the cumulative impact of numerous small changes in mission and circumstances was not perceived by those in the chain of command. Thus, there was no appropriate alteration of the explicit military instructions given the forces in Lebanon; the marines were left unprepared to deal with the evolving threat and no one in authority took prudent steps to guard against it.

Finally, the current system would have great difficulty managing the transition from peacetime to crisis to war. Those who would operate the forces in wartime are not always the same individuals who control them in peacetime. This is particularly true for the unified commands. The peacetime authority of the unified commander over his forces is limited compared to that of his component commanders. In a crisis or war, however, the unified commanders would have full operational authority, while many—although not all—of the component commanders would play a predominantly logistical and administrative support role.

Accordingly, to prepare for a crisis or a war, the peacetime command structure must change, with the relative influence of the unified commanders rising and that of the component commanders falling. This is exactly the wrong time to manage such a change.

PROPOSED REFORMS

The fundamental source of the problems outlined above is the inability of the joint military institutions to advise or lead in military planning, programming, and operations. We thus propose a series of reforms to bolster the role and influence of all three components of the joint military establishment: the chairman of the Joint Chiefs of Staff, the Joint Staff, and the unified and specified commanders. These reforms will also necessarily affect the roles of the service chiefs. They are designed to assist the secretary of defense to execute his duties more effectively and to provide the horizontal integration and coordination of individual service programs.

The essence of our proposal is fourfold: (1) to give greater authority for rendering military advice to the chairman of the Joint Chiefs of Staff supported by a stronger, more independent Joint Staff; (2) to have the chairman (assisted by the Joint Staff) take the lead in recommending cross-service budget priorities; (3) to augment the authority of the unified and specified commanders to influence the training, composition, equipping, readiness, and sustainability of their forces; and (4) to forge stronger links among the elements of the military command structure, such that the chairman (assisted by a Joint Staff which he selects and directs) can supervise the unified and specified commands effectively and represent their interests in Washington.

These proposals are intended to strengthen the influence of the joint military structure relative to that of the individual services in order to ensure that cross-service military advice and planning is available to civilian leaders and to improve the responsiveness and operational effectiveness of U.S. military forces. Nothing in these measures would undermine civilian control of the military. To the contrary, better professional advice and planning from military leaders would provide civilian officials with a sounder grasp of the implications and likely outcomes of the employment of military forces, thereby enhancing their practical control as a complement to their existing statutory authority. Likewise, more effective control of the deployed forces by the joint military command structure would increase the likelihood that the established policies and orders of civilian leaders will be carried out effectively. In short, the input of senior military officers to the civilian leadership is advice, not decisionmaking; it is clear that better advice and a better capability for carrying out the decisions of civilian leaders can only strengthen civilian control of the military establishment.

We have outlined below, by component, the specific agenda of reforms we think necessary to make the joint military establishment effective. These reforms constitute an integrated system with substantial synergistic benefits. Although each of the reforms independently would help address specific deficiencies, they should be implemented as a package in order to address the structural weaknesses that are at the core of the serious problems the U.S. military establishment faces today.

Chairman of the Joint Chiefs of Staff

As the only member of the JCS without a service portfolio, the chairman is uniquely situated to provide broad and independent military advice that cuts across service boundaries. Our proposal calls for a strengthened chairman with stronger, more experienced staff support and closer links to the other elements of the military command structure. We believe such a chairman would be better able to generate broad strategic alternatives, increase the relevance and mutual compatibility of contingency plans, and—most importantly—integrate the inputs of the uniformed services in planning, programming, and operations. Specifically, we propose the following measures.

Principal Military Adviser.   The National Security Act should be amended to make the chairman the principal military adviser to the president, the secretary of defense, and the National Security Council, supplanting the Joint Chiefs of Staff in the role they now play as a corporate body. The purpose of this provision is not to deny civilian leaders advice from multiple sources, but rather to ensure that they have an additional military perspective not tied directly to an individual service. The service chiefs would continue to provide advice to the service secretaries and to the chairman on all issues, and to the president and secretary of defense on issues of "crucial" national importance. The chairman, however, would have a unique position as the individual who presents an integrated, professional military perspective on all questions.

As the principal military adviser, the chairman would have the authority to offer cross-service advice and recommendations without obtaining unanimous service approval. In this context, the chairman should be required to consult fully with the other members of the JCS in formulating joint military positions. But the current situation in which each individual service has an effective veto on all joint issues would be eliminated. The chairman, supported by the Joint Staff, would have the ultimate responsibility for determining the joint position.

Chain of Command.   The chairman should replace the corporate JCS as the transmitter of orders from the civilian national command authorities to the operational commanders. In addition to clarifying the chain of command by replacing a committee with an individual, this reform would confirm the authority of the chairman as the representative of the operational commanders in Washington. To ensure civilian control, this change could be made by simply revising the 1958 secretary of defense directive that placed the JCS in the chain of command to support the secretary. If the change were to be accomplished by statute, however, it should be drafted in such a way as to avoid limiting in any way the constitutional authority of the president as commander-in-chief of the armed forces.

Role in PPBS. The chairman should play a more active role in the planning, programming, and budgeting system (PPBS) to ensure that civilian leaders are presented with alternative strategies to accomplish national security objectives within realistic fiscal constraints. Specifically, the chairman with the assistance of the Joint Staff should prepare force planning recommendations constrained by realistic projections of future resources, based on policy and fiscal guidance issued by the secretary of defense. The Report of the Working Group on Defense Planning and Resource Allocation addresses the chairman's expanded role in PPBS in much greater detail.

Deputy Chairman. To support the chairman, the National Security Act also should be amended to designate the director of the Joint Staff as the deputy chairman of the JCS. The deputy, who would be a four-star officer chosen from a different service than the chairman, would act for the chairman when the latter was unavailable. Currently, the chairman is the only senior executive—civilian or military—in the Department of Defense without a deputy. Designating the director of the Joint Staff to be deputy chairman would improve continuity in the direction of the joint military apparatus, both in its day-to-day activities and its management of crisis situations. A deputy would also free the chairman to interact more fully with the unified and specified commands in line with his recently legislated role as their spokesman on operational requirements and the even greater expansion of his role proposed in this report.

Joint Staff

The Joint Staff is crucial to this proposal for a more active and independent joint structure in that it would provide the primary support for the chairman. The reforms enumerated below would enhance the effectiveness of the Joint Staff, encourage the most talented officers to seek Joint Staff assignments, and allow them to remain there long enough to operate effectively.

Chairman's Authority. The National Security Act should be amended to provide that the Joint Staff report directly to the chairman, rather than to the corporate JCS. The chairman also should be assigned authority to manage the Joint Staff independent of the JCS.

Joint Speciality. Giving the chairman greater authority over the Joint Staff would only improve cross-service military advice if the military personnel system were also modified so that officers were attracted to, trained for, and rewarded for service in joint positions. Toward this end, we recommend that each service establish a "joint speciality" that selected officers could enter in addition to their traditional service specialties. These officers would be trained at existing joint schools and could spend up to one-half of their subsequent assignments in joint positions—the staffs of the unified and specified commanders, OSD offices and other civilian agencies, as well as the Joint Staff. In this context, it would be necessary to remove the remaining statutory restrictions on Joint Staff tenure and reassignments. To ensure that officers with joint specialties have adequate opportunities for promotion, an officer with a joint specialty should be included on promotion boards for colonels/captains and flag officers.

It is not contemplated that all joint positions would be filled by officers with a joint specialty, but rather that approximately one-half of these positions would continue to be filled by officers from other specialties. We believe that there should be a mix of officers with varied backgrounds and specialties in joint positions to ensure that these staffs do not become isolated or in any sense a general staff. A more detailed description of how a joint career specialty would operate is contained in *The Organization and Functions of the JCS,* a report for the chairman of the Joint Chiefs of Staff prepared by the Chairman's Special Study Group in April 1982.

Internal Procedures.   Joint Staff procedures should be revised to eliminate the necessity for service agreement to Joint Staff papers during any stage of their preparation. The Joint Staff, under the direction of the chairman, should have full control of the content of joint papers without service approval. The services, however, should continue to serve as important sources of information in the development of Joint Staff papers and should be provided opportunities to review and provide comments on them to the chairman.

Service Chiefs

The reforms described above would reduce the time spent on joint matters by the service chiefs, allowing them more time for the management of their respective services. The role of primary adviser would shift to the chairman supported by a stronger and more independent Joint Staff. The service chiefs, however, should retain the right, consistent with their mastery of the details of their own service doctrine and weapon systems, to advise on major issues with significant implications for the service. To ensure that service viewpoints continue to be well represented in joint decisions, we propose the following three measures.

Chairman's Requirement to Consult JCS.   The Joint Chiefs of Staff should continue to meet as a body to review Joint Staff products and advise the chairman. In formulating joint military positions, the chairman should be required to consult fully with the other members of the JCS. This would ensure that the chairman's recommendations to the secretary of defense and the president benefited from the expertise of all the service chiefs and would guarantee that the chiefs were informed of the content of the chairman's recommendations.

Corporate Advice.   On issues of crucial national importance, such as arms control treaties or proposed uses of military force, the chairman should be required to provide civilian leaders with the individual positions of all the service chiefs to the extent that they differ from his recommendation. It is our view that only a handful of the 2,000 issues that the joint military establishment addresses each year would merit such consideration. Although it would be the chairman's responsibility with the approval of the secretary of defense to designate which issues were crucial, the chiefs could influence that designation through the chairman's requirement to consult on all issues. Moreover, the president or the secretary of defense could request the advice of the full JCS on any issue they deemed appropriate.

Right of Dissent.   Because the chairman would no longer be obligated to represent the corporate view of the JCS on all issues, any service chief should have the right to bring his dissent from the chairman's position to the secretary of defense or through the secretary to the president. In addition, the service chiefs would still have the option of presenting their views to civilian leaders through their respective service secretary. Finally, none of the reforms proposed in this report would limit the freedom service chiefs currently enjoy to testify before Congress.

Unified and Specified Commands

The unified and specified commanders are the primary operational commanders of U.S. forces in wartime. To perform this operational role adequately, these commanders require more peacetime authority over the training, readiness, sustainability, composition, and equipping of the forces that they would command in war. Increased CinC influence on these matters is essential if the forces in the field are to be well prepared for combined-arms and multi-service operations. Moreover, it is clear that the ability of the theater commanders to plan such operations is inadequate and must be improved. Necessary reforms can be divided into two areas.

Authority over Component Commands.   Although the National Security Act grants the unified and specified commanders "full operational command" of the forces assigned to the combatant commands, it leaves the definition of that phrase to the JCS. In our view, the JCS have defined "full operational command" too narrowly. The component commanders should not be service representatives with independent authority. Instead, the relationship between a unified commander and his service component commanders should be that of a commander and his deputies for air, land, and sea operations. Specifically, the JCS guidelines that require a CinC to exercise operational command only through the component commands and those that allow the component commander to select subordinate units to perform tasks assigned by the unified commander should be relaxed. Subject to approval by the secretary of defense, the CinC should have the authority to establish the operational chain of command in his theater and to select the units he believes necessary for a given military operation. Moreover, the CinC should be given greater authority in the selection of the members of his own staff.

Training and Readiness.   The influence of the CinC in this area can be improved by increasing his control over three vital resources: money, information, and personnel.

(1) *Money.* The Working Group on Defense Planning and Resource Allocation recommends a major reform in the defense budgeting process, giving the CinCs responsibility for preparing a significant portion of the annual operating budget of the U.S. military establishment. This would allow each CinC to have substantial influence over how operations and maintenance funds are spent in his command, and thus to affect the joint readiness of all the forces in the theater. The chairman would play a crucial role in the coordination and justification of these "readiness budgets." To perform this role, the chairman should be given statutory authority to supervise the unified and specified commands on behalf of the secretary of defense, in addition to his recently enacted authority to act as the CinCs' spokesman on operational requirements.

(2) *Information.* The CinC needs two kinds of information to improve the overall standard of his forces. First, the system of unit readiness reporting must be enhanced and expanded to include criteria related to performance of joint missions. Second, the training plans of the major forces in his theater should be forwarded to the CinC on a regular basis. The CinC should have the right to alter the training plans of the various components under his command to bring them into greater correspondence with one another and to maximize joint training.

(3) *Personnel.* The CinC should have more authority to select his staff and greater influence on their subsequent career advancement. Also, the planning staffs of the CinCs should be strengthened and improved. Establishment of a joint operations specialty in every service, as suggested above, should provide the necessary resources. The connection between the staffs of the unified and specified commanders and the Joint Staff should be tightened so that contingency planning better reflects national policy guidance and resource constraints. In this vein, a continuous flow of personnel between the CinC staffs and the Joint

Staff should be encouraged. Of course, opportunities for actual field experience should not be ignored in this process.

Roles and Missions

The distribution of roles and missions among the services has remained a point of controversy since before World War II. It is widely conceded that the current distribution of roles and missions, incorporated in the 1948 Key West Agreement, has permitted some military missions to be underfunded and others to be executed inefficiently. Both strategic sealift and strategic airlift fall into the • former category. Command and control, close air support, tactical airlift, and strategic nuclear strike forces fall into the latter category. Special operations, including forces for strategically significant raids and hostage rescue missions, have wandered between the two categories. Generally, they receive little attention, but occasionally become the focus of much uncoordinated activity from each service acting independently.

Nevertheless, the working group has refrained from proposing shifts in service roles and missions for two reasons. First, it is our judgment that roles and missions problems loom large because of the failure of the intended principal integrative forces in the command structure—the chairman of the JCS, the Joint Staff, and the CinCs—to deal effectively with them. If these institutions were strengthened as envisioned in this report, they would be in a position to review and act on the roles and missions issues. Additionally, given the pace of technology and the very large number of military problems that the United States could face in the coming decades, the group thought it unwise to recommend major changes in service roles and missions that might convey the illusion of definitive solutions. What is required is adaptability, and the reforms recommended earlier in this paper should help provide it.

The second reason why the working group has eschewed recommendations on redistributing roles and missions is related to the intense political controversy that such proposals inevitably generate. Given the scope of the other reforms recommended by the working group, and the strong possibility that these reforms can resolve many of the current roles and missions problems, it seems unwise to expend much political capital on the issue.

If the reforms recommended in this report cannot be implemented more or less as a package, however, it may be necessary to revisit the roles and missions issue. If the central integrating structure of the U.S. defense establishment cannot be strengthened, it may be wise to consider making the services both "provide" and "employ" U.S. military forces. In such an organization, each service would then require either control or strong influence over all the forces essential to whatever contingencies it had been assigned. This, in turn, would require major changes in roles and missions and perhaps, ultimately, significant restructuring of the services.

CONCLUSION

The reforms outlined above are not revolutionary. They would simply fulfill the intent of President Eisenhower's 1958 reforms by making the Joint Chiefs of Staff system and the unified and specified commanders the primary agents of integration in the military structure. This improved horizontal integration is essential if the U.S. military is to function effectively in the years to come. A strengthened, more independent joint military structure is a necessary, but not a sufficient, condition for improvement in the formulation and execution of defense policy. Reforms in the civilian defense structures, as well as the processes for resource allocation, weapon acquisition, and congressional oversight, are also imperative.

3 REPORT OF THE WORKING GROUP ON DEFENSE PLANNING AND RESOURCE ALLOCATION

Chair: John P. White

Members: Les Aspin   Robert W. Komer
                 Archie D. Barrett ·   Robert C. Moot
               · Antonia Handler Chayes   Robert B. Pirie
                 Edwin A. Deagle   Walter B. Slocombe
                 Andrew J. Goodpaster   Jasper A. Welch
               · Samuel P. Huntington

Rapporteur: William P. Mako

The fundamental conclusion of the working group is that the basic processes by which the Department of Defense formulates policy and allocates resources—particularly the Planning, Programming, and Budgeting System (PPBS)—are in need of a serious overhaul. PPBS has never fulfilled its promise of a multi-year resource allocation process that would proceed deductively from the setting of national defense priorities through the establishment of a multi-year program to the construction of the annual defense budget.

The model of PPBS as a series of interlocking functions, the output of one forming the input of the next, has never been achieved. The planning phase, particularly the joint military contribution, is not satisfactorily grounded in fiscal reality. It consequently produces policy guidance that is unrealistic, ambiguous, imprecise, and thus usually ignored. The programming and budgeting phases are repetitive and concentrate heavily on the first year of the Five-Year Defense Program, all but ignoring the future implications of programmatic and budgetary decisions. Moreover, programming and budgeting decisions are weighted too heavily in favor of modernization and force structure at the expense of sustainability and readiness. In this context, joint priorities are often neglected in favor of individual service priorities. Finally, PPBS lacks an evaluation and implementation phase. There is no systematic means of evaluating progress in implementing approved programs. PPBS is driven by single-year programming and budgeting decisions, which each service negotiates individually with the Office of the Secretary of Defense (OSD), and after the decisions are made, there is inadequate attention to implementation and evaluation.

The working group proposes six actions to restructure the Defense Department's planning and resource allocation systems.

1. *Strengthening* the chairman of the Joint Chiefs of Staff in order to supply what has been the missing element in the planning phase—integrated military advice constrained by realistic estimates of future budgets. To perform this role, the chairman requires the full support of the Joint Staff.
2. *Expanding* the role of the under secretary of defense for policy to include responsibility for program integration on a mission basis. To support him in this expanded role the under secretary's office would include an assistant secretary for each of the three major missions of the Department of Defense: nuclear deterrence, NATO defense, and regional defense.
3. *Merging* the programming and budgeting phases into a combined process that would retain a mission and programmatic orientation, while simultaneously establishing relevant budget inputs—pricing, scheduling, and so forth.
4. *Giving* the unified and specified commanders a larger institutional role within this merged program/budget process. Specifically, they would act with the chairman and the Joint Staff to prepare an independent program/budget request for the operational expenses of their commands.

5. *Establishing* a third under secretary of defense with broad policy oversight responsibilities for functions related to the readiness and sustainability of the operational forces.
6. *Adding* a fourth phase, evaluation, to the Planning, Programming, and Budgeting System. In this context, the Defense Department's accounting system would have to be updated to permit programming, budgeting, and execution to be done on a unified basis. This would allow decisionmakers to assess program outputs and accomplishments against given levels of resource inputs.

We also recommend shifting the defense budget process to a biennial cycle. We have not, however, included this issue in our report because the Working Group on the Congressional Defense Budget Process has addressed it at length.

BACKGROUND

World War II demonstrated what subsequent military encounters have confirmed: separate land, sea, and air warfare is gone forever. Modern warfare requires not only unity of operational command, but also unified and coordinated processes for strategic planning, force development, and resource allocation. Accordingly, since World War II, the United States has made a series of organizational and process changes to integrate its defense establishment more tightly.

U.S. military integration has clearly followed an evolutionary, rather than a revolutionary, development. Radical realignments, such as disestablishing the military departments or creating a multi-service general staff, were rejected during the postwar controversy over unification of the services and have since received little support in Congress or the executive branch. Instead, greater integration of the defense establishment has been achieved by complementing and balancing the service departments with two central structures, one civilian and the other military. On the civilian side, a central organization has been built around the secretary of defense, who has supplanted the individual service secretaries as the primary civilian authority in the department. On the uniformed side, a joint military structure was created, which includes the Joint Chiefs of Staff, the Joint Staff, and the unified and specified commands. The evolution of these two central structures dominates the history of American defense organization since World War II. This history has had two major phases: a period of structural reform that culminated in 1958 and a period of process reform that spans the years from 1958 to the present.

Between 1947 and 1958, four major reorganizations created and gradually expanded the role of the new central civilian management structure and the joint military structure. The National Security Act of 1947 established the position of secretary of defense with a mandate to exercise general direction, authority, and control over the activities of the defense establishment. In 1947, this establishment consisted of three executive departments headed by cabinet-level secretaries—the Department of the Army, the Department of the Navy, and the newly created Department of the Air Force. The 1947 Act also formally recognized the existence of the Joint Chiefs of Staff, which had been operating since 1942.

In 1949, Congress amended the Act to establish the Department of Defense (DoD) and to enlarge the Office of the Secretary of Defense (OSD) to include a deputy secretary and three assistant secretaries. At the same time, the Departments of the Army, Navy, and Air Force lost their cabinet rank, as Congress reduced them from executive departments to military departments—but with the proviso that they be separately administered. The 1949 amendments also created the position of chairman of the Joint Chiefs of Staff but endowed its occupant with only the authority to preside over JCS meetings as a nonvoting member.

President Dwight D. Eisenhower made further changes in the defense establishment in 1953, under the provisions of a 1949 law that gave the president authority to reorganize the executive branch subject to congressional veto. Eisenhower abolished several of the interservice boards, assigning their authority to the secretary of defense. To carry out these new functions, six additional assistant secretary positions and a general counsel of equivalent rank were added to the Office of the Secretary of Defense.

The structural reform of the Department of Defense culminated with Eisenhower's second major reorganization: the 1958 amendments to the National Security Act. Eisenhower's proposed changes had three broad objectives. First, he sought to clarify beyond doubt the authority of the secretary of defense. Thus, the 1949 requirement that the military services be "separately administered" was reduced to "separately organized." The 1958 amendments also granted the secretary of defense authority to coordinate all weapon research and development and to establish defense agencies to perform common service and support functions. Lastly, Eisenhower recommended that the Congress alter its procedures and appropriate all defense funds to the secretary of defense, rather than directly to the military departments. The Congress initiated the new procedure with the FY-1960 budget.

Eisenhower's second objective was to improve the quality of joint military advice to civilian leaders by granting more authority to the chairman of the Joint Chiefs of Staff, in particular giving the chairman full authority over the Joint Staff. Eisenhower also sought to increase the size of the Joint Staff. Congress raised the statutory limit on the Joint Staff from 210 to 400 but refused to grant the chairman the independent authority Eisenhower requested. The 1958 amendments limited the chairman's authority over the Joint Staff to managing it on behalf of the JCS and assigning it duties jointly with the JCS. Without independent authority and staff, JCS chairmen have been unable to impose a unified, national perspective on JCS analyses and recommendations. The chairman's role has been limited to brokering compromises that reflect each service's individual interests.

Finally, Eisenhower sought to ensure unified operational command by separating the combatant commands from the services. Specifically, he proposed and Congress enacted a new division of labor between the services and the combatant commands. The services, organized along traditional distinctions among air, land, and sea warfare, would perform the maintaining functions of recruiting, organizing, training, and equipping the armed forces. The unified and specified commands, organized along geographic and functional divisions, would operate and lead the forces in the field.

In line with this new military division of labor, two chains of command were established. The administrative chain of command ran from the president to the secretary of defense to the military departments and then to the individual service components of each unified or specified command. The operational chain of command ran directly from the president and secretary of defense to the unified and specified commanders, with the JCS acting as the secretary's military staff for operations. The allocation of operating funds, however, did not follow the change in operating command. Instead, the secretary of defense, with his new authority for all defense funds, elected to continue the allocation of operating funds down the administrative chain, thus effectively hobbling the ability of the commanders in the field to provide leadership commensurate with their new responsibilities.

The current defense structure remains essentially the same as that enacted in 1958. This is not to say that the defense establishment has remained static, but rather that the changes made since 1958 have focused instead on management procedures, particularly the resource allocation process.

Prior to 1961, the individual military departments prepared their budgets with relatively little program guidance from the secretary of defense, whose role was limited to issuing broad functional guidelines to the service departments and reviewing their budget requests. When the total of the individual service budgets exceeded the department's ceiling, across-the-board cuts were usually made to attain the requisite lower figure. The secretary had little capability—and, in most cases, little inclination—to review the programmatic aspects of the military department's budget submissions.

This approach to resource allocation had several often-noted weaknesses. Annual budget decisions were largely unconnected to plans and programs that were mission-oriented and multi-year in their focus. The budget process concentrated almost exclusively on the upcoming year, despite the considerable consequences current decisions had for future years, and looked at matters in functional terms—personnel, procurement, research, and so forth. Operating programs were developed by the "maintaining" departments, not by the operational commands. Moreover, the services prepared their budgets largely independent of one another, giving little priority to joint programs or the support needs of the other services. The secretary of defense had little analytic capability either to make choices among competing service program proposals or to ensure that the separate service programs fit overall national strategic priorities.

Determined to be a more active participant in making budget and force structure decisions, Secretary of Defense Robert McNamara instituted the Planning,
Programming, and Budgeting System (PPBS) in 1961. PPBS divided the resource allocation process into three phases. The planning phase was intended to
♦ provide an integrated overview of U.S. defense priorities to guide the development of programs. The programming phase sought to evaluate specific alternatives in each mission area and establish a multi-year program (five-year defense
plan) for meeting those priorities. The budgeting phase was then intended to be
limited to the more precise pricing and timing of the first year of the approved
program. To provide the analytical staff necessary to evaluate alternatives and
review service plans, McNamara established the Office of Systems Analysis within
the Office of the Secretary of Defense.

Despite McNamara's efforts, program and budget decisions remained largely
divorced from formal plans. Overall national planning was either absent or too
general to be useful. Within the Department of Defense, long-term strategic
planning remained the province of the Joint Chiefs of Staff. Their recommendations, however, were of limited value because they were unconstrained by
realistic fiscal guidelines and represented only a compilation of the recommendations of the individual services, not an integrated plan to achieve U.S. security
♦ goals. In practice, the planning and programming phases were combined in the
Draft Presidential Memoranda (DPM) that the Systems Analysis Office prepared for the major force programs in the five-year plan. The DPMs laid out
military objectives, set forth a strategy, and analyzed alternative program choices
for meeting that strategy. After approval by the secretary of defense, the DPMs
became the basis for the services' budget requests. As before, the services controlled the resources and budgets for the operational commands.

Although subsequent secretaries of defense have not sought to exercise
McNamara's degree of detailed control over the defense program and budget,
PPBS has remained the framework for defense resource allocation decisions. The
basic elements of the system—three phases, program and budget guidance to the
services from the secretary, and the use of quantitative analysis to choose among
competing programs—have been retained, both by secretaries whose management philosophies favored centralized control and direction, and by those who
preferred a more decentralized approach. But the roles of the participants in the
processes, as well as the processes themselves, have evolved substantially since
McNamara's tenure as secretary of defense.

Melvin Laird, who became secretary of defense in 1969, made the first significant changes in PPBS. He abolished the DPMs and shifted the initiative for
program development back to the services. The Systems Analysis Office (later
renamed Program Analysis and Evaluation) no longer originated independent
program proposals but reviewed those the military services put forward in their
Program Objective Memoranda (POMs). Laird also issued program guidance
and multi-year budget ceilings for development of the service five-year programs.
These changes have become permanent features of PPBS.

The type of programmatic guidance provided to the services by OSD and the rigor of OSD's review of service proposals has varied with the management styles of subsequent secretaries of defense. The secretaries of defense in the Nixon and Ford administrations tended to follow Laird's model of decentralized management, whereas Harold Brown, President Carter's secretary of defense, assigned OSD a more active role.

Whatever the management style of the secretary, however, the JCS consistently has had little influence in any aspect of PPBS because it has been unable to provide military advice that recognized the reality of fiscal constraints. Without the ability to set priorities or make hard choices among services or programs, their input has remained of limited value.

Following the recommendation of the 1979 Defense Resource Management Study (chaired by Donald B. Rice), Secretary of Defense Brown formed the Defense Resources Board (DRB) chaired by the deputy secretary and including relevant under and assistant secretaries, as well as the JCS chairman. As conceived in the Rice study, the DRB was to review major programs, resolve the lesser issues, and identify those issues that deserved the secretary's attention. Over the course of the Carter administration, the DRB took an increasingly active role in deciding major programmatic and budgetary issues.

The Reagan administration made two significant changes in the functioning of the DRB. First, it not only used the DRB to examine resource allocation issues, but made it the primary decisionmaking body for the entire defense resource allocation process. Second, it has expanded both the membership and the scope of the DRB. Membership has been increased to include the service secretaries, in order to ensure representation of service viewpoints and to reduce appeals of DRB decisions. (Service chiefs also attend DRB meetings, but not as members.) Additionally, the commanders-in-chief of the unified and specified commands meet with the DRB semiannually to outline their operational needs.

Despite the numerous changes made over the years, structure and management processes of the Department of Defense are still deficient in several respects. Neither the structural reforms of the 1940s and 1950s, nor the procedural reforms of the 1960s, 1970s, or 1980s have attained their objectives fully. The basic organizational model contained in the National Security Act of 1947, as amended, has not been achieved in practice. The dominant organizations in the Department of Defense are the central civilian management (the secretary and his staff) and the uniformed military services. The latter exercise preponderant influence over both elements of the joint military structure: the Joint Chiefs of Staff system and the unified and specified commands. Neither an effective joint military perspective nor independent military advice is offered in the planning and resource allocation processes. Although there have been some notable exceptions, the civilian service secretaries generally exercise limited influence over their respective services and, in addition, have little impact on the decisions of the central civilian management. Accordingly, issues regarding both maintaining and operating functions are resolved between the Office of the Secretary of Defense and the leaders of the uniformed services. The joint military structure and the civilian service secretaries are only secondary players in both types of issues. In particular, the authority and responsibility for the operating functions assigned to the unified and specified commanders have not been augmented by authority over the allocation of resources to forces under their command.

These structural imbalances adversely affect each phase of the Planning, Programming, and Budgeting System. Below we examine each phase of PPBS, emphasizing the problems we consider most serious and proposing structural and procedural reforms to correct them.

STRATEGIC PLANNING

In the view of the working group, a major weakness of the U.S. national security machinery has been its inability to establish and adhere to a coherent defense
• strategy, especially in the conventional area. As a consequence, strategic priorities are often ill-defined and military means are inadequately linked to policy ends.

In theory, the model of the strategy-formulation process is straightforward.
• First, the president acting through the National Security Council (NSC) apparatus establishes the political objectives for which the United States would risk conflict or employ armed force. Second, the president and the NSC set priorities among those objectives and match them with the most effective means—military or otherwise—for their achievement. Finally, the Defense Department should prepare programs and budgets to generate the military capabilities necessary to execute the strategy within established resource constraints.
• In practice, this model is simply not workable. Strategies are seldom, if ever, formulated in such an explicit or rigorous form. Moreover, potential military needs will always exceed available resources; therefore, an iterative process that balances goals and priorities with available resources must be pursued. But even this practical iterative approach has not been developed.
• There are many and varied causes for the failure of the nation's leaders to formulate a clear strategy that would provide meaningful programmatic direction. Our highest political leaders have consistently seen potential political and
• foreign policy liabilities in being too specific. A detailed, clearly stated strategy must exclude, by necessity, some foreign policy objectives or military capabilities that have domestic and international consequence. If trouble breaks out in an area the strategy has excluded (witness Korea in 1950), presidents fear being held accountable for the results. Finally, presidents simply have limited time to devote to the details of formulating a strategy and translating it into even the
• broadest defense priorities. As a consequence, strategic guidance has been limited in most cases to very general objectives—deterring nuclear war, containing Soviet expansion, and maintaining treaty commitments.

The working group recognizes that reform of the structures and processes of the Defense Department cannot address the broad political and foreign policy sources of these strategic planning problems. Nevertheless, we believe that two organizational deficiencies within DoD contribute to these planning inadequacies: (1) the lack of integrated, cross-service military advice and (2) the gap • between the strategic purposes of the Department and the organizational structure of the Office of the Secretary of Defense.

Inadequate Cross-Service Military Advice

The military establishment does not provide broad strategic alternatives that are adequately formulated for civilian consideration. Nor do civilian leaders receive relevant, timely, and unambiguous military advice from a cross-service perspective when considering alternative priorities and policies within fiscal constraints.

Currently, the primary JCS contribution to the Defense Department planning • process is the Joint Strategic Planning Document (JSPD). The JSPD, which initiates the planning cycle in PPBS, defines the scope of the military threat and recommends a force to meet that threat. The JSPD, however, is not a resource-constrained document. Accordingly, its recommended force structure is much larger than the United States can sustain within peacetime defense budgets. Although the JSPD has value as a benchmark to assess the risks inherent in adopting smaller force structures, it contributes little to the programming and budgeting processes since it makes no recommendations as to the tradeoffs necessary to construct the annual defense program within established budgetary contraints.

These problems clearly derive from the JCS system, not the individual military officers who serve in it. Civilian leaders have consistently expressed satisfaction with the advice they receive from JCS members individually. But both civilian decisionmakers and senior military officers have sharply criticized the formal position papers of the JCS—their institutional product—as ponderous in presentation, predictably wedded to the status quo, and reactive rather than innovative. More important, the JCS have often been unable to act at all on issues that run close to important service interests or prerogatives. Paramount among these issues are the establishment of defense priorities and the allocation of defense resources.

These deficiencies in the JCS system have a common source. The rules, procedures, and structures of the Joint Chiefs of Staff and the Joint Staff institutionalize the overriding goal of the military services to preserve their independence of action. The National Security Act, as amended, intended the joint organizations to be the principal military agents of integration. Instead, as the Working Group on Military Command Structure explains in more detail, an independent, cross-service perspective has been lacking because of service dominance over the views and loyalties of the JCS members themselves and

Joint Staff procedures that give each service an effective veto over all recommendations. Each service chief is put in the untenable position of having to be both an advocate, defending his own service interests and programs, and a judge, providing advice to civilian leaders from a broader, department-wide perspective. The chairman is less subject to this institutional conflict, but he lacks the staff and the authority to provide integrated, cross-service advice to civilian decisionmakers. Institutional constraints also prevent the Joint Staff from operating as an independent military staff. Instead, it is essentially a committee of service representatives operating under procedures that seek positions that all members will accept.

OSD Organization

Accordingly, the Office of the Secretary of Defense has had to assume primary responsibility for ensuring that defense planning is linked to subsequent programming and budgeting decisions. But OSD is poorly organized to perform this crucial function effectively. First, planning is separated from programming and budgeting within OSD. The under secretary of defense for policy has responsibility for preparing the Defense Guidance, which is the major planning document in PPBS. But the responsibility for ensuring that service programs conform to the guidance lies elsewhere, with the office of Program Analysis and Evaluation and the assorted functional offices in OSD, such as research and engineering, manpower, and acquisition and logistics.

This organizational separation of planning from programming and budgeting is exacerbated by a second, perhaps more serious, problem: the large gap between OSD's structural configuration and the major strategic purposes of the Department of Defense. The dominant organizations in OSD are oriented along functional lines: research and engineering, manpower, health affairs, and so forth. OSD thus has a very limited capability to support the secretary in integrating the separate service programs in major mission areas. At the broadest levels, most strategists would agree that the United States has three major missions: (1) strategic deterrence—that is, to deter nuclear attacks on the United States and its allies; (2) NATO defense—that is, to deter and, if necessary, defend against an attack on European allies; and (3) regional defense and maritime superiority—that is, to control the seas when needed and to project U.S. forces where necessary to defend vital interests in other parts of the world, notably Northeast Asia and the Middle East/Persian Gulf area.

The most striking deficiency in the current OSD organization is the absence of senior officials or single offices with overall responsibilities for any one of these three strategic missions. Individual officials and offices are responsible for parts of each mission, while the under secretary for policy has a general responsibility for all the missions. OSD has individual officials responsible for research and engineering, command and control issues, and even for health affairs. But the secretary of defense lacks a senior aide with responsibility for strategic deterrence, for NATO defense, or for regional defense and maritime superiority. Even though these are the major strategic purposes of American defense policy, they are virtually the only important interests without institutional representation in the Department of Defense.

This limited organizational ability to integrate the overall defense effort along mission lines contributes to the disconnection of planning from programming and budgeting. OSD has not been satisfactorily able to translate strategic planning guidance into defense resource priorities. This is not to say that OSD does not influence allocation decisions; it does. But instead of establishing general policy guidelines and monitoring their implementation, OSD relies on detailed involvement in individual programming and budgeting decisions to produce an overall military plan inferentially.

The imbalance in OSD organization between functional and mission emphasis has also contributed to the inadequate recognition of coalition factors in the defense planning and allocation processes. Any optimum strategy must explicitly take into account the contributions of U.S. allies and examine burden-sharing tradeoffs between U.S. and allied resource allocations. With the exception of the short-lived establishment of a high-level adviser on NATO affairs in the late 1970s, the Department of Defense has lacked senior officials oriented to coalition planning.

Costs of Planning Weaknesses

The inability of the U.S. military establishment to provide integrated, timely, and useful advice has combined with the gap between OSD's structure and the department's strategic purposes to produce significant weaknesses in the U.S. strategy-formulation process. These weaknesses have political and military costs that the nation can ill afford.

The first of these costs is the so-called strategy-forces mismatch, in which U.S. declaratory policy on the use of force consistently outruns U.S. military capabilities. Given the global interests of the United States, it is not surprising that our foreign policy goals and interests exceed our available military power. As a result, difficult choices and tradeoffs must be made in planning and developing U.S. military forces. Our declaratory policy will, and probably should, exceed our ability to apply military power. To do otherwise would needlessly forgo important national interests. But a sound strategy that provides direction and priorities to our military planners is essential. The lack of a clear strategy and purpose for our defense establishment undermines the confidence of our allies, reduces public support for defense spending, and may weaken our ability to deter aggressive acts on the part of potential enemies.

Second, the absence of a comprehensive, joint military strategy contributes to the development of suboptimal and disjointed military strategies by the individual services. The military services require a clear strategy and priorities on which to base their plans. The lack of such direction gives each service the latitude to spend money according to its own priorities. Since the resources available in peacetime can seldom address all the nation's security needs, the service priorities are always defensible. Nevertheless, lacking strategic guidance with a national perspective, the service-determined plans are often inconsistent, neglect some essential military requirements, and direct scarce resources away from higher priority uses.

Finally, the lack of overall, mission-oriented guidance for allocating defense resources among competing claimants results in poor force planning. There are no sound criteria for saying either "no" or "enough." This contributes to an excessive number of new program starts, resulting in more weapon systems being developed and produced than can be sustained efficiently within peacetime budgets.

Recommendations.

1. The Joint Strategic Planning Document (JSPD) should include fiscally constrained force planning recommendations prepared by the chairman of the Joint Chiefs of Staff with the assistance of the Joint Staff.
2. The role of the under secretary of defense for policy should be expanded to include responsibility for program integration on a mission basis. To support him in this role, the under secretary's office should include an assistant secretary for each of the three major missions: nuclear deterrence, NATO and North Atlantic defense, and regional defense.

Improved Cross-Service Planning

The working group believes that if the planning advice of the joint military structure is to be meaningful, it must be constrained by realistic estimates of future resource availability. Accordingly, the JSPD should propose forces that can be supported within the fiscal guidance established by the president and secretary of defense. In this manner, civilian decisionmakers would receive integrated, cross-service advice on the tradeoffs required by limited defense resources. These resource-constrained recommendations should be additions to, not replacements for, the comprehensive and unconstrained assessments of U.S. defense needs that the JSPD already contains. The working group sees value in retaining the unconstrained planning force as a baseline to judge the risks of fiscally constrained forces.

It is the judgment of the working group that the Joint Chiefs of Staff, as presently constituted, are not able to provide integrated, resource-constrained planning input. The service chiefs cannot be expected both to defend and to judge their service programs and priorities. Accordingly, we recommend a new division of labor in the joint military structure. The service chiefs should concentrate on constructing and justifying their service programs, in the context of the guidance provided by the secretary of defense. The chairman should be made responsible for formulating the JSPD's new fiscally constrained program recom- • mendations. The chairman should also provide advice to the secretary and the Defense Resources' Board on the adequacy of service programs in meeting overall national military priorities. To give the chairman the necessary statutory authority, the National Security Act should be amended to provide the chairman with specific authority to offer independent military advice.

In this context, it should be noted that this working group has limited its recommendations on the JCS system to the resource allocation process. Questions about whether the chairman needs further authority or should exercise a broader role in other areas are addressed by the Working Group on Military Command Structure, which is examining all JCS issues in more depth. To provide the chairman with staff support for these new duties, the working group recommends that the Joint Staff be placed under the exclusive authority of the chairman. Concomitantly, the Joint Staff should be organized as an independent military staff, abandoning the elaborate procedures for coordinating all documents with each service at multiple levels.

Restructured OSD

To strengthen the link between national defense planning and resource allocation decisions, we recommend that the office of the under secretary of defense for policy be realigned and its responsibilities expanded to include program integration on a mission basis. Such an expansion would constitute a logical extension of the under secretary's current responsibilities, which include the integration of defense plans and policies with overall national security objectives. In essence, we propose extending these integrative responsibilities to include programmatic and budgetary decisions. The under secretary for policy • would retain responsibility for coordinating preparation of the Defense Guidance, but would assume greater authority in the program and budget review phases of PPBS.

To support the under secretary in this expanded role, we propose that three assistant secretaries be established with broad responsibilities for each of the major strategic missions of the department: nuclear deterrence, NATO and North Atlantic defense, regional defense. The principal objective of this realignment would be to connect mission-oriented defense planning to the force development and acquisition processes. Each of the mission-oriented assistant secretaries would have responsibility for coordinating all Department of Defense activities related to a specific strategic purpose. These would include long-range planning, as well as force development and operational planning.

The specific division of labor between the three assistant secretaries might be defined in a variety of ways. We envision that the assistant secretary for nuclear deterrence would have cognizance over all strategic offensive and defensive forces, as well as all missions in space. The nuclear deterrence office also would coordinate the department's efforts regarding strategic arms control negotiations.

The assistant secretary for NATO and North Atlantic defense would be generally responsible for issues connected with European defense, including both U.S. conventional forces and theater nuclear forces allocated to that purpose. It would take the lead in mobilization planning, since the requirements for a major contingency in Europe dominate decisions on that process. Finally, the assistant secretary for NATO would develop Department of Defense positions on arms control negotiations involving nuclear and conventional forces in Europe.

The assistant secretary for regional defense would have responsibility for overseeing plans and programs for military contingencies in East Asia, the Middle East/Persian Gulf area, Latin America, and other Third World regions. This office would also have responsibility for coordinating military assistance programs for these regions. Most counterinsurgency and special operations forces would fall within the purview of this office.

To carry out their functions, the mission-oriented assistant secretaries would require staffs trained to oversee the translation of policy into force requirements, programs, and budgets. The objective would be to enable the policy office to ensure that the secretary's goals and priorities were reflected in the programs of the individual military departments. Under this scheme, the offices of the assistant secretaries for international security policy and for international security affairs would be abolished, all of their functions being absorbed by the three new mission-oriented assistant secretaries. This realignment, however, would not undercut the basic responsibility of the under secretary of defense for research and engineering to oversee the development of weapons and equipment. Nor would it reduce the need for an effective program analysis and evaluation (PA&E) staff to coordinate the department's analytic and programming efforts on behalf of the secretary.

In some ways, the establishment of a strengthened and mission-oriented office of the under secretary for policy follows from developments already underway in the department. Over the past 25 years, the ability of the secretary of defense to integrate the plans and programs of the military departments has been enhanced with the additions of the offices of program analysis and evaluation, net assessment and the under secretary for policy. Moreover, during the Carter administration, the secretary had an adviser for NATO affairs. In the Reagan administration, the assistant secretary for international security affairs has been generally responsible for matters concerning the Third World, while the assistant secretary for international security policy has handled NATO matters, strategic forces, and arms control negotiations.

Continuing this evolution toward establishing offices in OSD at a relatively senior level that have broad responsibilities for the major strategic missions of the department would have several important benefits. By closing the gap that exists between strategic purpose and organizational structure, the realignment along mission lines should reduce micromanagement by OSD by focusing the staff on the major strategic issues, allowing greater delegation of the details of program management to the individual services.

The assistant secretaries for the three strategic missions clearly would compete with each other for resources to perform their missions. This competition, however, would be constructive, because it would concentrate attention on the crucial issues of priority among the core missions of the department. Similarly, the existing rivalries between the services would be channeled along more constructive lines—competing to develop the most cost-effective ways to achieve the strategic missions. In other words, the services would continue to do all they do today, but their activities would be directed to objectives more clearly related to national purposes. Finally, the establishment of assistant secretaries of defense with regional responsibilities—for NATO and North Atlantic defense and for regional defense—should promote more explicit consideration of potential allied contributions and burden-sharing tradeoffs both in drafting the Defense Guidance and the subsequent construction of the defense program.

The working group considered proposals that would restructure OSD further, aligning all its functions under three mission-oriented under secretaries. We concluded, however, that such a proposal might make it more difficult for the secretary of defense to deal effectively with other government agencies and lead to duplicated efforts within the department. More important, we see a continued need for strong, department-wide oversight in functional areas, such as manpower and research and engineering. Accordingly, we believe that a hybrid OSD structure would be most effective, with the under secretary for policy oriented along mission lines and the rest of OSD focusing on specific functional areas.

PROGRAMMING AND BUDGETING

Role of Operational Commanders

The Department of Defense has not followed the basic management principle that responsibility, authority, and resources should flow through the same channel. Military operational command flows from the president to the secretary of defense through the JCS to the unified and specified commanders (CinCs). Resources, however, flow through the military departments to the individual service components of the operational commands. The CinCs, who command all deployed U.S. armed forces, have little influence in the resource allocation process. As a consequence, their budgetary priorities—which tend to focus on readiness, sustainability, and mobility—are slighted in favor of service priorities for larger force structures and more weapons.

Although the CinCs have opportunities to articulate their requirements to the JCS and the Defense Resources Board personally, they lack an institutional role in the resource allocation process. The Program Objective Memoranda (POMs) prepared by the services are the basis for the program and budget review and the primary military recommendations that are constrained by realistic projections of available resources. The CinCs have little influence on the POMs. Inputs to each service POM regarding the needs of the operational forces come not from the CinCs, but from the service components in each command. The CinCs thus have little opportunity to consider tradeoffs among the operating needs of their service components. Moreover, the budgetary request for readiness and sustainability funds that the component commands submit must compete at the service level with requests for modernization programs and expanded force structures. The individual services typically have tended to favor modernization and expanded force structure over readiness and sustainability in making the initial program tradeoffs.

In short, despite the fact that they command all deployed U.S. armed forces, the unified and specified commanders lack adequate authority because they do not have an institutional role in the resource allocation process. They lack control over the resources of their component commands and do not have the ability to determine and monitor the levels of readiness and sustainability for their forces.

Recommendation.

The unified and specified commanders, acting with the chairman and the Joint Staff, should prepare an independent program and budget for the operational resources of the forces within their commands.

The division of the Department of Defense into force-maintaining and force-employment structures should be reflected in defense programming and budgeting. Accordingly, the working group recommends that a separate program and budget be established for the operational forces, submitted by the unified and specified commanders under the direction of the JCS chairman.

Under this proposal, each service would continue to produce its program and budget for procurement, research and development, training, and associated operations and personnel costs. The service programs and budgets, however, would not include the in-theater costs of the service component commands of the unified and specified commands. Instead, a separate readiness program and budget would include such items as operations and maintenance, military construction, and family housing for the unified and specified commands.

The development of the readiness program and budget would parallel that of the service programs and budgets and be based on program and budget guidance from the secretary of defense. The specified commands and the service components of the unified commands would prepare program/budget submissions.

These submissions, however, would not go to the military departments. Instead, the unified commanders would review and approve their subordinate commands' submissions, and then the submissions of the nine unified and specified commanders would go to the Joint Staff. This would initiate the third step in which the Joint Staff would prepare an integrated readiness program and budget submission for review and approval by the chairman. The Joint Staff would have to be expanded to handle this new duty, but service military staffs could be reduced commensurately, because their program and budget submissions would now exclude these functions. Finally, the readiness program and budget would be sent forward for OSD review at the same time and under the same procedures as the service programs and budgets. Any program/budget changes that resulted from review by the DRB and the secretary of defense would be staffed back down the same system.

Within the DRB and later before Congress, the chairman, supported by the Joint Staff, would represent the interests of the unified and specified commands. Accordingly, the working group supports the recent amendments to the National Security Act that made the chairman the CinCs' representative on resource allocation issues.

In terms of the congressional budget structure, it would be necessary to establish an account for unified and specified commands under each relevant appropriations category. Funds would be appropriated to these accounts to cover all of the costs of the unified and specified commands as included in the readiness budget. Finally, the chairman would allocate funds to the CinCs, who in turn would sub-allot funds to their component commands.

Oversight of Readiness and Sustainability

In 1977, the Department of Defense sought to locate responsibility for policy matters concerning the provisioning, supply, and support functions of the armed services under a single OSD official, the assistant secretary for manpower, reserve affairs, and logistics. The objective was to establish an official below the secretary of defense who could integrate the large number of related policies that affect the readiness and sustainability of the combatant commands. This objective was never fully achieved, however. Congress insisted that the assistant secretary for health affairs continue to report directly to the secretary of defense rather than through the assistant secretary for manpower, reserve affairs, and logistics. Subsequently, Congress created another special interest office within OSD with the establishment of a separate assistant secretary for reserve affairs. Finally, the department recently established a separate assistant secretary for acquisition and logistics.

The result of these developments is that OSD oversight of the functions that support military operations is broken up among several assistant secretaries, with integration too often forced up to the level of the secretary of defense. As a result, the secretary is faced with making the many detailed tradeoffs and rationalizations necessary among these areas—a time-consuming task that he simply cannot perform effectively in view of the many other demands on his time. Moreover, creation of these additional assistant secretaries has led to an even larger OSD staff, created new coordination problems, and further stretched the secretary of defense's already too broad span of control.

The lack of a high-ranking OSD official with responsibilities for oversight of readiness and sustainability has also contributed to the inadequate attention given these operational concerns. Since the primary role of the military departments is to recruit, train, and equip the forces, their natural institutional bias is to elevate force structure priorities of modernization and expansion above operational concerns of readiness and sustainability. We believe that responsibility for operational support functions within OSD must be less fragmented in order to ensure that balanced tradeoffs are made between force structure and operational concerns.

Recommendation.

A third under secretary of defense for manpower and readiness should be established with broad policy oversight responsibilities for functions related to the readiness and sustainability of the operational forces.

This new office would oversee the various functions related to the provisioning, supply, and support of the operational forces. These functions would include manpower, installations, logistics, reserve affairs, and health affairs. In organizational terms, we recommend the retention of the assistant secretary for manpower, with the proviso that he report to the secretary of defense through the new under secretary. If the assistant secretaries for health affairs and for reserve affairs are retained (which we do not recommend), they also should report through the new under secretary rather than directly to the secretary of defense. With regard to the new assistant secretary for acquisition and logistics, we take no position on the desirability of separating procurement from research and engineering. We do believe, however, that responsibility for installations and logistics should be shifted from the acquisition office to the new under secretary for manpower and readiness.

We believe that creating a new under secretary for manpower and readiness is an essential complement to our earlier proposal for the CinCs to play a larger role in the programming and budgeting processes. The under secretary for manpower and readiness will have the mandate and capability to review the expanded inputs from the CinCs for the secretary and ensure that the approved recommendations are reflected in the department's program and budget.

• Finally, as will be discussed in a later section, we recommend that program evaluation receive far greater emphasis than it currently does. Pulling together the various OSD offices that focus on operational support functions would provide an institutional sponsor for many of these expanded evaluation capabilities.

Disjunctures Between Programming and Budgeting

The rationale for the division of the resource allocation process into three identifiable phases (planning, programming, and budgeting) rests in large part on the concept that the programming process would serve to translate military plans into specific budget requests. In practice, however, programming and budgeting have evolved into competing, rather than complementary, processes.

As originally intended, the programming phase was to be the forum where senior decisionmakers would evaluate alternative programs and approve a rolling five-year defense plan (FYDP). The budgeting phase would then be limited to costing out the first year of the approved program in detail. Instead, the budgeting phase has developed into a separate decisionmaking process, in which many of the issues ostensibly decided in the programming phase are reopened in the budget phase. In cases where the secretary has been heavily involved in the programming phase, major decisions often survive throughout the subsequent budget review. But even when the secretary makes a firm decision, major issues are frequently raised again during the budget phase. For less visible issues, decisions made during the programming phase often are changed significantly at budget time, even when the underlying conditions supporting the original decision remained unchanged. This pattern of revisiting programming decisions in the budgeting phase effectively undermines the programming process, wasting much effort by senior civilian and military officials and destroying the overall integrity of the process.

The wasted effort that results from competing programming and budgeting processes is exacerbated by recurrent gaps between the overall fiscal levels used to guide the preparation of the defense program and the actual level of funds Congress eventually appropriates. In fact, there are three so-called fiscal gaps.

The first fiscal gap is between the numbers forecast for the second through fifth years of the five-year defense plan (the outyears) and the budgets Congress finally approves for those years. As a consequence of overly optimistic assumptions regarding both future budgetary levels and program costs, more programs are packed into the FYDP than can be funded fully when each outyear becomes the budget year. Given the virtual political impossibility of terminating a major program after it has entered full-scale development, the overflow is accommodated by stretching out development and production schedules and reducing the number of weapons purchased for all programs. The result of these practices is often higher unit costs, inadequate quantities of crucial weapon systems, and the slower introduction of current technologies into U.S. combat forces than might otherwise be possible.

The second fiscal gap is between the fiscal guidance assumed by the Defense Department at the beginning of the annual program cycle in the spring and the actual fiscal guidance the Office of Management and Budget (OMB) provides late in the fall when the budget is finally constructed. When the department negotiates with OMB, it tends to adopt a very aggressive stance, seeking high fiscal guidance in order to accommodate as many programs as possible. Although the department does not know in the spring what the actual guidance will be, it does know that its planning number is probably on the high side. Having put together a program under optimistic assumptions, however, the Defense Department is faced in the fall with cutting back programs to meet the OMB budget mark.

This problem is compounded by the fact that the Defense Department programs funds in different terms than it budgets and allocates them, and the link between the two processes is inadequate. Programs are developed in terms that emphasize their outputs or missions, such as strategic nuclear forces or airlift. In contrast, budgets are formulated in terms of inputs or resources, such as personnel, operations and maintenance, and procurement. The FYDP, which arrays each of the major force programs in terms of its budget inputs, is intended to be the crosswalk between the programming and budgeting phases. It is not sufficiently flexible or detailed, however, to permit officials to translate readily between budgets and programs. As a result, it is difficult for decisionmakers to evaluate the longer-term program implications of the inevitable budget cuts that take place toward the end of the process.

The third fiscal gap results from differences between the budget the president submits and the actual funds Congress authorizes and appropriates. In part, this problem is inherent in the constitutional separation of powers; the legislative branch can and should assess the president's budget request in light of its own assessment of budgetary priorities. Still, in practice, the congressional budget reviews have become so repetitive and detailed as to cause excessive reprogramming of funds and frequent readjustment of production schedules. Such budgetary instability lengthens the acquisition cycle, raises the cost of defense programs, and undermines the value of multi-year defense plans.

Recommendation.

Merge programming and budgeting into a combined process that retains a program and mission orientation, but simultaneously establishes relevant budget inputs.

To promote the matching of resource inputs to program outputs and the linking of both to defense objectives and missions, the working group recommends integrating programming and budgeting procedures. Under this proposal, the programming and budgeting phases would be merged at each stage of the process: (1) the issuance of guidance by the secretary of defense, (2) the preparation of program and budget requests by the military departments, and (3) the review of those requests by OSD. The mechanical adjustments needed to unify programming and budgeting will have to be set forth in some detail, but the general prescription is clear: to put programming and budgeting in the same, consistent context with a common, uniformly interpreted nomenclature.

This proposal contemplates programmers and budgeters acting in a coordinated fashion in preparing and reviewing the unified program/budget requests. The institutional machinery for this cooperation already exists. DRB membership includes all relevant officials, and the three military departments currently have the equivalent of program/budget review committees with constant membership. This machinery, however, will require a revised budget format in which each appropriation justification includes matching program and resource data:

1. The national goals and OSD program objectives being supported.
2. The force units or activities being funded, and their relation to goals and objectives.
3. The performance measures for tracking progress toward program objectives.
4. Planned outcomes, in terms of quantitative performance measures and resources consumed.
5. Interservice support.
6. Outyear funding requirements.
7. Current and past-year performance and resource consumption.
8. Resources used and requested, expressed in standard appropriation terms.

The intent of this justification framework is to develop program and budget requirements up through service and command channels so that the integration begins at the operational level and remains integrated throughout the process.

Merging programming and budgeting would make the defense resource allocation system more efficient by reducing repetitive decisions. It also would provide greater constancy to program decisions. Moreover, merging programming and budgeting should help alleviate the problems caused by gaps between the fiscal guidance used to prepare the program and the final budget that the president submits to Congress. Considerations involving fiscal policy and the state of the economy dictate that the president will not make final decisions on the size of the defense budget until shortly before it must be submitted to Congress. Merging programming and budgeting would accommodate rather than seek to reverse this imperative. With budget inputs integrated into program categories, defense decisionmakers would be able to evaluate better the ramifications of late adjustments in the defense budget total. Similarly, the program impact of congressional alterations in the president's budget would be understood better. This, in turn, would reduce the likelihood that these budgetary adjustments would unbalance the program.

The case for merging the programming and budgeting process is compelling under the current system. The merger would be even more necessary, however, if the earlier proposals for enhancing the roles of the Joint Chiefs of Staff and the operational commanders in the resource allocation process are adopted. These proposals would add important new players to already overtaxed programming and budgeting processes. By merging the two processes along the lines described above, PPBS should be sufficiently streamlined to absorb these new inputs effectively.

EVALUATION

- Evaluation is the orphan function in the current resource allocation process. Insufficient attention has been devoted to program evaluation and to the review and feedback procedures necessary for such evaluation. In theory, PPBS should
- be a circular process with accounting and performance data from one cycle serving as the planning base for the earlier phases of the next cycle. In practice, PPBS essentially starts fresh each year, with little systematic attention given to the evaluation of past program decisions. Major weapon programs that have high congressional visibility are an exception to this generalization, in that their cost and performance tend to be monitored more closely. But PPBS has never included an explicit and comprehensive system for measuring and reporting progress in implementing approved programs. Perhaps the best example of this problem is the failure over many years and administrations to carry out planned programs to enhance readiness and improve our sustaining capability.

Adoption of more comprehensive and systematic evaluation systems is hindered by several problems. First, the Defense Department accounting base is inadequate to support effective evaluation. DoD financial reports provide a mass of information, but the financial data in these reports are inconsistent, incomplete, and untimely. The source of many of the problems is the department's reliance on accounting systems that operate almost exclusively on an obligation basis. Under this system, an economic event is measured when the resources are "obligated"— that is, when orders are placed or contracts awarded.

This emphasis on obligational authority is understandable in terms of DoD's fiduciary responsibilities, since Congress grants obligational authority in approving the defense budget. Obligation-based information, however, does not provide an adequate financial picture of the Defense Department's activities for decisionmaking or for monitoring implementation. The effect of the current accounting system is to focus all attention on the purchase of new assets and the obligations to be incurred during the current year, rather than on the total resources used and costs applied over a longer period. In other words, controls are at the point of purchase or order placement, with little or no subsequent monitoring of the effective use of the resources being acquired.

Obligation-based accounting also skews the process by which the Defense Department estimates the prospective costs of new weapons. This process is based largely on a parametric pricing system, which forecasts the cost of a new system by using the historical costs of similar items adjusted to account for design changes, assumptions about the economy, and a few other variables. Since an obligation-based accounting system does not record costs as resources are consumed, it cannot provide complete and current costs to form the basis for parametric pricing. Instead, weapons-cost estimators must rely on contractor estimates and cost submissions for the historical cost base. When this cost base is inaccurate, as has often been the case, cost estimates for new programs are inaccurate and cost overruns will be inevitable.

Obligation-based financial information also distorts the evaluation of program effectiveness and management performance. Generally, program inputs in terms of obligations are not comparable to program outputs until the program is completed. For example, the entire cost of a navy ship may be obligated in the first year, but the ship will not be completed for seven years. An obligation-based accounting system records the entire cost in that first year and does not monitor how those resources are expended over the seven-year building cycle. In short, obligation-based input/output comparisons are misleading and cannot provide a rational basis for evaluating programs.

Evaluation of program implementation is blocked by a second problem: the poor linkage between the programming process and the budgeting and accounting process. As was noted in the programming/budgeting section, programming is done in terms of outputs (forces and missions), while budgeting and accounting are done in terms of inputs (appropriations categories); there is no satisfactory bridge between the two. The audits, reviews, and evaluations that do take place focus on inputs, assessing variations from planned obligation and outlay rates. This type of fiscal accounting, oriented to fiduciary responsibilities, does not provide adequate measures of the effectiveness with which programs are executed. Program decisions are generally based on comparisons of estimated capabilities associated with alternative resource allocation decisions. But reporting systems tied to budget input categories provide relatively meager reflections of the actual defense capabilities purchased.

A third obstacle to effective program evaluation is the lack of sophisticated management information systems. There are areas, such as recruiting and retention, in which the Defense Department has developed effective management information systems. But there are numerous instances in which such systems are either incomplete or nonexistent. For example, there is no integrated system to measure equipment maintenance requirements and activity at various echelons. Accordingly, it is difficult to measure backlogs accurately or to determine whether excess capacity exists.

The lack of integrated performance measures is particularly severe with respect to combat readiness. There are many detailed reports on the operational readiness and warfighting capabilities of U.S. combat forces, but these reports focus on unit, rather than joint theater or command-wide, capabilities. Not only are these reports conducted and routed through service channels, but the services use differing standards to measure unit readiness. Accordingly, senior decisionmakers have no systematic measures of readiness and must rely entirely on the personal judgment of the operational commanders and the chairman of the Joint Chiefs of Staff.

Better feedback is needed to monitor program execution and to make appropriate adjustments to past decisions. The lack of a systematic evaluation system denies decisionmakers the ability to assess program outputs and accomplishments against given resource inputs. Financial and management reports are not tailored to produce the kinds and levels of information on program outputs that would enable management to relate achievements to goals and objectives.

Recommendations. Evaluation should be the fourth phase of the Planning, Programming, and Budgeting System. In this context, the working group recommends three specific reforms:

- Conduct programming, budgeting, and execution processes within a unified accounting structure.
- Supplement the current obligation-based accounting system with reporting on an accrual basis.
- Improve management information systems to enable decisionmakers to evaluate progress toward identified objectives.

The Department of Defense requires an explicit evaluation process that systematically reviews the progress made in implementing programs and introduces that information into subsequent planning, programming, and budgeting phases. This evaluation system would, in effect, be a fourth phase of PPBS that would complete the allocation cycle, linking goals and objectives to performance standards.

Much of the value of merging programming and budgeting would be lost without parallel improvements in the accounting system. The new system should record the use of resources in the same manner as they are planned, programmed, and budgeted. In this way, the reported status of the current year's programs and budgets could provide the performance and cost basis for decisions in the planning cycle for future years. In addition, the system could readily track changes in the projected total cost of programs, thereby contributing to future planning.

The underpinning of the revised accounting system, its chart of accounts, must be an updated and expanded program element structure. Program elements are the basic building blocks of the defense budget—planes, tanks, ships, army divisions, and so forth. Under the working group's proposal, this structure would be redefined and expanded to include the full scope of resource inputs, program outputs, and performance measures. Each element or account would be defined precisely and included in an authoritative chart of accounts that OSD would issue for use throughout the resource management process.

The Defense Department also needs to update and improve its accounting system in order to provide complete, accurate, and timely cost information to decisionmakers. Specifically, the accounting system must record the use of resources on an accrual as well as an obligational basis. The accrual basis has four benefits that are not available with obligation based methods:

- *It provides a basis for input/output comparisons.* The accrual basis measures inputs in terms of resources consumed to provide an output. Therefore, input/output relationships may be formulated, budgeted, and monitored in terms of actual results. This type of information is critical for accurately evaluating programs and program managers.
- *It provides a basis for forecasting costs of future weapons programs.* By recording costs when resources are consumed, accrual accounting methods would supply the Defense Department with a better historical cost base on which to conduct the parametric pricing system.
- *It focuses decisions in terms of total resource usage.* Under the accrual basis, the consumption of resources paid for in prior and future years is considered in annual budgeted program costs. Therefore, an annual accrual budget lays out a plan for using existing resources as well as those that will be acquired currently. This is a far more comprehensive approach to managing defense resources.
- *It measures financial position.* Financial position refers to the resources required to pay for past activities that have not yet been funded and the resources available for that purpose. This information is critical when evaluating the long-range effect of programs.

The accrual basis is the most comprehensive method to budget and account for federal programs. Cash basis and obligations basis information is also important for management of cash, debt, and outstanding orders. Cash and obligations alone, however, do not provide the means to monitor financial position or the use of available resources. Their use is also limited in evaluating program effectiveness.

Finally, the Defense Department should adopt comprehensive management information systems in order to assess performance in such crucial areas as equipment maintenance and combat readiness. Since these systems will have to be individually tailored to specific program needs, the details of their implementation are beyond the scope of the working group.

4 REPORT OF THE WORKING GROUP ON WEAPONS ACQUISITION

Chair: Jacques S. Gansler

Members: Robert Art
                 Eugene J. D'Ambrosio
                 Dale Church
                 John Ford
                 Ronald Fox
                 Rowland Freeman
                 Dave McCurdy
                 Joseph Shea
                 Marvin Stern
                 George Sylvester
                 Robert F. Trimble
                 Robert Wertheim

Rapporteur: Janne Nolan

INTRODUCTION

Historically, national security policy and programs have been left largely to "experts." However, with growing popular awareness of the threat of nuclear war, with hundreds of billions of dollars now being spent annually for defense in peacetime, and with the widespread perception that the United States is no longer the single dominant military power in the world, there has come increasing public involvement in, and dissatisfaction with, national security policy and budget making. If the nation is simultaneously to "get its money's worth" from resources allocated to defense, strengthen national security, and develop public confidence in the Department of Defense, four adverse trends in weapons acquisition must be addressed.

The first of these is *increasing concern about the choice of weapon systems themselves*. There is a perception that the existing institutional structure does not provide for the selection and development of the most cost-effective weapons. The extensive debates over the MX missile and the B-1 bomber typify this concern. The issue was not whether these weapon systems were desirable but, rather, whether they represented the best way (among many possible alternatives) to enhance the nation's security. Similarly, there has been much debate—but, again, no clear consensus—over the priorities for expanding the current force structure: whether a 600-ship navy, more army units, or more air force fighter wings should have highest priority. These questions of strategy, and the resultant weapon selections, are compounded by interservice rivalry for resources and still further complicated by the opportunities for revolutionary changes in force structure that are offered by technological change. Moreover, proposals for dramatic technological change often fall into an ambiguous region between traditional service identities, leaving the technology without a strong institutional sponsor. For example, theoretically at least, the navy could carry out its mission of sea control with reconnaissance satellites and land-based missiles. But such concepts are so foreign to traditional notions of naval operations that they receive little attention.[1] Instead, we continue to concentrate on building improved versions of traditional platforms—ships, planes, and tanks.

Further, the armed services insist that each item of equipment be the best possible. This contributes to the second of the adverse trends—namely, *rapid growth in the cost of defense equipment*. The United States has kept its military equipment at the forefront of the technological state-of-the-art, but the cost of this increasing performance has been increases of around 6 percent per year in the price of each unit, even after adjusting for inflation and the higher unit price associated with the lower quantities typically purchased now.[2] The cost of a single ship is currently measured in hundreds of millions and even billions of dollars, an individual plane in the tens or even hundreds of millions, and an individual tank in the millions. Accordingly, if real unit costs continue to rise at past rates, the nation will be able to buy fewer and fewer weapon systems each year under any realistic projection of resources likely to be available for defense.

Recognizing the difficulty of buying enough weapons within the dollars available, the armed forces historically have been optimistic in estimating the likely cost of these weapon systems when first requesting funds for their development. Their hope has been either that costs will in fact be unexpectedly low or that more money will become available in the future. More cynically, some suggest that unrealistically low cost estimates reflect a bureaucratic tactic whose purpose is to get the development program started, deferring the problem of how to pay for it. Indeed, as weapons are actually developed and procured, far too often their actual costs have been significantly higher than the initial estimates. This program cost growth historically has averaged between 50 and 100 percent of the original cost estimate of each weapon system.[3]

Naturally, if there are only a certain number of dollars available for buying a given system and its costs double, we can only afford to buy half as many. Thus, although the United States has been buying extremely capable weapon systems, the total result of cost growth from generation to generation and between initial estimates and final price tags has been fewer and fewer systems bought each year. For example, in the 1950s the United States bought around 3,000 fighter planes each year; in the 1960s, the number purchased declined to 1,000 per year; and in the 1970s, the figure was only 300 fighter planes per year. (Norm Augustine has pointed out that, by the year 2054, a continuation of this trend would result in our building one fighter plane per year.)[4] There is, however, a minimum quantity of weapon systems that is absolutely crucial to the successful completion of any military mission, especially as the Soviet Union has been steadily improving the quality of its weapons, while still maintaining equipment stocks and production rates that are very high by American standards. Thus, these cost-induced reductions in the quantity of U.S. weapon purchases could be devastating.

The increasing cost of U.S. weapon systems also adds to the third of the undesirable acquisition trends—namely, a *lengthening of the acquisition cycle*, the time required to move from the initiation of development through to the completion of production. Part of this lengthening is due to the increasing complexity of modern weapon systems, but two more important causes are (1) stretch-outs resulting from an increasingly burdensome and indecisive managerial and budgeting process, and (2) stretch-outs resulting from cost growths and budget reductions. It used to take five to seven years to acquire a weapon system, but new systems now often take twelve or even fifteen years to move from exploratory development to initial deployments in the field. Even after development is complete, the high costs of each weapon mean that only a few can be purchased per year, so that the deployment of any significant number is delayed still further. An added effect of lengthened acquisition cycles is reduced efficiency in the acquisition process and, therefore, still greater unit costs and still lower quantities. Thus, the lengthening acquisition cycle has a compound military effect. First, it results in a decline in America's technological advantage over the Soviets, since most of the systems deployed in the field are older designs; and, second, the longer cycle itself causes higher costs and, therefore, reduced quantities.

Adding to these undesirable weapon system acquisition trends, and to a considerable extent being caused by them, is the fourth of the adverse trends—*worsening problems in the U.S. defense industrial base*. With the long-term decline in rates of production, one would expect to see the industrial base drying up. In fact, during the shrinkage in defense procurements in the early 1970s (the annual procurement account dropped from $44 billion to $17 billion, at constant prices, from 1969 to 1975), the large prime contractors remained in business by building equipment at very low rates (e.g., one aircraft per month in an extreme case), while suppliers of parts and subcontractors were allowed simply to disappear.

A series of reports in 1980 all indicated significant problems in the U.S. defense industrial base.[5] These studies identified areas of substantial inefficiency for normal operations in peacetime, as well as critical bottlenecks (e.g., in selected critical parts and production equipment), such that there was almost a total lack of capability to respond to any emergency condition with a surge in production. For example, it was reported that it would take over three years for an existing aircraft production line to increase its output significantly.

Reversing these four undesirable acquisition trends can be accomplished neither quickly nor easily. The complexity and magnitude of the defense acquisition system does not lend itself to simple solutions. Rather, correcting these problems requires the implementation of broad reforms; in effect, "cultural changes" in the way the Defense Department does its business are needed. Yet, these must be accomplished without destroying those current management practices that are constructive. The latter is a point that must not be overlooked. In contrast to the general tone of public debate, the Department of Defense is generally believed by professionals in the procurement business to be one of the best managed government agencies. Numerous studies have shown that defense cost overruns are generally lower than those of comparable programs managed by other federal and state agencies.[7] There is little question, however, that there is much room for improvement. If Americans are to get the maximum military capability for each dollar they allocate to defense, the need for such improvements is urgent.

REQUIRED AREAS OF CHANGE

Four broad sets of changes are required to reverse the undesirable trends in the Department of Defense's acquisition practices. In priority order, these are:

- 1. *JCS Reform* The establishment of an improved joint military mechanism for allocating resources over the long term and for developing weapon system requirements.
- 2. *Budget Reforms* The development of means to import greater stability in programs and budgets.

3. **Procurement Reforms** The placement of greater emphasis on acquisition techniques (incentives) that can help to drive down the cost of weapon systems.
4. **Industrial Revitalization** The placement of greater emphasis on the importance of the health and responsiveness of the defense industrial base.

Obviously, there is a strong interrelationship among these four recommendations, and thus synergistic benefits would result from the implementation of all four changes. It is, however, equally important to note that each type of reform faces political obstacles to implementation, and thus there might be a tendency to try only the easier—and less significant—parts of each. Therefore, it again must be emphasized that without all four of these interdependent and broad structural changes, the system would likely remain in its current deficient state.

Improved Methods to Allocate Resources and Set Requirements

At present, weapons and other equipment are selected almost solely by each military service acting independently. The army, navy, air force, and marines each choose the systems that appear best suited for their unique historical missions, according to their own perceptions of requirements. Thus, the armed services design the structures of their forces as if they intended to fight *independent* land, sea, air, and amphibious wars. For example, during the Grenada operation of 1983, the fact that the radios of different services operate differently inhibited direct communications among them during the conflict. Most military experts agree that future battles will be fought with integrated forces, so clearly weapons and equipment should be selected to complement one another and to maximize the combined capabilities of the armed forces.

Unfortunately, those who have the responsibility for planning how wars will be fought—the Joint Chiefs of Staff and the commanders of the unified and specified commands (CinCs)—do not develop weapon requirements, approve the selection of weapon systems, or establish priorities for resource expenditures among the various competing demands. Thus, the Office of the Secretary of Defense, with frequent advice from the Congress, has assumed the responsibility for imposing some coherence upon the uncoordinated procurement programs of individual services.

In the opinion of this working group, the people responsible for planning for war (not the individual services) must be given a greater voice in determining the overall distribution of military resources, setting individual weapon requirements, and selecting the systems to be acquired. Specifically, the chairman of the Joint Chiefs of Staff should be made responsible for developing a long-range, integrated defense resources plan—with appropriate guidance and oversight from the secretary of defense, and with the assistance of the CinCs, the services, and the defense agencies. (The inputs from the CinCs are particularly important in helping to achieve the proper balance between resources allocated to maintain the readiness of the forces to fight and resources used to modernize or expand the force structure.)

The chairman would recommend to the secretary of defense a long-range strategy and budget—with an allocation of dollars to specific mission areas, including explicit quantity/quality tradeoffs, and with recommendations for the relative allocations to force modernization and force readiness. This long-range plan would conform with and respond to the national security objectives that were established by the Congress, the president, and the National Security Council. The secretary of defense would provide both fiscal and policy guidance; it is essential that the long-range strategy and resource plan be established within realistic fiscal projections. The secretary of defense also would review, approve, and oversee the implementation of the long-range plan. Such a plan would tie weapon acquisition decisions more closely to national security strategy. It also would help to direct defense resources toward satisfying military missions with the most effective weapon systems and efficient force structures, all with due consideration to the posture and equipment of U.S. allies. The services could then concentrate their efforts on recruiting, organizing, and training people, and equipping the forces.

To implement this change, the current Joint Staff should report to a strengthened chairman of the Joint Chiefs (rather than to the JCS as a corporate body) and should assume a role more independent of the services, as President Eisenhower proposed in 1958. With these changes, the Office of the Secretary of Defense could then return to its proper emphasis on policy and oversight.[8]

Greater Program and Budget Stability

The second broad change required to achieve the full benefit of dollars allocated to defense is to impart greater stability to the defense programming and budgeting process. The United States is one of the few nations in the world, if not the only one, to operate its defense establishment on an annual budget cycle. Single-year defense budgets encourage the services, the administration, and the Congress to meet annual total budget limits by stretching out purchases of individual weapons over several years—a far less difficult action than actually cutting an entire weapon program. Such stretch-outs are shortsighted, as they force contractors to produce equipment at inefficient rates of production, causing higher unit costs and the overall procurement of fewer systems. For example, the three-year production stretch-out of the F-15 aircraft in the mid 1970s resulted in a two billion dollar increase in program costs (excluding the effects of inflation). Eighty-three fewer fighter aircraft were purchased than would have been possible—for the same dollars—had the original plan been adhered to.[9]

Congress could make a significant contribution to controlling procurement costs by adopting a multi-year defense budget.[10] Two- or three-year budget cycles would introduce the greater stability necessary for contractors to plan more efficient production rates and lower the unit costs of new systems. Furthermore, the stability of multi-year budgeting would encourage the application of multi-year procurement contracts—a far more efficient technique. Finally, and most important, multi-year budgets would encourage the Defense Department and the Congress to consider more carefully the long-term fiscal and strategic implications of procurement decisions. Naturally, multi-year budgets could be reviewed annually for changes in world conditions.

It should be noted that the Congress' annual budget resolutions actually have three-year budgets contained in them, but only the first year is binding on the executive branch, while the second two are considered "targets." Making these outyear targets binding as nominal budgets, with the president permitted to submit amendments as the economic picture changed, would introduce a major element of the needed stability without requiring radical changes in procedures.

A second beneficial congressional reform would be to reduce the number of committees that are involved in the defense budget process. In 1983, Defense Department witnesses testified on the 1984 budget before ninety-six committees and subcommittees; 1,306 witnesses provided 2,160 hours of testimony. These redundant hearings are time consuming (for both defense management—civilian and military—and for the Congress) and focus excessive attention on the details of the budget, rather than on broader policy issues. Additionally, the many small changes that result from this process introduce great instabilities into defense programs and uncertainties about future funding levels and schedules. An air force study estimated that savings of 20 percent could be achieved, after a few years' time, by stabilizing the defense budget;[11] congressional reforms would help to make these savings possible.

The Defense Department itself also could help achieve greater budget stability. The department might begin by recognizing how much it hurts itself by not making realistic total program cost estimates. Historically, the cost associated with the uncertainty of developing new weapons incorporating advanced technologies has not been included in most initial program estimates; potential price tags look more attractive without these contingency dollars. This is a problem throughout the various levels of the Defense Department, as well as in the Congress. There is no question, however, that there are major uncertainties in the development of weapon programs and that factors to cover these risks must be included if costs are to be estimated realistically. (This is basically a management issue, not a cost-estimating issue.) It must be emphasized that realistic program cost estimates are critical to the achievement of stability in the defense acquisition process. Of course, once having established realistic total program budgets, it is equally important to adhere to them strictly. As a complementary need, affordability analyses must be completed, based on realistic estimates of the total budgetary resources that will be available in the future, since even a well-planned and well-run program cannot succeed unless the dollars are available to fund it. Naturally, if realistic program cost estimates were used, it would result in fewer programs in the total budget than currently exist. Each of the programs that survived, however, could be managed more efficiently and, in the end, more equipment could be procured for the same amount of money.

Three techniques that should be used in establishing long-term, stable programs are:

1. Start a full-scale development program only if the technology already has been demonstrated, firm requirements have been established, and relevant operational concepts have been settled.
2. Recognize that, historically, a commitment to full-scale development has been a commitment to production. There have been no programs cancelled by the services, and very few cancelled by any other authority subsequent to a decision to begin full-scale development. Thus, any program plan and associated affordability analysis should be based not only on development costs, but also on the assumption that the system will enter production on a timely schedule and at efficient production rates. The intelligent, low-risk, well-planned use of "concurrency" (i.e., some overlap between development and initial production) may actually save money by making possible a smooth transition from development into production.
3. The Defense Department should be provided with greater reprogramming authority to permit necessary managerial flexibility, including an ability to reprogram among funding categories. But this authority should only be provided within broad mission areas and for programs that have been fully authorized. In this way, the Congress could review budgetary requests on the basis of both new programs and requirements for different mission areas, but the executive branch could better manage the programs within these broad categories.

If these three techniques were utilized—as complements to the major stability thrusts of multi-year budgets and realistic program cost estimates—cost growth would be far smaller and risks could be minimized.

Incentives to Reduce Costs

Turning to the third of the broad acquisition reforms that would be desirable, we come to specific procurement reforms, the types of measures with which most discussions of "getting more bang for the buck" normally start. In the opinion of the working group, to make any progress in improving the efficiency and effectiveness of the defense procurement system, one cannot begin with a new set of detailed regulations intended to control costs in the unique defense market. Rather, progress must begin by changing the cultural environment. Specifically, *incentives* for improved performance must be created for individuals involved in the acquisition process, both in the government and in industry. Directives requiring lower costs cannot achieve their objectives; incentives encouraging lower cost systems can make a difference.

The working group recommends eight specific techniques toward this end. In the interest of space, the techniques are noted briefly. Quantitative backup data are available from members of the group.

1. Enhanced Professionalism Since experienced government managers are crucial to the successful acquisition of new, multibillion dollar, high-technology, high-risk weapon systems, incentives must be created for the retention and, especially, the promotion of effective military and civilian personnel in the agencies that manage the acquisition process. Currently, this is largely not the case, although the air force has made some significant strides in this area recently. Until the personnel system is reformed, it will be difficult to get and keep the most capable people in the acquisition process.

2. Continuous Alternatives In the nondefense world, the maintenance of some form of continuous alternative (e.g., competition between two suppliers for the same product or between two different products for the same mission) is normal practice. Such competition provides continual incentives for lowering costs and improving performance. The Department of Defense must design measures to shift from its current mode—a single competition for the initial award of a development program, with subsequent sole-source contracts for procurement of the product throughout its lifetime—to some form of continuous competition. Although this technique is not always practical, it should always be considered and efforts made for its achievement. Where it is not possible at the weapon system level, then it should be used for critical subsystems. Studies have shown that when the Defense Department has acted to promote continuous competition, average program cost savings of 25 to 30 percent have been realized along with significant performance improvements.[12]

3. Profit Obviously, industry is motivated to enhance its profit margins. The Defense Department, however, follows the unproductive practice of negotiating a contractor's profit margin each year regardless of how its costs in prior years have compared to stated plans. In fact, on production programs the base used is that of the previous year's cost; as the profit margin, expressed as a relative term, tends to remain constant, the higher the costs, the higher the profit. A better approach would be for the government to allow a higher profit margin in subsequent years if costs fell below those that had been expected in prior years. Thus, if costs rose one year, the contractor would receive a smaller profit the next year; but if costs fell in one year, the contractor could be assured that his profit margin would rise in negotiations for next year's contract.

4. Price Elasticity   The military services' incentives to achieve lower costs could be enhanced by a policy that permitted the services to buy larger quantities or improve the performance of those particular systems for which unit costs fell below expectations. In short, part of the cost savings would be returned to the services for the acquisition of greater military capabilities. This is not now the case. If costs are reduced, the relevant program office now loses the money. Instead, savings could be used to improve the performance of systems (e.g., through increased reliability testing), to buy more of them, or to pay for needed product modifications. This (price elasticity) technique was tried successfully by former Secretary of Defense James R. Schlesinger when he offered the air force a choice between a larger number of the lower-cost F-16 aircraft or a smaller number of the more expensive F-15s.

5. Baselining   Another technique to reduce costs would be for each service to establish an internal "contract" on each program that specified performance parameters, annual budgets, quantities, schedule, support plans, and so forth. If this contract were signed at a high level—for example, the secretary of the service—and rigidly adhered to, program managers would know precisely to what they were committed. Historically, such contracts have existed only rarely, although the air force has recently implemented this technique. (For example, the air force is now trying to discipline itself to operate within the $20 billion estimate for 100 B-1B aircraft.) Normally, the government changes its mind frequently on both program requirements and budgets, which creates great turmoil and instability in the programs and allows industry to renegotiate contract costs. Baselining would tend to reduce this turbulence and thus to control costs. However, the concept can only work if the government's program manager is given sufficient authority to reject changes suggested by other staffs.

6. Subsystem Demonstrations   More efficient major weapon programs require that high-risk, high-cost subsystems incorporating new technologies (e.g., radars, engines, computers) should, whenever possible, be developed independently of the complete weapon system and be tested fully prior to a commitment to include them in the overall system. This would reduce the cost risk of major weapon system development programs and reduce the time necessary to complete them. When new subsystem technology has been demonstrated, it can be quickly inserted into the overall program and brought into the field. This "modification" approach already has proven to be an extremely efficient way of developing new weapon systems (both in the United States and other countries), but the Department of Defense acquisition and budget processes are structured primarily around the development of complete weapon systems.

7. *Design-to-Cost* In the commercial world, new technology is used simultaneously to lower equipment costs and to improve the performance of new systems. In the defense world, technology is used almost exclusively to maximize performance. It has been estimated that achievement of the last few degrees of performance tends to raise costs by 30 to 50 percent, correspondingly reducing the number of weapons that can be acquired. If unit cost were made an important design criterion along with performance, the Department of Defense could take advantage of new technologies both to improve the quality of its equipment and to increase the quantities it is able to purchase.

Similarly, an important, early design consideration must be the development of innovative techniques to reduce the costs of logistics. Today, support costs are prohibitively expensive; their reduction must be recognized as an early, engineering design task, not something to be fixed later.

8. *Promoting Nontraditional Concepts* In order to encourage new technology to be used to improve overall military effectiveness in ways that cut across historical service roles and missions, it is necessary for the services and the Defense Advanced Research Projects Agency to allocate funds for nontraditional systems and technology. Such nontraditional technologies remain, otherwise, underfunded, as the institutions that control the research process consider them to be a lower priority. If a special allowance were made for nontraditional systems—and the money not considered as service money (i.e., charged to OSD)—a form of internal competition could be set up between improvements in traditional systems and innovative ways of accomplishing the same task. To create the proper incentives, it is desirable that separate organizations be created within each service to pursue these nontraditional approaches.

Implementation of these eight changes would make a major difference in the way the Defense Department accomplishes its business. Because this would be such a significant "cultural change," it will be difficult not only to initiate the effort, but also to apply the continuous follow-up that would be necessary to assure its implementation. The effort, however, is well worth making.

Revitalizing the Defense Industrial Base

The fourth of the broad changes required to improve the efficiency and effectiveness of the defense acquisition process is to change current perspectives on the defense industrial base. Historically, the assumption has been that a normal, free market has been operating in this area that adjusts to changing conditions to achieve economic efficiency and strategic responsiveness to the nation's defense needs. Unfortunately, this has not actually been the case, the principal reason being that in most instances the overall defense market is unique—consisting of one buyer and, in many instances, only one supplier.

Under these unique conditions, the Defense Department, as the only buyer, has an obligation to concern itself with the health and responsiveness of the defense industry. In order to do this, it needs to have some organization responsible for and in a position to take action to ensure the industry's health. At times, such an office would encourage establishment of second or even third producers of important equipment. At other times, it might encourage the awarding of a contract in a form that would achieve greater labor stability. At still other times, it might investigate the critical lower tiers of the defense industry to ensure that similar efficiency and responsiveness are attained in the supply of critical parts. The United States is the only nation in the world that does not treat its defense industry as a vital national resource. Today, the Defense Department does not have the means to achieve these ends, either at the prime contractor level or at the critical lower tier levels. Specifically, what the department lacks is *visibility* into the conditions of the industrial base. This visibility could be provided by gathering data for given industrial sectors regarding competition levels, labor force stability, potential bottlenecks, capital investments, foreign dependency, research and development prospects, capacity utilization, surge capability, and integration of civil and military production.

When provided with this data on the health and responsiveness of the industrial base, the Defense Department can include in its major acquisition and budget decisions such considerations as the best time and location to start up a new production line, the need for a second supplier, and investment requirements for a rapid production surge in the event of a crisis.

Today these supply-oriented decisions are not part of the acquisition process, because the necessary data base is missing. With it, far greater efficiency and effectiveness could be achieved in this unique marketplace. Additionally, industrial responsiveness could be made a more significant part of the overall U.S. national security posture.[13]

IMPLEMENTATION

Achievement of these four broad changes in the way the Defense Department does its business requires both organizational and procedural changes. Rather than elaborating on these in detail, consider instead the highlights for each of the critical organizational elements:

- • *Strengthened JCS Chairman, CinCs, and Joint Staff.* To achieve the unified, military long-range planning required and the establishment of an improved mechanism to select among the various possible weapons and resource alternatives, significant changes are required to strengthen all elements of the joint military institutions. With such a change, the military would be in a position to integrate strategies, technological opportunities, resource constraints, and mission funding into a coherent long-range plan.

- *Shift in role of OSD.* Instead of focusing on the details of programs, the Office of the Secretary of Defense should shift to its proper role of providing defense policy guidance and oversight. This would strengthen the civilian control of the military, by focusing civilian oversight on the broader policy issues and away from total absorption in the infinite detail of each of the separate service budgets.

- *Clearly defined service roles.* Currently, there is ambiguity as to who is responsible for the management of the acquisition process (OSD or the services). This should be defined clearly as the role of the services. Each service chief and secretary should be held fully accountable for managing the development, procurement, training, and support of the personnel and the equipment of their respective services.

- *Shift in role of Congress.* As with the Office of the Secretary of Defense, the role of Congress should shift from its frequent, multiple, line-item reviews to the broader aspects of a multi-year defense budget and national security policy, and continued oversight of the effective management of defense resources.

Overall, the result of these shifts in organizational focus for each of the major components of the defense acquisition system would result in more centralized decisionmaking—but more decentralized implementation responsibility—while still maintaining the critical oversight role of OSD and the Congress. This contrasts significantly with an alternative proposal of moving toward a single, centralized acquisition agency for all of the Defense Department. Given the size of the defense establishment, the necessary close ties and continuing tradeoffs between operational capabilities and resource management, and the long history and existing organizations within the services for acquiring weapon systems, the working group believes that the less revolutionary approach contained in this report could more easily be implemented and would be equally—or more—effective. A total restructuring and reorganization within the Department of Defense, as envisioned in proposals for a central acquisition agency, might take years to achieve and might in the end create a system that is even less efficient because of its size.

Naturally, the greater role being proposed for the chairman of the Joint Chiefs of Staff would result in more joint programs being implemented among the services and greater interoperability and standardization among them. This is both a desirable and logical consequence of the proposed change, resulting in greater equipment commonality and thus a lowering of both acquisition and support costs. Shifting to a single buying agency for the full Department of Defense, however, might have the disadvantage of eliminating much of the diversity and many alternative ideas that currently exist within the various service development agencies, which have the distinct advantage of encouraging the development of technological alternatives. It is believed that the U.S. market (unlike that of our European allies and other countries who have shifted to a single buying agency) is large enough to allow the separate service development agencies to operate efficiently and effectively. But it is necessary that the decisionmaking process, in which major acquisition commitments are made, be far more centralized, as would be achieved by the proposed recommendations.

Consistent with this set of organizational changes, there would be a corresponding set of procedures that would naturally follow (e.g., for the chairman of the Joint Chiefs, the generation of a long-range plan; and for the services, the implementation of actions to assure enhanced professionalism of acquisition managers). Such actions would have to be taken for each of the broad reforms noted above and for the specific subcategories within them.

It again must be emphasized that it will take time and political will to implement these necessary changes. Today, many on Capitol Hill and in the Pentagon are attempting to achieve procurement reform in a piecemeal fashion—from spare parts "task forces" to a growing number of detailed procurement laws and regulations. Such measures are often necessary, but they obscure the requirement for fundamental change in the way the Defense Department does its business. If the four broad thrusts described in this report were accepted and implemented—JCS reform, budget reform, procurement reform, and industrial revitalization—their combined effects, over time, would result in needed improvements in the defense acquisition process and would simultaneously enhance the credibility, with both the Congress and the public, of DoD management. Our nation's security requires these changes; the taxpayers deserve them.

NOTES

1.   For a more extensive discussion of the emphasis on and resistance to technology in traditional and nontraditional weapon systems refer to J.S. Gansler, *The Defense Industry* (MIT Press, 1980), pp. 97–109. For an excellent historical perspective, see Elting Morrison, *Men, Machines, and Modern Times* (MIT Press, 1966).

2.   Defense Systems Acquisition Review Council Working Group, "Final Report, Weapon Systems Costs," 19 December 1972. See also "The Defense Industry," p. 16, for a more recent update.

3.   The higher range comes from both a GAO study of 1972 (Comptroller General of the United States, "Acquisition of Major Weapon Systems," DoD report B-163058, July 1972) and a 1979 report (House Committee on Government Operations, "Inaccuracy of DoD Weapons Acquisition Cost Estimates," 16 November 1979). It was again reconfirmed as slightly over two in one in 1981 by the Air Force Systems Command, "Affordable Acquisition Approach," 9 February 1983. The lower range comes from attributing more of the cost growth to inflation effects.

4.   Norman Augustine, *Augustine's Laws* (American Institute of Aeronautics and Astronautics, Inc., 1982).

5. House Armed Services Committee, Industrial Base Panel Report (Chairman, Richard Ichord), "The Ailing Defense Industrial Base: Unready for Crisis," 31 December 1980; Defense Science Board Task Force Report on industrial responsiveness, (Chairman, Robert Fuhrman), 21 November 1980; the Air Force Systems Command Statement on Defense Industrial Base Issues, (General Alton Slay), 13 November 1980; J.S. Gansler, *The Defense Industry* (MIT Press, 1980).

6. For a fuller discussion of this strategy shift, see J.S. Gansler, "Industrial Preparedness: National Security in the Nuclear Age," *Military Engineer* (Nov.–Dec. 1983):483–90.

7. For example, "System Acquistion Performance of U.S. Government Agencies," Department of Defense Memorandum (Pyatt, OSD, 14 April 1976).

8. Reorganization of the Joint Chiefs of Staff is discussed at length in the Report of the Working Group on Military Command Structure. Also, see Archie Barrett, *Reappraising Defense Organization* (National Defense University Press, 1983). See also, T.L. Heyns, ed., *Understanding U.S. Strategy: A Reader* (National Defense University Press, 1983), especially the two articles on reform of the Joint Chiefs of Staff by General David C. Jones, USAF (Ret.), p. 307, and by General Edward C. Meyer, USA (Ret.), p. 327.

9. For a detailed discussion of schedule stretch-out, its effects, and possible corrective actions, as well as the specific F-15 example, see Air Force Systems Command, "Affordable Acquisition Approach," 9 February 1983.

10. For a detailed discussion of multi-year budgeting see the Report of the Congressional Working Group. Also refer to J.S. Gansler, "Reforming the Defense Budget Process," *Public Interest Magazine* (Spring 1984).

11. For a discussion of the effects of instability, see "Affordable Acquisition Approach."

12. For a brief summary of some examples, see J.S. Gansler, "There's Precedent for Pentagon Thrift," *L.A. Times*, 2 October 1983. For more details, see L.W. Cox and J.S. Gansler, "Evaluating the Impact of Quantity, Rate and Competition," *Concepts: The Journal of Defense Systems Acquisition Management* (Autumn 1981).

13. For a more detailed discussion of the needed industrial base actions, see J.S. Gansler, "Can the Defense Industry Respond to the Reagan Initiatives?" *International Security* (Spring 1982):102–21. Also, for a discussion of the importance of industrial responsiveness today, see J.S. Gansler, "Industrial Preparedness: National Security in the Nuclear Age," *Military Engineer* (Nov.–Dec. 1983):483–90.

5 REPORT OF THE WORKING GROUP ON THE CONGRESSIONAL DEFENSE BUDGET PROCESS

Chair: Alice M. Rivlin

House

Les Aspin   Willis D. Gradison
Anthony C. Beilenson   Dave McCurdy
Ed Bethune   Norman Y. Mineta
Butler Derrick   Leon E. Panetta
Norman D. Dicks   Joel Pritchard
Newt Gingrich   Samuel S. Stratton

Senate

William S. Cohen   Nancy L. Kassebaum
J. James Exon   Sam Nunn

Rapporteur: John J. Hamre

The steering committee of the Georgetown Center for Strategic and International Studies' Defense Organization Project realized early in its deliberations that congressional procedures for review of the defense budget reflect and reinforce many of the impediments to effective policymaking and management in the Department of Defense. Indeed, criticisms of procedures for defense decisionmaking in the Defense Department and the Congress reflect many common themes: lack of attention to strategic planning and opportunities for addressing basic issues of defense policy, unrealistic outyear resource projections, excessive micromanagement, too little attention to evaluation, too frequent revisiting of decisions on weapon systems, and too little continuity and stability in resource allocation decisions. Changing the way that Congress makes defense policy would not only improve efficiency on Capitol Hill but would also encourage and reinforce reforms in the Pentagon.

As a result, the steering committee formed a separate working group to examine how the Congress reviews the defense budget, establishes overall policies for the department, and exercises oversight over the activities of the U.S. military establishment—and to suggest ways to improve those processes.

The principal recommendations are:

1. The Congress should move to a biennial budget for defense. Two-year authorizations and appropriations should be passed in the first year of each Congress. This reform is envisioned as part of the general shift of the Congress to two-year budgeting for all federal programs.
2. The role of the authorizing and appropriating committees should be differentiated more clearly. The authorizing committees should review the long-range plans of the Department of Defense, insist that they be based on realistic forecasts of available resources in the outyears, and debate the basic issues of overall defense policy that the plans reflect. The appropriating committees should focus their attention on the specific actions necessary to convert decisions on the defense program into a two-year defense budget.
3. Both the authorizing and appropriating committees should encourage objective evaluations of defense programs and utilize the second year of the congressional session for oversight activities.
4. If biennial budgeting is not attained, the Congress should shift from annual reviews of major weapon systems to authorizing and appropriating funds at the major decision milestones in the acquisition cycle (e.g., advanced development, initial production, full-scale production).

EXISTING PROBLEMS

No legislature in the world devotes as much time, energy, and talent to decision-making on the defense budget as does the U.S. Congress. Nevertheless, almost everyone involved in the process expresses dissatisfaction both with the outcome of all this effort and with the procedures themselves.

The working group reviewed the experience of its own members and consulted additional members of Congress and outside observers. Papers prepared for the overall CSIS project, particularly ones by Robert J. Art and John J. Hamre (published in this volume), were also helpful.

Participants in this analytic process generally agreed on the following deficiencies in current congressional procedures for defense oversight.

Work Overload

The members of Congress have too much to do. There are too many issues to debate and too little time to review each one in a thorough manner. Much of the excessive congressional workload results from the complexity of public policy issues that now confront the republic and from the character of national politics in recent years. But the members of Congress have contributed to the work overload problem by broadening the scope of their overview process while continually deepening the level of detail sought on each issue. One or the other—scope or detail—has to be sacrificed, at least some of the time, for there to be sufficient time (and energy) for careful and responsible oversight.

Duplication of Effort

Redundancy has become a serious problem in the congressional review process. Each chamber reviews the defense budget at least three times a year. In each chamber, each of the three annual reviews is controlled by a different committee. At the same time, the differentiation of functional responsibilities that once clearly distinguished each committee has become blurred. Authorizing committees increasingly encumber appropriations, while appropriating committees increasingly establish their own authorizations. Moreover, the question of how the budgeting committees can rationally establish overall budgetary levels without delving into the detailed questions traditionally considered by authorizing, and even appropriating, committees has never been answered satisfactorily.

To complicate matters, each committee has adopted its own style of organization and presentation. Compiling and cross-checking the same data through the three phases of the congressional process, to say nothing of accounting for differences between executive and congressional data formats, has become a clerical nightmare.

Reluctance to Make Final Decisions

Redundancies in the congressional process have reinforced the natural reluctance of politicians to make final decisions. It is always tempting to suggest that another court of appeal exists for difficult and controversial decisions; the redundancy of reviews in the congressional process makes this posture credible—and, indeed, the reality is that no decision is ever final. Defense contractors, military departments, and other claimants who lose in one phase of the process can appeal their fate in the next—or, at worst, in the opening phase of the next year's process, which usually follows the final phase of the previous year's process by only a few months. Weapon systems with weak rationales or spotty performance records can struggle from one hurdle to the next. Opponents and proponents alike can believe that time is on their side. Year after year, the same issues are debated but never resolved. The history of the MX missile is an extreme example of this deficiency in the congressional process.

Distortions Created by Artificial Planning Horizons

On average, it requires eight years just to develop a new weapon system; that same weapon is then placed in production for an additional number of years. This suggests that planning horizons should be quite long. Decisions to develop and then to produce a weapon system should be accompanied by the firm designation of funds necessary to finance the program, a decision to be reviewed only upon strong evidence of problems or radically altered circumstances. But, like the executive branch, congressional budgetary decisionmaking is heavily oriented toward the next year's budget. Although the Congress insists that the Defense Department produce long-term plans, it takes seriously—and reviews in detail—only the plan for the next year. This focus on a single year permits more programs to be initiated than can actually be afforded. The long-term fiscal implications of new program starts are only rarely factored into evaluations; but, once started, weapon programs rarely die. The result is far too many claimants for the limited weapon acquisition funds that are available in a given year—and repeated decisions to stretch out or otherwise delay existing programs that inevitably lead to inefficiencies and higher unit costs.

Inability to Debate Major Issues

The overwhelming workload, the redundancies in the process, and the excessive attention to the details of programs all inhibit serious congressional attention to broad questions of the overall direction and content of U.S. security policy. The Congress is so immersed in the fine points of the defense program that it lacks the time, the resources, and the orientation to execute its oversight role effectively by engaging in a substantive dialogue with the executive branch on fundamental policy decisions. It is lost in the trees of defense decisionmaking, unable to make out—far less to influence—the broad outlines of the policy forest. The executive branch reinforces this tendency by avoiding discussion of major long-run defense issues with the Congress, while simultaneously bemoaning congressional micro-management.

A STRATEGY FOR CHANGE

These problems in the congressional defense budget review process are not the result of deliberate decisions; they are a by-product of the political dynamics that have characterized executive-legislative relations for many years. Congress is an institution in which no one can guarantee the outcome of an issue, but almost everyone can influence its ultimate resolution. Repetitive procedures, and preoccupations with increasingly detailed levels of review, reflect the quest of individual members of Congress to maximize their ability to serve their constituents and increase their own influence over government policy. Any serious reform in the congressional process is difficult to achieve, because in the end it means that members of Congress have to yield some of their ability to serve narrow interests in the common interest of the nation's security.

Removing redundant steps in the process, for example, sounds simple in theory; however, it is not in fact, since different committees control those respective procedures. Deciding which of the three committees should give up authority, or at least circumscribe it within more narrow bounds, would be extremely difficult. Moving the entire system from an annual to a multi-year cycle may also be difficult, as such a step would imply a voluntary relinquishment of the power to review decisions yearly. Annual authorizations and appropriations have become crucial levers of influence on the administration. Moreover, as gridlock has developed in so many aspects of legislative activity in recent years, the annual defense bill—which for a variety of reasons is unlikely to be vetoed—has become a primary means of advancing legislative proposals that would otherwise perish in isolation.

For these reasons, reform in the congressional process might best be accomplished in conjunction with reforms in the organization and procedures of the Department of Defense. If the two branches can cooperate in a comprehensive approach to improving the methods used by the United States to defend its national security, existing institutions may be more easily persuaded that the sacrifices demanded of them were being matched by the sacrifices of others—all in the national interest.

Even so, any proposal for congressional reform must be realistic. Any suggestions to scrap existing institutions and procedures wholesale in favor of a totally new system would almost certainly meet overwhelming resistance. The challenge for reformers is to find feasible changes and practical measures that can contribute to "ideal" solutions in the long run. Reformers need a clear vision of the ideal in order to guide them in proper directions, but they also must be pragmatic in their expectations as to what might be accomplished in the short run.

OBJECTIVES OF REFORM

If designed and implemented properly, it should be possible to reform the congressional defense review process to accomplish the following four objectives:

1. To focus greater congressional and popular attention on major, long-range defense issues in enough time to affect their outcome.
2. To enable the Congress to exert closer policy guidance on the Department of Defense to assure that its preferences are implemented, and yet to remove the Congress from the detailed management of specific programs.
3. To reduce the congressional workload so that the tasks that are pursued are accomplished more effectively.
4. To help the Defense Department use its resources more efficiently and to provide greater stability in programs over the long run.

The ultimate goal of reform is to restore to the Congress an effective ability to carry out its primary responsibility of setting national purposes, establishing major strategies, and ensuring the efficient oversight of executive branch actions. Together, the president and the Congress must establish the broad strategic framework within which detailed policies and programs can be designed and implemented successfully. Four types of issues must be resolved in establishing that framework.

1. *National goals and resources.* What are we trying to accomplish in the world? In view of our economic situation and competing national demands, how many and what types of resources are we willing to make available to accomplish those objectives?
2. *National strategies.* What broad strategies should be employed to protect the nation's security and advance its interests in the near and long term?
3. *Manpower and procurement policies.* Are current policies of internal Defense Department management in harmony with the economy and with societal values and preferences, and yet still capable of ensuring a militarily useful return on investments?
4. *Major weapon systems.* How should funds made available for defense investments be apportioned among competing hardware demands?

Clearly, the Congress must survey national strategies and the adequacy of national resources to support them, but it need not do so every year. Ideally, the administration would set out at the beginning of its term a national strategy and a fiscally constrained, long-range plan to implement it, which the Congress would debate thoroughly and then leave in place unless drastic international changes required a re-evaluation.

Certainly, the Congress should review the details of budgets and weapon programs, but again it need not undertake such a time-consuming task every year for every weapon—far less three times per year. Ideally, budgeting would be accomplished on a multi-year basis—perhaps even a quadrennial budget could be established—and weapons would be reviewed only in conjunction with the three or four major decision milestones during their entire acquisition cycle.

The separation of authorizing and appropriating functions may have outlived its usefulness. Defense decisionmaking would be improved by consolidating the current authorizing and appropriating authority in a single "defense committee." This committee would first debate longer range issues and then translate its decisions into multi-year budgets. In between budget years, the defense committee would review and evaluate the ongoing defense program; in other words, it would have time to exercise serious policy oversight.

Together, these changes would greatly streamline the congressional review process and permit the Congress to refocus its efforts on the broad, longer run issues of policy and oversight that it is most capable, and most responsible, for determining. The implementation of this ideal reform is currently beyond reach, however. It would require a complete restructuring of the committee system and a shift of such magnitude in the budgeting process that we cannot assume it could be adopted at any time in the near future. As a result, the working group recommends a less drastic shift in congressional procedures, which would still remedy many of the deficiencies in the current system and be a first step toward more far-reaching reform.

A REALISTIC SOLUTION

The working group recommends that the Congressional Budget Act be amended to establish a biennial budget. In the first year of each new Congress, the administration would submit—and the Congress would debate, amend, and eventually approve—a two-year authorization and appropriation. In the second year of each Congress, the committees would direct their attention to the review, evaluation, and oversight of existing programs, with the authorizing committee concentrating on broad questions of defense policy and the appropriating committee paying most attention to the efficiency of program management.

This relatively simple step could greatly ease existing problems in the congressional defense review process. It would clearly impart greater stability in the defense planning process. It would ease the burden the process now imposes on members of Congress. It would assure that far greater efforts were directed at broad questions of oversight. It would permit more thorough consideration of budgetary issues when they were considered. It would permit greater attention to those long-run issues that are indeed of the greatest importance for the nation's security.

Obviously, this solution to deficiencies in the congressional review process goes well beyond the defense budget. Defense spending is an inextricable feature of broad fiscal policies and debates on national priorities. It thus would be desirable to shift the entire federal budget to a two-year cycle, which would have beneficial effects for domestic programs as well. Because the change would be comprehensive, it would require action by the entire Congress. But, ironically, it may be somewhat easier to accomplish such a sweeping change, in which the many members of Congress who do not participate on the armed services committees or defense appropriations subcommittees would have a say, than a change which would come solely under the purview of the specialized committees.

There has been considerable interest in the Congress in biennial budgets for many years. The number of members who have publicly supported the concept has grown with each passing year. The time to act may be now. The working group urges prompt action to establish a biennial federal budget. It is the single most important practical step to correct the grave problems now encountered in congressional handling of defense policy and programs.

A LESSER BUT STILL HELPFUL STEP

If it proves impossible to shift to a biennial budget, the Congress should consider shifting from annual reviews of major weapons to a system in which funds for major weapons are authorized and appropriated only when the development cycle reaches a major decision milestone.

In developing major new weapons, the Defense Department follows a procedure whereby each system is reviewed only at major decision milestones in its development. Approval to proceed beyond a milestone means that insufficient funds will be allocated to complete the next development phase, even though that phase may take several years. The Congress could create a similar system. Specifically, we recommend that the Congress authorize and appropriate multi-year funds for each major weapon system at four milestone decision points: (1) initial development, (2) full-scale development, (3) initial production, and (4) full production. As a weapon neared each milestone, the administration would request sufficient funds in the next year's budget to pay for the complete upcoming segment of the weapon's development or production, even though the funds would actually be obligated and expended over a several year period.

The system would work like ship authorizations work now. Most of the full cost of a new ship is authorized and appropriated in a single year, but the funds are actually spent over a period of several years. If a specific weapon were not planned to reach any milestone in a given budget year, there would be no need for the Congress to review it, unless some problem had been uncovered that required attention. Under this system, some weapons would still be reviewed yearly—notably those that had become controversial—but the presumption, at least, would be that annual reviews were no longer required.

To ensure that the necessary information would be available, the Congress would have to establish explicit reporting procedures for the department for each milestone. These documents would lay out optimal procurement patterns, life-cycle costs, inventory and force structure objectives, and test and performance parameters. The relevant congressional committees would similarly need to set forth procedures for milestone hearings, staff reports, and decisions.

This new procedure could concentrate the debate over weapon programs at those points in the development cycle at which key decisions were required. By conforming more closely to the decision procedures used in the Pentagon, the new system would reduce existing sources of inefficiency and misunderstandings. A milestone system also would move Congress away from its current tendency to review each decision several times each year. This would contribute to greater program stability and allow more effective long-term planning and more efficient program management.

Although a shift to a milestone system in authorizing and appropriating funds for the acquisition of major weapon systems would not accomplish nearly as much as would a shift to a biennial budget, it would be an important step in the right direction and bears further consideration.

6 REORGANIZING COMBAT FORCES

by

Morton H. Halperin and *David Halperin*

Every military operation of the United States since the Korean War has brought to light serious problems in the organization of the armed forces. Often the operation has been conducted using an ad hoc command structure. In other cases, the regular chain of command was used with serious adverse consequences. Despite the fact that a number of official and unofficial studies have documented these problems, there have been no major changes in the formal command structures since 1958 and no major changes in the allocation of functions among the services since 1948. Nor is the executive branch now giving any serious attention to fundamental changes.

This paper will seek to define these structural problems, show their impact on past events and current capabilities, point to an ideal remedy, and finally propose more modest and politically feasible steps forward.

Apart from the inherent difficulties and the inevitable need to make tradeoffs, two major obstacles block adequate organization of forces. The first is the present distribution of roles and missions, established by the 1948 Key West agreement and subsequent "treaties" among the services. This agreement prevents the procurement of equipment and deployment of forces for key supporting functions and precludes the establishment of coherent and ready units for vital contingencies. The second obstacle is the existing chain of command rules that Congress enacted into law in 1958 at the strong urging of President Dwight D. Eisenhower. Although the purpose of the changes was to strengthen the authority of the unified commanders, the 1970 Blue Ribbon Defense Panel concluded that the reforms had little or no impact.

The Key West structure grew out of a series of conflicts between the wishes of the navy and those of the army and its offspring, the air force. Following World War II, the army pressed the navy for unification of all forces into a single department. The navy, fearing that it would be swallowed up into the army structure, resisted. Soon after, the next struggle began: Should each service be given the right to acquire all the forces it needs to carry out its missions independently, or should the services endeavor to work together and thus prevent unnecesssary duplication of forces and equipment? The navy favored the first view; the army and air force, the second.

Unable to resolve this disagreement, the services turned to Secretary of Defense James Forrestal, who summoned the Joint Chiefs of Staff to the Key West Naval Base in March 1948 to hammer out a compromise. The result was just that, an uneasy compromise of the two positions rather than the acceptance of one or the other perspective and its application to all the services.

The navy got much of what it wanted: authority to carry out those air operations, including ground-launched missions, required for sea battles; authority to provide its own air transport; control of antisubmarine warfare, mine laying, and controlled mine field operations;[1] retention of the navy-based marine corps, and the authority to provide close air support for marine operations.

Although the navy insisted on self-sufficiency, the army and air force decided it was better to rely on navy resources and on each other than to seek similar independence. Thus, while the army retained primary interest in all land operations and control over sustained ground combat, it agreed to forgo development of organic close air support and tactical and strategic lift capabilities. For sealift, it would rely on the navy, and for close support and tactical and strategic airlift, it would rely on the air force, which maintained primary interest in air operations and strategic air warfare. Because the air force needed little help from the army to perform its primary functions, the army–air force pledge to cooperate was basically a one-sided promise. It also proved to be an empty promise.

Key West gave the navy and the air force responsibility for providing the army with crucial support functions but little incentive for doing so. The two services have had their own primary functions to carry out, their own forces to pay for, and their own doctrines to support. Thus they have only increased capabilities for these supporting functions when heavily pressured by civilian officials or when threatened by army moves to take the functions away. The result has been that the army—and the United States—has always lacked strategic and tactical lift capacity and combat air support sufficient to meet U.S. security goals. Prevented under the Key West structure from procuring the tactical lift and close support airplanes the air force will not provide (strictly speaking, the army can only provide its own lift within the combat zone), the army has been forced to rely on expensive and inefficient helicopters. And the army has found no remedy at all for its strategic lift problems. As many secretaries of defense and military experts have testified, provisions for these vital functions remain inadequate.[2]

Enforcement of the Key West rules has also ensured that some crucial military functions have not been provided for at all. For example, the navy controls sea operations, but the army and the air force control the forces trained and best equipped for missions deep into ground territory. Consequently, the United States has no ready force for a mission that requires flying off an aircraft carrier to such a ground mission. Key West also prevents the serious consideration of optimum basing modes for weapons. The MX provides a current important example: Although many experts believed that basing the missile on small submarines was the best way to enhance the survivability of U.S. nuclear forces, the option was never seriously considered by Pentagon officials. MX had been given to the air force, but Key West gave control of all submarines to the navy. The air force did not want to give up the program, and the navy did not want to take it.[3] In fact, U.S. possession of nuclear-armed submarines—perhaps the most valuable component of the strategic triad—required stretching of the Key West rules. The navy, interested in control of the seas and not in strategic air warfare, was initially reluctant to take on the Polaris program, and the air force was precluded from doing so by the agreement.

These are all simply illustrations of a basic problem: The functions and forces required for some extremely important missions are split between services by the Key West rules. In the MX case, this problem led to an unwise deployment decision. When the military is ordered into combat, the problem forces units that have not trained together or coordinated their equipment purchases to suit each other's needs to combine suddenly and go into action. Instead of relying on coherent permanent units, the United States frequently must deploy improvised coalitions of forces that must learn to work with strangers on the spot.

The unified command system has done little to counteract the problems created by the Key West division of roles and missions. The National Security Act gave the Joint Chiefs of Staff (JCS) authority to establish unified commands in strategic areas. By 1953, the military chain of command ran from the president to the secretary of defense, who was to consult with the Joint Chiefs, to the civilian secretary of the service responsible for the relevant unified command, to that service's chief, and finally to the unified commander before reaching the field. (In wartime, the service secretaries would be bypassed.) By 1958, President Eisenhower had decided that the chain was "cumbersome and unreliable in time of peace and not usable in time of war."[4] With the cooperation of Congress, he acted to shorten the chain by removing the service secretaries and chiefs. He also took the authority to establish unified and specified commands away from the Joint Chiefs and gave it to the secretary of defense, who also was empowered to determine the forces and missions of the commands. In addition, Congress gave the commanders of the unified and specified commands "full operational command" of all forces assigned to their commands.

These moves, however, did not eliminate problems with the unified command system. In fact, they did not even meet Eisenhower's goal of streamlining the chain of command, for on the day the act of Congress became effective, Secretary of Defense Neil McElroy promulgated a directive including the Joint Chiefs in the chain of command. The JCS has at times divided responsibilities for the unified commands among the individual service chiefs, in effect acting as if the 1958 change had not occurred. At other times, the Joint Chiefs have acted together in the chain or delegated responsibilities to their chairman.[5] Experience suggests that the chain remains inefficient or unusable in wartime and that the unified commanders continue to have inadequate control over the composition of the forces they must command in battle.

The unified commanders, or CinCs, are responsible for the military operations of command forces, but it is the individual services that procure equipment and devise and train units, and it is the secretary of defense who assigns these forces to commands. Although the secretary's role makes it more likely that the assignment of forces will have some coherence, it does not directly address the biggest problem: The training, equipping, and selecting of forces is not carried out by the individuals who are responsible for their command in combat. As a result, the unified commanders may be insufficiently familiar or comfortable with their forces.

Thus, in crisis situations the CinCs have often proved ineffective or have been ignored. Frequent disregard of CinCs in such situations seems to have encouraged further improvisational shifts in the chain. Once the official chain has been broken, why not continue to make changes? Excessive rigidity in chains of command may be unwise, but excessive disregard of chain structures has led to unacceptable confusion in recent cases. These structural problems with roles and missions and chains of command have displayed themselves in most U.S. military actions of the last twenty years.

In Vietnam, CINCPAC, the commander in chief of U.S. forces in the Pacific, was bypassed with regard to forces in the country. The commander of those forces, who always bore the title of Military Assistance Commander (Vietnam), reported directly to the JCS. Offshore air and naval forces, however, reported through CINCPAC to the JCS.

In addition, because of Key West, the army was prevented from procuring the airplanes it needed but was not getting from the air force. The army was forced to deploy thousands of helicopters, which most defense planners believe are inferior to small airplanes for close support and tactical lift and which cost more and use significantly more fuel than such airplanes. Because they are so difficult to maneuver and because they must be made with relatively light material to keep fuel costs down, helicopters are extremely vulnerable to enemy fire. According to one source, approximately 10,000 helicopters crashed or were shot down in the war. During the peak years of U.S. involvement, the army was losing about one-third of its Vietnam-based helicopter force each year. Yet despite this dismal record, the army continues to rely on its helicopters for all contingencies, including the defense of Western Europe. Aircraft that could be knocked out by Vietcong automatic rifles would not last long against Soviet tanks and fighter planes.

The Iran hostage rescue mission of 1980 was actually described above; it required flying off an aircraft carrier to a mission far inland. Lifting off from a ship offered U.S. helicopters the shortest safe flight path to their destination. Key West gave the navy all the aircraft carriers, and planners decided that moving army or air force helicopters to a navy ship might jeopardize the mission's secrecy. Thus they selected for the mission a navy helicopter equipped for minesweeping when army or air force aircraft crafts might have been better suited to the mission. Because they were using navy aircraft, the planners decided to use navy and marine pilots, even though army and air force pilots were better trained for such missions. And, the commander of the army rescue unit suggests that maintenance of the helicopters prior to their takeoff by a carrier crew that was unaware of their special purpose could have affected the performance of the helicopters.[6] It was, of course, helicopter failure that caused the mission to be aborted.

But helicopters and their pilots represent only one facet of what was wrong with the mission. The United States did not possess a ready force capable of carrying it out and thus had to rely on ad hoc planning and separate units and individuals who, in some cases, had never trained together or even met until the day of the mission. A few years prior to the rescue attempt, the army had created a counterterrorist unit, but that outfit had no organic transport or support; nor was it permanently connected to any transport or support units or to an operational chain of command. The planners had to assemble the remaining forces ad hoc, and, as the army rescue commander suspects, each service, and even groups within services, wanted "a piece of the action."[7] Thus the army counterterrorist Delta unit was joined not only by marine and navy pilots, but also by an army special forces unit trained in West Germany, an army Ranger unit, and an air force unit that provided the transport airplanes that landed at the Desert One rendezvous point.

Given the improvised composition of the force, no one should be surprised that the previously established chain of command was ignored or that the command situation on the ground was confusing. The planners created a special joint task force, whose commander took orders directly from Joint Chiefs Chairman General David Jones; the regional CinC was excluded. The joint task force commander gave orders to Delta's deputy commander in Egypt. On the ground at Desert One, command duties seem to have been shared between the Delta commander and the commander of the air force crew.[8] A military commission chaired by Admiral James L. Holloway III (Ret.) reported that several helicopter pilots said they did not know or recognize the authority of those giving the orders at Desert One. Both the Holloway commission and the Delta commander, in critiquing the mission, stressed the problems caused by ad hoc planning.

In Lebanon, in 1982, the United States deployed a marine force ill-equipped to deal with its main threats: terrorist attacks and sustained artillery fire. An army unit would have been better prepared to handle the artillery fire but would have had other limitations. The fact is that the United States had no ready force for this presence mission and thus no clear choice as to which forces to send in.

In addition, reports from both a Pentagon commission chaired by Admiral Robert L.J. Long (Ret.) and the House Armed Services Committee charged that weaknesses in the chain of command to the forces in Lebanon may have contributed to the security failures that led to the deaths of 241 U.S. servicemen. Perhaps because it was a relatively long-term operation or because no actual combat was anticipated, the chain to the marines actually followed the official rules. It began in Washington with the president and the secretary of defense acting through the Joint Chiefs. It then went to the regional CinC, the commander of U.S. forces in Europe, who is based in Mons, Belgium. From there the chain passed to his deputy, based in Stuttgart, West Germany. From Stuttgart, it continued to the European navy commander in Naples, Italy, and on to his deputy in London. From London, it at last passed to an operational commander, the U.S. Sixth Fleet commander in the Mediterranean. Both reports charge that officials in the upper levels of this long chain failed to exercise proper oversight authority over the forces in Lebanon. Commanders so far from these forces—both physically and in the chain of command—and who had so little control over the composition and training of these forces may not have been sufficiently concerned with the security and tactics of these marines. Yet the existence of so many layers of commanders may have convinced commanders closer to the action that their missions were being monitored adequately by more experienced officers.

It is quite possible that the convoluted upper levels of the chain contributed not only to lax security but also to an ambiguous chain of command situation in the theater. According to the House committee report, one chain extended from the Sixth Fleet commander to the amphibious task force commander stationed on a ship off Beirut to the marine amphibious unit commander at the Beirut airport. Another extended directly from the Sixth Fleet commander to the airport commander. The three commanders gave the committee conflicting and confusing accounts of the chain. In addition, the committee report asserts that the Joint Chiefs of Staff, the marine headquarters, and the European CinC did not know of the second chain of command directly from the marine commander to the fleet.[9]

The Grenada operation, in contrast to the preceding examples, seems to have accomplished its objective relatively smoothly. But the extremely limited capability of the opponent practically ensured the mission's success. In fact, the Grenada operation suffered from some of the same kinds of problems that plagued the failures that came before it. Once again the United States had no standing force designated and specially trained for the mission. Once again ad hoc planning was required, and once again a curious command situation arose. Two distinct forces invaded the tiny island: army Rangers backed by air force air support, and marines backed by navy air support. There was no single commander on the island for the two forces; the overall commander of both ground forces was a naval officer stationed offshore.

Key West has prevented the United States from making sensible procurement and deployment decisions and helped created a situation in which ad hoc planning, sometimes degenerating into bargaining among the services, is required for nearly every military action. The unified command structure has placed combat responsibility for forces in the hands of commanders who have little control over the designing, training, and equipping of these forces and has led to confused chains of command when ignored and cumbersome chains of command when observed. The best solution to these severe structural problems is to alter the structures dramatically.

The United States could reorganize its armed forces into self-sufficient units trained and equipped for specific missions, such as large-scale ground combat, control of the seas, strategic delivery of warheads, presence missions, limited applications of ground forces, and counterterrorist operations. Such units could be made services or commands and would be given no limits on the kinds of procurements they could request from Congress. No longer would turf rules prevent the services from carrying out their functions; such a reorganization would increase the probability that the incentives of the individual units and the defense requirements of the United States coincided.

The plan might lead to some large-scale duplication of military equipment; this was the army and air force argument at Key West. But it is not clear that the purchase of equipment needed to perform distinct missions constitutes duplication. Furthermore, the cost of such programs as strategic lift for ground forces might be offset by savings from such moves as a shift from helicopters to small planes for close support and tactical lift.

With these units trained, equipped, and ready for specific missions, ad hoc planning and interservice bargaining in a contingency could be drastically reduced. The president and the secretary of defense, with the advice of the Joint Chiefs of Staff, would in most cases be able to decide quickly which unit to deploy.

Furthermore, chains of command could be short, clear, and competent. Ready forces could have ready commanders, commanders who had participated in procurement decisions and in shaping and training the force. These commanders could report directly to the secretary of defense. Field commanders could report directly to them. Such a brief chain, including only top leaders in Washington and unit commanders with affinity for and intimate knowledge of their units, could be upheld even in crisis situations.

But faced with the real world no one would seriously argue that such fundamental changes could be instituted any time soon. With this model as an ideal, however, a determined executive branch, with the assistance of members of Congress willing to question the current structures, could take steps to increase the ability of U.S. forces to meet likely contingencies. We will first propose procedural means for instituting a process of reform and then discuss various substantive proposals that might be feasible.

The first step should be to bring Key West and chain of command issues out
of the closet. Public linkage of the current structure of roles and missions and
crucial military weaknesses might increase support for change in the Pentagon,
the Congress, and the media. A presidential statement would have the greatest
impact, but such a statement ought to be preceded by an effort by the secretary
of defense to induce the services to raise the issue themselves. If the message
came though the mouths of current service leaders, it might impress those politicians and observers who believe that only the military knows what is good for the
military.

The secretary of defense needs to conduct a full airing of the issues. A comparable effort by Secretary of Defense Robert McNamara at the beginning of the
Kennedy administration led civilian officials to pressure the services for improvement of strategic lift capabilities and eventually to air force procurement of
the C-5A. The secretary could bring in outside experts, but the focus would be
on service heads speaking independently and not through the Joint Chiefs. Disagreement and the articulation of differing service perspectives, not consensus,
would be encouraged. Interservice differences would be harnessed for constructive purposes if service leaders stated publicly that certain supporting functions
were inadequate and that rival services—and Key West rules—were responsible.
To encourage such statements and other relevant critiques, the secretary could
direct to service leaders questions such as the following:

1. If the Key West structure were to be reorganized, what changes would you
   recommend in assigning roles and missions?
2. How does your service currently make procurement and deployment decisions for functions that primarily aid another service, such as close air support and lift?
3. Are there important combat functions for which the United States currently
   has no ready force?
4. What changes would you make in the current unified and specified command structure? Are the current relationships between unified commanders
   and the forces they must direct in combat adequate?
5. Are existing chain of command arrangements adequate for combat or crisis
   situations?

If the chiefs of the military services were given the green light to challenge
each others' programs and expose Key West and command problems, they might
well respond candidly. Charges could bring countercharges, and the powerful
conspiracy of silence regarding roles and missions might crumble. Once weaknesses were brought to light and potential constituencies for their correction
awakened, significant substantive steps might be feasible. (Even if they were not,
the relevant actors might be convinced that only meaningful actions to make the
current system work more effectively would ultimately succeed in heading off
sweeping reforms.)

Three approaches for procuring adequate forces for supporting functions come to mind. One would be to do what has already been done with some airlift aircraft: Remove them from individual service budgets and invest procurement responsibilities in the deputy secretary of defense. Part of the reason the services try to avoid procuring equipment for supporting functions is that they fear Congress will not take into account these "contributions" to other services in determining their appropriate share of the overall defense budget. Spending on support functions raises a service's overall budget and may thus jeopardize congressional approval of the budget request for primary functions. If the deputy secretary made the request, politicians would be less likely to link increases in procurements for supporting functions to decreases in procurements for primary functions. Relevant service officials might no longer fear such linkage. They might cooperate fully with the deputy secretary and effectively train and deploy forces for supporting roles.

Another approach would be to allow one service to subcontract with another for procurement. For example, the army could order and pay for close support planes that would be developed, procured, and controlled by the air force. The army would include such aircraft in its Program Objective Memoranda (POM), but the air force would be the actual purchasing agent. The planes could be flown and maintained by crews made up of individuals from both services.

A third possibility would be to transfer incrementally key supporting functions from one service to another. If the services could not tolerate a dramatic revamping of roles and missions, perhaps they could accept a shift of the close air support function from the air force to the army. Clearly, all services would resist transfers of functions to other services, but if the secretary of defense and the Congress supported such changes, they might become politically feasible. Even if the ultimate result was not a shift of all supporting functions to the services that wanted them most, each step in that direction would enhance the ability of the United States to meet its security aims.

Some of the supporting function problems and other problems described above—the failure to develop certain types of forces, the need for ad hoc planning and emergency coordination of units that have never trained together, commanders' lack of control over the composition of their forces, and the weaknesses in current chains of command—should be addressed in a different way. The United States could set up small, self-sufficient units for specified functions *within the services* and have these units recruit individuals from other services and conduct operations under the command of the service chief reporting to the secretary of defense.

Applications of American military force in recent years have been, and are likely to continue to be, for the most part of limited scope and duration. Since the withdrawal of forces from Vietnam, U.S. military operations have never required more than small units. The U.S. military has attempted two rescue operations (one for the crew of the *Mayaguez* and the other in Iran), one presence mission in Lebanon, and one takeover of a tiny country (Grenada). Given the lack of political support for large-scale military intervention abroad and the apparent unwillingness of America's most powerful foes to provoke a major war, it seems likely that improving U.S. capabilities to deal with missions of relatively small magnitude could solve many of our most pressing problems. But dealing with this problem by setting up new unified commands, such as the counterterrorist unit created in the wake of the Iran failure, would not solve the problems we have identified.

Instead, the existing services could set up separate small units for counterterrorism, for presence missions, and for small-scale invasions, or, if they preferred, a single entity to carry out all three missions. But Key West turf rules might prevent the new unit or units—because they would remain in individual services—from procuring the forces they needed to carry out their mandates and from conducting combat operations without being integrated into a joint structure. Therefore, a slightly different alternative might be more feasible.

Small, special-purpose units could be set up within the services and within the Key West structure and still meet U.S. military goals—if the army, on the one hand, and the navy and the marine corps acting together, on the other, were permitted to develop such units. For example, each could set up a counterterrorist unit, but only the navy's could carry out missions involving an aircraft carrier. The units would have authority to recruit individuals from all services for long-term assignments. Air force planes would be permanently assigned to the army units. Thus the units would combine features of the current unified commands and specified commands. Like the specified commands, they would be directed by one service for a specific purpose. Like the unified commands, they would draw on the resources of all the services.

These permanent, self-sufficient units, which could grow out of existing special units within the services, could assemble and train their forces before a contingency arose, thus greatly reducing the need for ad hoc planning and the possibility of interservice bargaining in a crisis—and dramatically increasing preparedness. No longer would the United States send strangers to operate side-by-side on these missions. Each unit that was deployed would have been long rehearsed as a team, and would constitute a force with a coherent structure and shared perceptions and goals.

The unit commanders would be responsible not only for assembling, training, and equipping their units, but also for their command in the field. Though they would be authorized to draw on forces from all the services, they would not face the problems that cripple the current unified commanders.

Chains of command to these units could be simple and coherent. They could extend from the president and the secretary of defense to the relevant service chief and then to the unit commander. We would include the service chiefs because these units would be permanent parts of individual services, and it would be a mistake to alter the command structure as units moved into combat, which is the usual procedure under the present structure. There would be no intervening layers of unified commanders with less knowledge of and interest in the actions of the field forces. If resources under the control of unified commanders were needed as a backup, they could be made available to the combat unit. Under such a system, there might be little urge to bypass the chain and improvise a new one in a crisis. With the chain functioning smoothly at higher levels, the likelihood of confusion at lower levels might diminish.

Competition between army and navy units for potential mission assignments •
might lead to forces of very high quality. Civilian officials would have to protect the budgets of these units against the tendencies of the services to devote their funds to large forces. Civilian officials would also have to make clear that in a contingency, only one of the two units would be deployed. Otherwise, the problems of ad hoc planning and interservice bargaining and uncoordinated forces might remain. The chairman of the Joint Chiefs of Staff could be given authority to make an independent recommendation as to which force should be used in each instance. The decision as to which of the two forces to employ would be made easier by their service affiliations and limitations: a mission requiring carriers or a beachhead landing would go to the navy unit, while one requiring rapid airlift or defense against sustained artillery would go to the army unit.

The establishment of small, specialized units within the existing military services would greatly increase the ability of the United States to meet likely contingencies and to deter foes from taking steps that would make U.S. military action likely. Creation of these units could significantly improve the coherence and readiness of American forces without the need for a dramatic and perhaps politically impossible overhaul of command structures and service roles and missions.

NOTES

1. This last duty was shifted to the navy from the army by direction of the secretary of defense on 24 May 1949.
2. See our "The Key West Key," *Foreign Policy* 53 (Winter 1983–84):114–30.   •
3. Ibid.
4. Quoted in Alice Cole, et al., eds., *The Department of Defense: Documents on Establishment and Organization, 1944–1978* (Washington, D.C.: Office of the Secretary of Defense, Historical Office, 1978), p. 180.
5. See Archie D. Barrett, *Reappraising Defense Organization: An Analysis Based on the Defense Organization Study of 1977–1980* (Washington, D.C.: National Defense University Press, 1983), pp. 124–25.
6. Col. Charlie Beckwith, USA (Ret.) and Donald Knox, *Delta Force* (New York: Harcourt Brace Jovanovich, 1983), p. 285.
7. Ibid., p. 225.
8. Ibid., pp. 258–80.
9. U.S. House of Representatives. 98th Congress. 1st Session. Committee on Armed Services. *Adequacy of U.S. Marine Corps Security in Beirut* (Washington, D.C.: U.S. Government Printing Office, 1983), pp. 43–54.

7 CONGRESS AND THE DEFENSE BUDGET
New Procedures
And Old Realities

by
Robert J. Art

INTRODUCTION

In the decade of the 1970s, the U.S. Congress underwent profound changes in both the makeup of its members and the style of its operations.[1] The changes in both makeup and operations occurred because the broader political environment within which Congress existed had also changed. On the one hand, the decline in the appeal and cement of America's political parties brought to Congress individuals who were less beholden to their parties, who were more skeptical of the traditional purposes of New Deal government, who wanted to open up the procedures of Congress to the public, who were impatient to make their impact on public policy quickly felt and were therefore less tolerant of the traditional mores and rights of seniority, and who were more questioning of the wisdom of the presidency and therefore less willing to defer to it.[2] On the other hand, these individuals entered an institution in which the members already there had become disabused of congressional deference to the presidency and had concluded that Congress' political power vis-à-vis the executive had suffered. The cast of the new members reinforced the existing predispositions of an institution looking to enhance its political power. In the 1970s, then, changes in member makeup abetted changes in operating style.

The changes in congressional operations adopted in the 1970s served the interests of both the institution collectively and the members individually. As such, these changes were at cross-purposes. The reforms that enhanced the power of Congress in relation to the president centralized it; those that enhanced the power of the individual member decentralized it. In the former category were measures that strengthened the leadership of each house, that increased the expertise and staff size of congressional committees, and that enabled Congress to deal more effectively with both the growth in federal spending and the president's impoundment of appropriations. In the latter category were measures that weakened the powers of committee chairmen, that increased the number of subcommittees, and that gave more personal staff to each member.[3] In the 1970s, then, Congress responded to the larger political forces acting on it by adopting new modes of operation that simultaneously enhanced and weakened the institution's ability to function collectively.

Because of the contradictory nature of congressional reforms in the 1970s, an assessment of their net effects is difficult. Both the individual members of Congress and the subcommittees they chair have more staff, and, consequently, both may be better equipped to take initiatives than before and to produce higher quality public policy. But what is good for each member or subcommittee singly is not necessarily good for the Congress collectively.[4] Individual initiative does not automatically translate into collective action, no matter how good the initiative. More legislation introduced does not thereby mean more legislation passed. More individual entrepreneurship in a horizontally structured institution can be as much a recipe for paralysis as it can be for more effective collective action. It can also mean greater congressional constriction of executive flexibility and greater confusion in policy if initiatives are condoned but not coordinated.

The one reform in congressional operations in the 1970s that clearly embodied both the centralizing and the decentralizing trends is the Congressional Budget and Impoundment Control Act of 1974.[5] With this act, Congress tried to centralize its treatment of the federal budget, but it did so in a way that was designed not to alter fundamentally the traditional functions and prerogatives of the legislating, taxing, and appropriating committees. The purpose of the act was to enhance Congress' power in federal budgetmaking vis-à-vis the presidency. That required Congress to create a mechanism to do what its appropriating and taxing committees had failed to do: To gain control over congressional spending and to relate spending and taxing to one another. But the members of Congress who wanted this in order to deal more effectively with the president also wanted to retain their prerogatives and "platforms of power" (their committee and subcommittee chairs) in order to serve their individual interests. Congress had to be better able to stand up to the president but not at the cost of trampling its members in the process. Thus, with the 1974 Act, Congress superimposed a new process on a pre-existing structure.

The purpose of this paper is to look at how the 1974 Act has affected Congress' treatment of one policy area—namely, the defense budget. In my analysis, I shall stress two fundamental themes: Neither the current operation of the new budgetary process nor the present congressional treatment of the defense budget is entirely satisfactory.[6] Today, the former requires a seemingly exorbitant amount of the members' time without having significantly improved the timeliness of budgeting; the latter has become heavily mired in programmatic details with high redundancy among the two defense committees. Many members complain that budgeting crowds out other important business. The budget committees set the spending priorities among national needs, but they do not and cannot deal with the fundamental issues of defense policy. Both the new budget process and the congressional treatment of defense appear to suffer from a preoccupation with next year's budget. Neither gives sufficient attention to the basic questions and the longer term perspective.

None of this should surprise us, however, because, first, "money is policy" • and, second, annual budgeting is a powerful congressional tool for closely controlling executive action. Annual budgeting, when combined with the more activist, skeptical, aggressive, and better staffed Congress of the 1970s and 1980s— the "new" Congress, that is—has produced the world's most potent legislature. Nevertheless, the question remains: Has annual budgeting for defense, with detailed annual authorizations and with heavy redundancy among the two defense committees, become counterproductive? In short, has annual budgeting for defense become incompatible with the new Congress?

In order to deal with this fundamental question, I shall answer three separate questions: (1) Has the 1974 budget act substantially altered the way Congress has traditionally dealt with the defense budget? (2) has the 1974 Act ameliorated or exacerbated the dysfunctions traditionally inherent in the defense budgetary process? and, (3) if matters are not satisfactory, is it a radical restructuring that is required or only a small change at the margins?

The first section of this chapter briefly describes the salient features of the 1974 budget act. The second section sets forth three attributes of the new Congress' treatment of defense and analyzes how the 1974 budget act has affected congressional defense budgeting. The third section describes the five traditional budgetary dysfunctions in the defense field and argues that the new Congress has left these virtually untouched. The fourth section offers three broad proposals to improve congressional decisions in defense budgeting.

SALIENT FEATURES OF THE 1974 ACT

With the 1974 Budget and Impoundment Control Act, Congress created two new committees, a new budgetary timetable, and a new process overlaid on the existing authorizing, taxing, and appropriating processes.[7] Potentially, the 1974 Act created two supercommittees—the Senate and House Budget Committees. The ability of these two committees to put Congress' fiscal house in order would depend upon their ability to exercise control over the budget process. That, in turn, would require their taking some power away from the authorizing, taxing, and appropriating committees. Authorizing committees would no longer be permitted to subvert the appropriations process through "backdoor spending" stratagems.[8] The appropriations committees would no longer be permitted to bust the budget by allowing their subcommittees to determine independently the next year's budget authority in their areas of purview. Delay in passage of the budget would be ended by adherence to a strict timetable and by adoption of one aspect of advanced budgeting—namely, the authorization of programs at least one year in advance of the fiscal year to which they first applied. Congress would no longer be permitted to allow its oversight responsibilities to slide, because the authorizing committees would be required to fulfill them either by contracting them out or by requiring the executive agencies to conduct evaluations of their programs. The new budget act, in short, went against the grain of nearly thirty years of congressional budgetary practices.

It did so, however, in a circuitous and ambivalent fashion. The appropriations committees would be strengthened against the authorizing committees because backdoor spending by the latter would be proscribed. But appropriations would also be weakened because the budget committees would be the ones to determine the overall level of federal spending. The authorizing committees would be strengthened because they would conduct oversight more effectively and were urged to report new authorizing legislation a year in advance. But they would be weakened vis-à-vis the appropriations committees because they could no longer commit the government to spend unless funds were first appropriated. The appropriations committees would give up the power to determine the level of federal spending, but they would control all spending once the total was set. The authorizing committees would give up backdoor spending but not their detailed annual reviews of executive spending requests. And the budget committees would set overall spending and taxing targets and also determine national priorities by fixing firm ceilings among the general functions of the government, but they could not legislate policy, become involved in the details of programs, or appropriate funds.

It was how they handled this difficult task—setting overall targets and functional ceilings without getting into the details of programs—that held the key to how effective the budget committees would be. The federal budget is broken down into over 1,200 program accounts. These are aggregated in the federal budget into nineteen functional spending categories, such as national defense, international affairs, energy, transportation, health, and so forth. The Congress passes thirteen appropriations bills, none of which is equivalent to one of the nineteen functional categories. The latter are set at a high enough level of aggregation such that each category cuts across and incorporates the jurisdictions of two or more appropriations subcommittees and generally several (of the sixteen in the House and thirteen in the Senate) authorizing committees. The national defense function, for example, includes the Armed Services Committees (for the Department of Defense and military construction bills), Interior and Insular Affairs (for the naval petroleum reserves), the Energy and Commerce (House) and Energy and Natural Resources (Senate) Committees (for atomic energy defense activities), and the Select Intelligence Committees (for intelligence). Funds for the national defense function are found primarily in the appropriations bills for the Department of Defense, for military construction, and for the Department of Energy.

The substantive rationale for the budget committees' use of these broad functional budgeting categories, which are the ones used by the president in formulating his budget and choosing his priorities, was that Congress, through its budget committees, was supposed to think broadly about the federal budget, not only about the spending and taxing totals, but also about the allocation of monies among the general functions of the government. The political rationale for the budget committees' use of these presidential categories was that the committees would be less likely to come into conflict with the legislative and spending committees if they avoided going into their business in detail and, instead, stuck to deliberating and determining the overall targets and functional ceilings.

The 1974 budget act, in short, created a giant shell game. The budget committees could set the functional categories and thereby constrain, to a degree, how the federal government would spend its dollars. But only by severely limiting the overall dollars allocated to a specific functional category could they affect the choices of the legislative and appropriating committees and, even then, only indirectly because the latter would still be free to make the specific detailed program decisions.

Because the budget committees could not with political impunity "line-item" (go into program details), they had a dilemma: How could they allocate resources *among* priorities without making some determination about how the funds would be spent *within* each of them? For example, for the national defense function, they are supposed to decide whether to recommend new budget authority for $275 or $310 billion for the next fiscal year, but not to determine whether the MX should be procured or how many, whether the next aircraft carrier should be nuclear or conventional, whether NATO should substitute conventional for nuclear weapons, how many men and women should be in the air force, or what should be the pay increase for the military.

This dilemma, which I term the macro/micro problem, is especially acute in the national defense function, because nearly all defense spending is discretionary (not fixed by previous law but rather subject to annual authorization), and big ticket items like the MX readily affect the total. In an era of concern about the deficit, the combination of a large number of big ticket items in the defense budget and the discretionary nature of defense spending makes it especially difficult for the budget committees not to go into some of the details of defense. If, however, assumptions about the details of spending within each category were made and then made known to the relevant defense committees, the budget committees could be accused of line-iteming. But if no assumptions were made or were made within the committees but not made known outside of them, the committees could be accused of pulling numbers out of the air. In short, if the numbers the committees picked had credibility, political conflict would ensue. But if the numbers the committees picked had no credibility, the charge of political irresponsibility would be leveled.

The two budget committees have not entirely avoided these two pitfalls because they are inherent in the task the committees are required to perform. In order to minimize them, the two budget committees have tried to be circumspect in their treatment of defense spending. The House Budget Committee has gone into the specifics and programs of the defense budget in greater detail than has its Senate counterpart, but it has tended to keep those details within the confines of the committee. The Senate Budget Committee has tended to take a more macro approach by determining how much should be allocated to defense as opposed to non-defense programs. Both committees, though, have resorted to ingenious political devices to make spending judgments about some fairly specific aspects of the defense budget but in ways that appear not to intrude upon the prerogatives of either the armed services committees or the defense appropriations subcommittees.[9] Neither budget committee, however, has dealt effectively with the major policy issues embedded in the defense budget because neither is constituted substantively or politically to do so. Neither has the requisite staff or mandate. Rather, the effects that each has had on defense spending, as we shall see, have been indirect: It is how the existence of the budget committees and the new budgetary process have affected the operating styles of the two traditional defense committee actors that is the key to understanding the ways in which the budget act has affected Congress' treatment of defense.

The last feature of the 1974 Act of concern to us is the timetable it established (see Table 7–1). Once the president submits his budget to Congress, the authorization committees have only about two months to review his requests. By March 15, they are to report to the budget committees their recommendations for budget authority and outlays. The appropriations committees are to do the same, but their estimates must by nature be more tentative, because floor action on authorization bills has not yet taken place. By April 15, with inputs from the authorizing, appropriating, and revenue committees, the budget committees are to report for floor action their "First Concurrent Resolution," which sets targets, not binding ceilings, for spending, taxing, and the functional categories. By May 15, Congress is to take action on the recommendations of their budget committees and set the targets of the First Resolutions. During the summer, authorization and appropriations bills are reported out; each house takes action on them; and each budget committee is to monitor those committee actions to see whether they are within the guidelines set by the First Resolution. By September, action on all appropriations bills is to have been completed. By September 15, Congress is to pass a Second Concurrent Resolution that sets binding ceilings. If the appropriations and revenues bills are not in harmony with it, the appropriating and taxing committees are to reconcile their bills to make them consistent with the September 15 action. By September 25, this reconciliation process is to be complete;

Table 7-1. Congressional Budget Timetable Established by the 1974 Act.

By November 10	President submits current services budget
By 15 days after Congress convenes (in January)	President submits his budget for next fiscal year
By March 15	All standing committees submit views and recommendations to budget committees
By April 1	Congressional Budget Office submits report on overall economic and fiscal policy, alternative budget levels, and national budget priorities to budget committees
By April 15	Budget committees report first concurrent resolution on the budget to their Houses
By May 15	Committees report bills authorizing new budget authority to their Houses
	Congress completes action on the first concurrent resolution
By 7th day after Labor Day	Congress completes action on bills and resolutions providing new budget authority and new spending authority (appropriation and entitlement bills, respectively)
By September 15	Congress completes action on second concurrent resolution
By September 25	Congress completes action on reconciliation bill or resolution or both that implements second concurrent resolution
October 1	Fiscal year begins

Source: Committee on the Budget, House of Representatives, *The Congressional Budget Process: A General Explanation* (December 1982).

and Congress has thereby passed the budget for the next fiscal year, which begins on October 1.

The purpose of the new timetable was to deal with the most mundane but operationally disruptive aspect of Congress' treatment of budgeting in general. As Schick put it in 1976:

> During the past decade, there has not been a single fiscal year for which all regular appropriations were enacted prior to July 1. During five of the years since 1965, Congress has failed to enact a single appropriation measure before the fiscal year began and in none of these years were more than two of the regular appropriations passed by July 1.[10]

Congressional delay was due, not only to the increasing complexity of governmental programs, but also to Congress' delving into them in ever greater detail. With the decline in permanent, and the consequent rise in annual, authorizations, the number of congressional actors involved in the yearly budget process expanded; and each actor took a more detailed look at presidential requests.[11] Such looks caused delays in the authorizing committees' reporting out their bills to the floor, and that, in turn, caused delay in the passage of appropriations bills. In turn, those delays led to increasing use of continuing resolutions, hurriedly passed without full member knowledge of what was in them. The lateness in passage of the appropriations bills ironically and perversely began to defeat the whole point of annual authorizations: closer congressional scrutiny over, and control of, presidential spending. The technique of annual authorizations was subverting itself. By shifting the start of the fiscal year to October 1 and by mandating a tough timetable, the budget act was supposed to achieve timeliness in congressional budgeting. As we shall see, it has not.

ATTRIBUTES OF THE "NEW" CONGRESS

There are three attributes that describe how Congress currently deals with the defense budget. First, the armed services and defense appropriations subcommittees overlap heavily in their functions but remain fairly uncoordinated in their actions. The defense appropriations subcommittees are doing more legislating; the armed services committees are doing more budgeting. Both continue to operate autonomously from one another. This raises the question of whether the original rationales of specialization of function and division of labor through separate authorizing and appropriating committees still makes sense for defense. Second, the financial and programmatic review of the annual budget by both committee actors has become quite voluminous and detailed. Each house changes well over 60 percent of Pentagon line-item requests. This raises the question of whether matters have proceeded to the point where micromanagement has set in— that is, whether Congress is now trying to manage rather than oversee the Pentagon. Third, although Congress is now engaged in both financial and programmatic oversight, its conduct of more general policy oversight remains tenuous and highly dependent upon the initiatives of a few individuals. This raises the question of whether general defense policy oversight can be systematically built into the congressional budgetary process.

Has the 1974 budget act produced these three attributes or simply reinforced them? Clearly, the answer must be "reinforced." In each area, the 1974 Act has not substantially altered what Congress had previously done for well over fifteen years. If it has done anything, the act has entrenched further these three patterns of behavior. In this sense, the consequences of the new budgetary procedures have been negative and contributory, not positive and primary.

Redundancy among Committees

The redundancy between the armed services committees and the appropriations defense subcommittees began when the armed services committees adopted the technique of annual authorizations in 1959 for the procurement segment of the defense budget. Subsequently, they expanded its application to the other parts of the budget. Annual authorizations began for two reasons: Competition between armed services and appropriations for control over the details of the defense budget and the desire of the former to exert more control over the Defense Department. The pattern of the armed services committees before 1960 had been to take a rather general look at the nation's defense policies through annual posture hearings.[12] But once they adopted and expanded the scope of annual authorizations, they became more immersed in the details of the yearly budget and thereby began to compete with the defense subcommittees. Table 7–2 details the growth of annual authorizations since 1960. Clearly, as the table shows, use of this technique predates the 1974 Act; and it was nearly complete in its expanded application by 1970, five years before the act came into force.

Table 7–2. Growth in the Scope of Annual Authorization of the Defense Budget.

1959	Authorization required for the procurement of aircraft, missiles, and naval vessels.
1962	Authorization required for all research development, testing, or evaluation of aircraft, missiles, and naval vessels.
1963	Authorization required for all research, development, testing, or evaluation carried on by the Department of Defense.
1965	Authorization required for the procurement of tracked combat vehicles.
1967	Authorization required for personnel strengths of each of the Reserve components as a prior condition for the appropriation of funds for the pay and allowances for the Reserve components.
1969	Authorization required for the procurement of other weapons to, or for the use of, any armed force of the United States. (Essentially this covers heavy, medium, and light artillery; anti-aircraft artillery; rifles; machine guns; mortars; small arms weapons; and any crew-fired piece using fixed ammunition.)
1970	Authorization required for the procurement of torpedoes and related support equipment.
1970	Authorization required for the average annual active duty personnel strength (termed "end strengths") for each component of the armed forces.
1982	Authorization required for the Operations and Maintenance Account.
1983	Authorization required for Other Procurement (includes items such as trucks and electronic gear, which affect the readiness of the forces).

Sources: J. Ronald Fox, *Arming America: How the U.S. Buys Weapons* (Graduate School of Business Administration, Harvard University, 1974), p. 122; Interviews.

The budget act not only failed to retard the advance of annual authorizations and detailed reviews, but it may even have abetted both. The reasons why tell much about the nature of the current competition between armed services and the defense subcommittees. The explanation begins with the final extension of annual authorizations to the entire defense budget by including the Operations and Maintenance (O&M) and Other Procurement accounts in 1982 and 1983, respectively. Traditionally, the defense subcommittees had carefully scrutinized the O&M account, while the armed services committees had largely ignored it. But a combination of factors in the early 1980s pushed the House Armed Services Committee to argue for extension of annual authorizations to this area too. Its Senate counterpart went along, although reluctantly.

There were four factors at work. First, in the last few years, House Armed Services had become concerned about the fate of the O&M and Other Procurement accounts because both contained items that affected the readiness of the forces to go to war and their sustainability once in war. If the defense subcommittees continued to have a free hand in these accounts, then it would be they—not the armed services committees—who would determine the state of readiness of the forces. Second was the calculation that "we might as well do this and finally extend our review to the entire budget." Because we scrutinize everything else, why exclude these two areas? Third was the House Armed Services Committee's calculation that the House Defense Subcommittee, faced with the need to cut defense to lower the deficit, would naturally concentrate the bulk of its cuts in an area over which it had an almost exclusive purview. Fourth, finally, was the fact that cuts in the O&M appropriations account produce nearly an equal cut in outlays. Appropriations are the monies the federal government is legally obligated to spend. Outlays are the monies actually spent in any given fiscal year. Not all monies appropriated for a given fiscal year are necessarily spent in that year. Only 10 percent of the appropriations for R&D, for example, are spent in the given fiscal year for which they are appropriated. Because it is outlays that determine the size of the federal deficit in any fiscal year, cuts in the O&M account are more effective for deficit reduction than are cuts in the R&D or procurement accounts. As such, in periods of large deficits, cuts in the O&M account are very attractive.

Taken together, these factors—intense pressures to cut because of high deficits, the tried and true budget cutting technique of axing where you can easily ax, and the fear of House Armed Services that the O&M account would bear more than its fair share of cuts—suggest the strategic reason for extension of annual authorization to the two remaining accounts: Namely, "defensive protection by preemption." What better way for the committees to protect the entire defense budget from appropriations' cuts than to justify in more detail each of its parts? What better way for the armed services committees to protect readiness than to intrude into that area and attempt to create floors below which the defense subcommittees could not go?

A key staff member of House Armed Services, who helped push for annual authorizations of these two accounts, summarized the rationales well:

> In 1980–81, we deliberately went for annual authorization of O&M. Stennis (then chair of Senate Armed Services) said we have too much annual authorizations and not enough time for broad policy and did not favor the move. But we realized that when you come to the end of the year, O&M is the 'billpayer.' Appropriations has to cut to hit the budget outlay number and they do it with O&M. There are natural lobbyists for procurement and R&D, but no one was lobbying for readiness. Our theory was that since there was no constituency for readiness, we would create our own. Hence we set up the readiness subcommittee [of House Armed Services]. That tactic works in the House because a member has only one major committee, and he will develop the subcommittee he sits on as his constituency and speak for it. We decided later that we needed to authorize annually Other Procurement, which includes non-combat items like trucks and electronic gear. We realized that it was not just O&M that affected readiness, but a whole lot of other items that we were not dealing with.

The final two extensions of annual authorizations in the early 1980s were products of the situation in which the armed services committees at the time found themselves. If the budget act had any effect, it was to provide an extra push for inclusion of the O&M and Other Procurement accounts into the annual authorization process. But it did so indirectly. Through its procedures, the budget act forced Congress to confront explicitly deficits when spending exceeded taxing. In an era of especially high deficits, the budget act focused, and made politically more potent, the effects of fiscal stringency on spending in general and on readiness in particular. In this manner, the act contributed to hastening the last two steps in annual authorizations, but it alone did not produce them.

Detailed Scrutiny and Action

Similarly, the level of detailed scrutiny and action on the defense budget predated the 1974 Act. Detailed congressional changes to the defense titles began in the early 1960s and continued ever since. In the 1960s, the advent of annual authorizations was probably the single most important factor in producing more detailed and voluminous reviews by *both* committee actors. Annual authorizations pushed the armed services committees into a closer scrutiny of the budget. And once they did so, the defense subcommittees were required to follow suit and take action on the larger number of line items on which the authorizing committees themselves had taken action. In the 1970s, both disillusionment with the imperial presidency and the antidefense mood of the country after Vietnam pushed Congress into ever more detailed scrutiny. But the single most important factor in enabling the Congress to engage in more detailed action on the defense budget was the expansion in the staff capability of the two defense committees. But, again, that expansion predates the 1974 Act. In the Senate and House, respectively, the size of staff for the appropriations committees was: in 1947, 23 and 35; in 1957, 31 and 54; in 1967, 40 and 56; in 1971, 41 and 74; in 1975, 72 and 84. Comparable figures for the armed services committees are: 1947, 10 and 10; 1957, 27 and 18; 1967, 19 and 29; 1971, 25 and 32; 1975, 30 and 28.[13] The growth in staff reflected a gradual coming of age of a more assertive and active Congress.

Tables 7-3 and 7-4 illustrate in one fashion the impact of more detailed annual reviews. Using a few years of the 1960s as a benchmark, these two tables record by year the number of pages in the reports of the armed services and appropriations committees on the defense authorizing and spending bills. Although counting the pages of these reports may seem a trivial exercise, it provides a measure of the change over time in committee review activity. Both show a dramatic increase from the 1960s.

These reports have increased in size for two reasons: first has been an increase in the number of titles included in the authorization and appropriations bills; second has been an increase in the number of items reviewed in each title, especially for the procurement and the research and development titles. The number

Table 7-3. Number of Pages in Appropriation Committees' DoD Reports.

Fiscal Year	House	Senate	Total
1960	83	31	114
1961	74	47	126
1964	70	69	129
1965	51	52	103
1968	67	71	138
1969	68	56	124
1970	102	141	243
1971	119	221	340
1972	139	210	349
1973	256	204	460
1974	239	173	412
1975	171	207	378
1976	358	302	660
1977	226	277	503
1978	387	295	682
1979	446	217	663
1980	493	219	712
1981	398	227	625
1982	315	137	452
1983	259	157	416
1984	298	205	503

Sources: For fiscal years 1972-78, Robert L. Bledsoe, "Congress and the Defense Budget: Portent of Change?" unpublished paper, 1978; for the other fiscal years, the House and Senate Appropriations Committees' Report on DoD Appropriations.

Table 7-4. Number of Pages in Armed Services Committees' Reports: DoD Authorizations.

(major reports only)

Fiscal Year	House	Senate	Total
1965	63	17	80
1969	91	31	122
1970	176	70	246
1971	95	121	216
1972	107	140	247
1973	115	177	292
1974	150	205	355
1975	132	190	322
1976	185	191	376
1977	169	204	373
1978	160	163	323
1979	163	158	321
1980	186	166	352
1981	171	242	413
1982	228	197	425
1983	233	222	455
1984	332	526	858

Source: Armed Services Committees Yearly Reports on DoD Authorizations.

of titles included in the two defense bills has increased from 4 in FY 1971, to 7 in FY 1977 to 10 in FY 1985. The increase in the number of items reviewed in the research and development and procurement accounts has increased dramatically, as shown by the increase in the number of pages devoted to the two accounts in House Armed Services Committee reports on authorization bills:

Fiscal Year	Procurement	RDT&E
1975	85	74
1979	156	172
1983	204	159

As would be expected, the largest number of pages in the authorization reports are devoted to the procurement and RDT&E accounts. Although the detail concerning each item considered has shown no increase over the years, clearly both the number of titles reviewed and the number of items per title considered have increased. It is in this way that the committees have increased the level of their detailed review.

Perusal of Tables 7-3 and 7-4 reveals the following patterns: (1) a significant increase in review activity in the 1970–75 period, which coincided with a significant increase in the size of the staffs of congressional committees; (2) a decrease in the early 1980s in the review activity of the defense subcommittees; (3) a continuing increase in the activity of the armed services committees; and (4) a dramatic increase in review activity of armed services for fiscal year 1984, which probably signified the full impact of the addition of two more accounts for annual authorization.

I have no explanation for the second pattern, but I do for the others. In the mid-1970s, the addition of more staff enabled the armed services committees and the defense subcommittees to look at more programs. In the late 1970s and early 1980s, the pressure to cut the deficits, the need to protect the defense budget from those pressures, and the greater activity that the entrenched habit of detailed scrutiny naturally brings (the more closely one looks, the more problems one finds) all produced more careful scrutiny by armed services. Compared to the early and mid-1960s, the amount of review activity in the 1970s and 1980s is truly dramatic.

There is other quantitative evidence that corroborates this picture. Robert Bledsoe found that for the fiscal year 1976–83 period, the two armed services and the two defense subcommittees together made over 10,000 line-item changes in the eight budget requests submitted to Congress, or, on the average, about 1,250 per year.[14] In a careful review of Congress' action on the fiscal year 1984 defense budget, *Armed Forces Journal International* found the following: Of the 731 line items in the DoD request to the armed services committees, the House made adjustments in 424 of them; the Senate, in 450. Of the 1,129 line items in the DoD request to the appropriations committees, the House made adjustments in 766; the Senate, in 710.[15] Finally, for each fiscal year, the comptroller's office of the Pentagon puts out a memorandum on "Actions on Recommendations in Congressional Committee Reports and Related Authorization and Appropriations Acts," in order to keep track of the actions required and recommended by the authorizing and appropriating committees and the actions taken by DoD to meet them. The memorandum for fiscal year 1984 ran to 942 pages and encompassed 624 items in the congressional reports that required special action. These items varied greatly in how many subitems each contained and ranged from elements like the MX missile that had many subitems to the Publications Management Center at Osan, Korea, which had few. The number 624 considerably understated the number of items Congress changed.[16]

The picture suggested by the quantitative data is confirmed by the judgments of many congressional participants. The following is a selection of a few views:

> The budget cycle drives the Congress, and the Congress drives the executive branch to such an obsession that we don't have time to think about strategy. We never had a strategy hearing since I've been in the Senate.[17] (Senator Sam Nunn of Senate Armed Services)
>
> I can argue that it [the new budget process] is a failure, a failure because Congress had consistently failed to meet most of the deadlines, a failure because I think Congress

has become mesmerized with the budget process to the detriment of other responsibilities and considerations. It spends so much time on budget matters that we really fail to adequately provide the kind of oversight that I think is necessary. We have failed to have the kind of debates that are essential on national issues such as foreign policy and defense.[18] (Senator William Roth, Chairman of Government Operation Committee)

From January through December, we are consumed by the annual budget. Many members of the Committee feel that the system is working so poorly that something has to be done. The issues are fought over and over and the level of detail is too great. Tower [then Chairman] said to the Committee in 1983: "I want to see us get out of details." We tried but we got back into the "weeds." (a Staff member of Senate Armed Services)

We don't talk about strategy or tactics to my satisfaction in Armed Services. I think we should be involved in strategy. I don't want to micromanage. . . . We should be concerned with a proper overall defense policy and its match with our foreign policy. What the hell is seapower strategy? All they talk about [on the Committee] are ships and where they are going to build them. There is too much line iteming and detail on Armed Services. (a Member of the House Armed Services Committee)

Things have gone too far, not in terms of getting into the knickers of the services, but in the sense that it [detailed review] consumes too much attention of Representatives and Senators. We don't do enough of the long term policy. But there is a natural constituency for concentrations on weapons systems in the here and now. It is difficult for Members to focus on the big issues because of the lack of time, because of the need to get reelected, and because of the fact that constituency service, not policy oversight, is what is necessary today to stay in office. How to get them to focus on policy, not programs, is the problem. (a recently retired staff member of House Armed Services with many years of service on the Committee)

The negatives of the 1974 Act are that it has so encumbered Congress and its members that they have no time to deal with anything except the budget process. We now have at least eight different committees in the Congress overseeing defense and that means we have enormous redundancy. It is easier to expand Congress than to streamline it.[19] (a Staff member of Senate Armed Services)

Congress' treatment of the defense budget is not microscopic. The defense budget is simply too large and complex for that. Nor is any of the above to say that many items in the budget do not require close scrutiny. Many do because they are built on compromises that may make bureaucratic but not military sense. If the Pentagon policed itself better, Congress would not have to scrutinize it so closely. But clearly the review by Congress is detailed when compared to what the institution did twenty or even ten years ago.

Slighting of Policy Oversight

The third attribute of the new Congress' treatment of defense—the slighting of sustained and systematic policy oversight—is a more difficult matter to assess.

It is easier to measure the amount and degree of financial and programmatic oversight because each involves items, whether they be dollars or discrete programs, that can be counted. General policy oversight is more qualitative and synthetic in character. Whether it is now being done systematically, and whether it has gotten better or worse, cannot be determined simply by counting how often it has occurred or presently occurs,[20] Inevitably, also, one's views about Congress' effectiveness in policy oversight hinge partly upon one's views about the adequacy of the executive's defense policies. Dissatisfaction with the latter usually brings calls for more of the former. Satisfaction with the latter usually brings resistance to the former. Gauging congressional performance in policy oversight, then, is highly subjective.

Policy oversight differs from both the financial and programmatic varieties, although it can encompass elements of both. Fiscal or financial oversight means: Can we spend the money on this particular program efficiently? Program or programmatic oversight means: How well is this particular program being managed and how many of the systems do we need? General policy oversight means: What are our military requirements and commitments? What size, types, and mix of forces do we require to accomplish the missions that we have set and are the missions themselves the correct ones?

In theory, a nation first fixes its commitments and requirements; then it determines the size, shape, and mixture of the forces it needs; in turn, it selects particular weapons to constitute those forces; and finally, it makes certain that the programs are being well managed. Matters never work out that neatly, but somehow all these steps should occur if resources on defense are to be spent intelligently. Obviously, in considering the financial and programmatic aspects of the defense budget, Congress inevitably does some general policy oversight. But the crucial point is how and when. At some point in its deliberations, the Congress must consider, apart from the financial and programmatic considerations, the broader policy contexts that inevitably constrain the financial and programmatic reviews. To consider how many of a given weapon to buy and whether the program is being managed efficiently without considering first whether the weapon is needed and how it fits into the larger force structure is equivalent to managing the details without thinking about where they are taking you. It is difficult to discuss the details of a program without touching upon the broader policy context; but it is easy to deal with the financial and programmatic details without carefully scrutinizing the broader policy contours. In the defense realm, general policy oversight is most analogous to what in the Pentagon are called "force structure" or "force design" issues. These issues are the links that connect national military commitments to the size and character of the nation's military forces.

Most analysts who have studied the congressional defense role have argued that in force design issues and general policy oversight, Congress does not do well. Over the years, the continuity of their critiques is remarkable:

1962: The major cause for Congress' lack of incentive [to play the role of coordinate budget-maker] . . . would appear to lie not so much in the desire to avoid responsibility as in the expectation that there is little to be gained from trying to exercise it. The role of coordinate budget-maker can be justified constitutionally, and it is feasible enough intellectually (provided the committees would limit themselves to a review of the high-policy choices involved), but politically the part is not very remunerative. Political conditions are normally such that Congress is little motivated and poorly set up to second-guess the President and make its own judgments stick.[21]

1966: Congress' record indicates, however, that it has been better disposed in its organization and procedures, and in its collective intellectual grasp of strategic problems, to respond to executive initiative than to mitigate the deficiencies of executive branch leadership by its own forceful and enlightened entry into defense policy. Congress has been slow to propose policies which compensated for the shortcomings and oversights in those offered by the executive branch.[22]

1977: The result of these past [until 1975] changes has been increasingly effective congressional oversight in virtually every aspect of defense policy save one: force design decisions. . . . In our view, these are the most critical decisions, because they drive the defense budget, dominate the design of weapon systems, and define the kinds of wars the armed forces will be able to fight. Congress at present simply does not have the institutional mechanisms to examine force design questions, with the result that oversight of overall defense policy is limited.

We conclude that, in its present form, the new budget process is unlikely to correct this institutional weakness in Congress. The main reason is that there still do not exist in the Congress procedures for examining defense planning and budget issues in the context of more than one year.[23]

1977: The temptation . . . [is] to try to manage the details of a specific program rather than wrestle with the more complex issues of policy and direction for our national defense posture. . . . The net result is not enough emphasis on the major policy issues and too much emphasis on detailed project management.[24]

1984: Members of [House] Armed Services do get into policy but only obliquely. For example, on the Lehman power projection or sea control issue. We made a decision in favor of the former by authorizing a 600-ship navy, but we did it this way: We justified a carrier by stating the policy behind it rather than the reverse. We did not debate which policy we needed and then determined the best weapons systems to achieve it. The members of the Committee thus back into policy. We debate policy when we attack or support specific weapon systems, but it should be the other way around. We should debate policy first and then determine which systems to procure. The hearings are program focused. If you say to the committee members, "have policy hearing first," you will get the big Pentagon brass there; but the members' questions are either parochial or programmatic.[25]

Although I argued above that counting is not a reliable way to determine the frequency and effectiveness with which Congress engages in policy oversight, at least we can do a little to measure the frequency of it. The argument that follows, however, is merely suggestive, not definitive.

Robert Bledsoe has tried his hand at counting and the results are interesting.[26] For the FY 1976–83 period, he counted, coded, and collated all the dollar changes that the four defense committees made in the procurement and R&D titles as they were listed and explained in each committee's report on the annual defense bill it voted out. The three categories into which he grouped the changes were management, fiscal, and policy. The match between what he terms fiscal and what I term financial is nearly complete. His category of management is also encompassed by my financial category. For what he calls policy, about seven of the twelve coding statements involve what I judge to be matters of general policy oversight, or force design decisions. That is, roughly 60 percent of his coding statements are equivalent to my policy category; the remaining 40 percent are equivalent to my programmatic category.

Below are the results of Bledsoe's heroic effort to code the several thousand changes in line items into one of three categories that he employed:

	Policy	Fiscal	Management
House Armed Services	40%	43%	17%
Senate Armed Services	31%	53%	16%
House Appropriations	25%	66%	9%
Senate Appropriations	20%	75%	5%

According to Bledsoe's reckoning, then, fiscal oversight constituted the largest single category of changes for *all* four committees. The most policy or programmatic-oriented was House Armed Services; the most fiscally oriented, Senate Appropriations. Neither of the armed services committees engaged in an overwhelming amount of policy oversight when measured by the rationales for making funding changes in the Pentagon's line-item program requests.

We can manipulate Bledsoe's data as follows. If we combine his fiscal and management percentages into what I call financial oversight and split his policy category—60 percent for general policy and 40 percent for programmatic oversight—his findings would look like this:

	Policy	Program	Financial
House Armed Services	24%	16%	60%
Senate Armed Services	19%	12%	69%
House Appropriations	15%	10%	75%
Senate Armed Services	12%	8%	80%

Obviously, this is a somewhat arbitrary, but not wholly unreasonable, manipulation. It yields three interesting conclusions. First, Bledsoe argued that the dollar changes made by all four committees in the line items that appeared in the procurement and R&D titles were dominated by what he called fiscal reasons.

When we rearrange his data to fit my categories, the nonprogrammatic and non-policy basis of all four defense committee actions looms even larger. When dealing with programs, committee actions are primarily financial in nature. Second, to the extent that the two armed services committees have concentrated their actions in the fiscal/financial category, whether measured by his figures or mine, we have some tangible evidence that these committees increasingly have become budgeteers, and thereby, that the overlap between what they do and what the defense subcommittees do is great. Third, the more financially based the actions taken by the four committees, the more the Congress is trying to manage, if not micromanage, the Pentagon.

Obviously, Bledsoe's data, and particularly my manipulation of it, should be interpreted cautiously. What we are dealing with are actions on specific programs in the authorizing and appropriating bill reports. This data excludes the more general policy oversight that occurs in the other activities and hearings of the committees. Nevertheless, the results are suggestive in that they do measure the types of considerations that govern committee activity on line-item programs.

How has the budget act affected policy oversight of defense? The answer seems to be, "little, and if at all, adversely." Congress has not implemented two suggestions of the 1974 Act—advanced authorizations and multi-year budgeting—each of which would require it to take a longer term focus. To the extent that it would have to focus beyond the next fiscal year, Congress would be forced to be more policy-oriented, because such a perspective requires a concentration on the more fundamental parameters of a situation and an eschewing of the short-term details. By failing to force Congress to institute these two advanced budgeting techniques, the act has not enhanced Congress' capability to look beyond the next budget year. By absorbing more of the time and resources of the Congress on the annual budget exercise, the act has probably diminished its capability to look beyond it. Either way—in its failure to enhance or in its success in detracting—the budget act has not improved the institution's ability to focus its energies on the broad contours and longer term horizons.[27]

None of this is to argue that the defense committees do no significant policy oversight. Notable examples in recent years are Senator Sam Nunn's requirement that the Pentagon review NATO's tactical nuclear stockpile, which paved the way for some later significant changes in NATO's nuclear doctrine and forces; the SALT II hearings and Congress' opposition to ratification of the treaty; recent actions to control antisatellite weapons; recent hearings on Pentagon reorganization; and the recent study report by the House Appropriations Committee on the poor state of readiness of the military forces. Moreover, measured by the number of hearings conducted per year, the armed services committees are among the most active overseers in the Congress today. They rank above every committee except agriculture and appropriations in the number of hearings held.[28] Policy oversight does occur. Some of it is quite important and has far-reaching effects.

What we are dealing with here, however, is not an either/or situation but a question of the proper balance between policy oversight and budgeteering. No matter how large the staffs of the armed services committees are, it is impossible for them to do both equally well. If the members of those committees wanted to do more policy oversight and less budgeteering, under the present procedures of the budget act, they could. As we saw, the act in fact intended this. That they do not is a matter of their choice.

Things were not always this way, however. In analyzing how the armed services committees acted nearly forty years ago, Huntington described the situation as follows:

> The House and Senate Armed Services Committees were preeminent, combining extensive interests in both policy and administration. The House military appropriations subcommittees used the budgetary process for the detailed probing of military administration. The Senate military appropriations subcommittee attempted a more general consideration of military policy.[29]

Before the advent of budgeteering by armed services, there was a division of labor among the defense committee actors. And when the armed services committees spent little time on the budget, they had more to give to matters of policy. The dangers for Congress of too great a focus on budgeting and detailed management were presciently put forward by Kolodziej in 1966:

> Once embarked on such a course [too close an examination of defense activities], it [Congress] would be quickly ensnared in an intricate web of minute facts. Its energies would be quickly sapped, and its attention deflected from the policy considerations presumably underlying administrative action. . . . Quite possibly lost in the sea of budgetary numbers and administrative minutiae would be the objectives to be served by the defense establishment and the political costs and benefits which might result from using different kinds and combinations of physical force as a response to foreign political and military challenges. Congress would have traded the substance of governmental power for the trappings of it.[30]

Although the situation is not now as severe as Kolodziej predicted, it is not as good as Huntington once portrayed. Why? The answer lies, not simply with the continual growth of annual authorizations, not simply with committee rivalry within Congress, not simply with the assertiveness of the new Congress, but also with the political incentives of members today to conduct policy oversight. To understate the matter, they are low. Policy oversight does not enhance a legislator's "credit-taking" posture; it does not garner him electoral votes; nor can it be tied directly to control over executive action. Policy oversight risks being too general and diffuse in its impact, both on a legislator's career advancement and on those objectives he holds for public policy.[31] As Seymour Scher perceptively put it over twenty years ago: "Congressmen tend to see opportunities for greater rewards in the things they value, more from involvement in legislative and constituent-service activity than from participation in oversight activity."[32]

Policy oversight requires disciplined analysis, perspective, time to reflect, and detachment from the agency one oversees. All of these are commodities in short supply in the harried and increasingly specialized Congress of today. Less attached to parties than they once were, today's members must rely more on their own individual efforts to gain attention and electoral advantage. They are constantly on the make for "the quick fix." They have to be shown, as Michael Malbin puts it, that "an issue will make them look good" before they will take it on.[33] The only thing worse than taking on an issue that will not make a legislator look good is taking on one that will make him look bad. Most issues of general policy oversight, however, involve long-standing and fairly intractable problems, ones in which the risk of looking bad is high. The penchant for the quick fix makes legislators conservative in their choice of how they spend their political resources. To tackle an intractable problem takes both political courage and a secure incumbency. If many members possess the former, most do not believe that they enjoy the latter. They are constantly running hard both to discourage competitors for their seats from running and to beat those who choose, nevertheless, to do so.[34]

Thus, the political incentives on the Hill today are biased toward the short term—specific programs that can be grabbed, manipulated, changed, and sold. The Hill is an arena of highly politicized entrepreneurs, each of whom is in a condition of "self-help," where he must rely on his own efforts to succeed. In such an arena, risks are carefully weighed because the costs of failure can be high—electoral death. Intractable issues are eschewed unless they cannot be avoided or unless the opportunity for political credit can be seized. In this environment, the bias is against policy oversight because the incentives are loaded against it.

In defense, the problem is even more acute. Nearly the entire budget is discretionary because it is authorized annually. That gives legislators lots of details and programs to manipulate every year. The temptation is too great to resist. Moreover, it is easier intellectually to think about the specifics of a given program than it is to analyze the larger purposes into which the program fits. The latter involves questions of military contingency planning and force structure mixes for which there are no seemingly definitive answers. It is all rather open-ended and slippery. When there is something specific to act upon, when there is political benefit and minimal cost in doing so, or when taking action has the appearance, even if not always the reality, of "solving" a problem, legislators will act. But the type of action that, to use Warner Schilling's phrase, "creates a climate of opinion" is more difficult to justify and take credit for because it does not have tangible, immediate, easy-to-point-to results.[35] That, however, is precisely what policy oversight involves.

A central reason behind the decision of Senate Armed Services Chairman Richard Russell to push for annual authorizations in 1959–60 was the failure of the committee to engage in effective policy oversight. Because the general hearings in which the Senate Armed Services Committee had engaged in in the 1950s were not tied to specific legislative action or budgetary decisions, the senators on the committee did not take them seriously. The more concrete the issue, the greater the attendance level and vice versa. The armed services committees set out on the path of annual authorizations precisely because their members felt that general policy reviews were ineffective and put them at a disadvantage with the appropriations defense subcommittees, which actually controlled policy because they had say over the details of spending. In short, annual authorizations were begun because policy oversight had failed. Or, that was the view at the time.

The situation appears to be the same today, if the views of staff from the armed services committees are correct:

> For the policy hearings, the Members ask us: "Do we have to do this?"; or, "Why are we doing this?" Only when they have to do something [specific] will they come. Tower got their attention and attendance [on Senate Armed Services] when he focused on how the Pentagon is organized by getting them to realize that it might make a difference in what they [as Committee members] did. (House Armed Services)
>
> We tried to have major overviews and how that affected our force posture, but the Senators don't turn out. They are used to hearings for the bottom line, where hardware decisions are going to be made.[36] (Senate Armed Services)

Policy oversight, then, is difficult to obtain, not because legislators are not smart enough to do it, not because they do not have the time to do it, not because they do not have the staff to do it, but because they do not want to do it. If more policy oversight of defense is to occur, the political incentives to do it will have to be strengthened.

DEFENSE BUDGETARY DYSFUNCTIONS

Historically in defense budgeting, there have been five general problems that have seemed impervious to solution: (1) buying into programs, (2) one-year-at-a-time budgeting and neglect of longer term planning, (3) duplication of missions and redundancy in weapons among the services, (4) neglect of missions that are not traditionally done or desired by the services, and (5) ranking of investment in weapons and personnel ahead of readiness and sustainability. Each of these budgetary dysfunctions has persisted because there are powerful bureaucratic and political incentives that sustain them.

Buying into Programs

The most pernicious may be the first. Buying into a program is a device to obtain what is not affordable. Real costs are understated in order to make what is expensive appear cheap. Over the years, weapon systems have cost on the average nearly twice what they were initially estimated to cost, no matter what were the techniques used to produce more realistic estimates, no matter what were the controls devised to hold down costs during development. Ronald Fox once quoted a program manager as saying: "If we told the truth to Congress, we would never get our programs approved. So we have to understate the cost and overstate the performance."[37] In short, people lie. Everyone plays the game. The contractors do it to the services because they need the business. The services do it to the OSD because they need the weapons. The OSD and the services do it to the Congress because they have made bureaucratic deals. And the legislators do it to themselves because of the needs to serve the interests of constituents, to avoid the appearance of being soft on defense, or to avoid taking responsibility for refusing a weapon the military says is vital for national defense.

Buying into programs is a perfectly rational strategy for the services. The peacetime defense budget, no matter how large it is, is never large enough to field the forces that would be necessary in a major war. What one therefore does in peacetime is to acquire the skeletal forces that would be needed for a war. In weapons acquisition, this means developing high quality weapons in peacetime so that they can be available for large-scale manufacture in war. But performance advances are expensive, and the services want both big advances in their weapons and large numbers of them. Forced to choose, they will go for the former over the latter; but even here, they still ask for greater numbers than ultimately the budget can support. Their gamble is this: Should war come, the funds will be forthcoming to buy all the quantities needed for the state-of-the-art weapons that had previously been developed. In peacetime, therefore, the services accept what they regard as *temporary* cuts in quantity in order to get *permanent* advances in quality.[38]

Buying into programs serves the short-term interests of all the participants but not necessarily the long-term interests of the nation. For the net result is that more systems are started than ultimately can be afforded at the planned quantities. Once development begins, moreover, the budgetary squeeze is usually made even worse because still greater advances in performance are sought and often acquired during development than initially planned for. That means a greater per unit cost and a corresponding reduction in the number of units ultimately bought. As a consequence, since the end of World War II, each generation of major new weapons has been produced in fewer and fewer quantities. Finally, although more systems are started than the budget can support, the Pentagon and the Congress agree to stretch out production and produce fewer of each system rather than cancel any system once started. In addition to fewer systems at the end, this tactic has led to uneconomic rates of production. Thus, more money is ultimately spent for fewer systems, and along the way, the funds have been inefficiently spent.[39]

One-Year-at-a-Time Budgeting

Focusing on the current year and neglecting long-term planning stems from the overweening preoccupation with the annual budget. The PPBS system used by the Pentagon (the Planning, Programming, and Budgeting System) neglects planning for programming and budgeting. At the initial stages of the PPBS cycle, planning documents are prepared, but most participants think they are not worth the paper on which they are printed. The incentives to think about plans for the medium term, or anything beyond the next fiscal year, are low, because the Congress itself concentrates almost all its energies on the next fiscal year. Thus Congress' practice of "one-year-at-a-time budgeting" produces the exact same result in the Defense Department. Why should the Pentagon make elaborate plans for the next several years and engage in the tough bureaucratic fights necessary to produce them when no one on the Hill will take them seriously? Finally, the practice of buying into programs biases the entire system against forward planning. For the latter goes against the grain of the former. Forward or multi-year planning, in which items are realistically priced, would undercut the ability to understate costs and buy in.[40]

Duplication, Redundancy, and Neglect in Missions

Duplication in missions, redundancy among weapon systems, and neglect of nontraditional service missions are all parts of the same package.[41] Each of the services has been committed to certain missions that it regards as essential to its essence. Each has also undertaken secondary missions in order to assist in accomplishing the primary ones out of a distrust that the other services will provide sufficient forces to accomplish the secondary mission. For example, the army has developed a large air force through purchase of helicopters to provide itself with close air support on the battlefield. Close air support has ranked in air force priorities a poor fourth next to strategic bombing, air superiority, and tactical interdiction. And yet most outside analysts agree that helicopters are not as effective as close air support aircraft over the battlefield. Airlift and sealift, as another example, have never been highly valued by either the air force or the navy, with the former preferring combat missions and the latter power projection; yet both are essential to get the troops where they need to be. Most outside analysts, as well as the Joint Chiefs of Staff themselves, agree that the nation has woefully inadequate air and sea lift capability to meet the needs of a major contingency.

Reconciling national needs with service preferences has been a difficult management task for the secretary of defense. It has been magnified by the protection that each service receives from its supporters in the Congress. And, of course, duplication, redundancy, and the failure to provide for national, as opposed to service, needs wastes money.

Slighting of Readiness and Sustainability

Finally, readiness and sustainability have too often taken second place to investments in personnel and new weapons. Traditionally, there has not been an adequate lobby for readiness either in the Pentagon or on the Hill. Faced with the usual peacetime austerity, the services understandably have put weapons and personnel first, again gambling that the skeletal forces of peace can be quickly fleshed out for war. The secretary of defense, the Joint Chiefs, and the unified and specified commanders have often been advocates for readiness; but the services have retained great discretion over how the funds allocated to them are spent. As a consequence, maintaining an adequate level of readiness has been an uphill battle. And the Congress, as we saw earlier, has readily cut readiness in order to reduce outlays for deficit reduction purposes.

The recent study by the House Appropriations Committee amply documents the case for the current situation. After three years of the largest peacetime increase in defense spending since 1945, an increase that began with President Carter's fiscal year 1980 budget, the state of readiness and sustainability of the forces looked like this:

> DoD and Army studies show that the Army does not have the men and materiel to sustain combat operations in a major contingency.
>
> U.S. Naval fleet readiness to defeat a Soviet multidimensional . . . threat is seriously degraded by existing equipment, logistical, and manpower deficiencies. These deficiences exist not only in the U.S. Navy's ability to defend itself against a "first strike salvo," but in its ability to sustain full combat air and surface operations for more than a week's duration.
>
> USAF forces are not capable of conducting sustained conventional war operations against the Soviets.[42]

Running through this three-volume report is the theme that readiness has suffered because of neglect of the more mundane aspects of warfare: shortages of spare and replacement parts for existing weapons, shortages of ammunition for both training in peacetime and the high rates of expenditure expected in a modern war, shortages of qualified maintenance personnel, and shortages in flying, steaming, and other training exercises.

A degree of skepticism must accompany the reading of this report. It is based primarily on interviews with theater and base commanders, all of whom are traditionally conservative in their requirements (they want a lot) and each of whom, if war comes, must implement contingency plans that require more than any peacetime budget could ever sustain. Nevertheless, many of these readiness problems are long standing; and this report simply documents them in their most recent reincarnation. Therefore, even if we discount the conclusions of this report a bit, it nevertheless clearly illustrates the short shrift that readiness and sustainability almost always receive in peacetime.[43]

Attributes, Dysfunctions, and the Budget Act

The 1974 budget act has had no ameliorative effect on any of these dysfunctions. It would have been naive to expect otherwise. The act created a set of procedures for Congress to do its budgeting better, not a set of solutions to spend defense dollars more wisely. Just as was the case for the manner in which the act failed to ameliorate the attributes of the new Congress in its treatment of defense, so too has the act been neutral in its effects on the traditionally dysfunctional aspects of defense budgeting. Budgeting procedures per se cannot override powerful political forces.

What should be clear, however, is that the three attributes of the new Congress have exacerbated these budgetary dysfunctions. Budgeteering by the armed services committees and detailed line item scrutiny by the authorizing and appropriating committees, done often rightly in the belief that the Pentagon does not have its own house in order, simply reinforces the one-year-at-a-time focus that pervades the Pentagon. And that, in turn, does little to counteract the tendencies for buying into programs and for slighting readiness. Lack of sufficient policy oversight abets duplication, redundancy, and neglect of important but nontraditional service missions. In short, there is little about the general manner in which the new Congress deals with the defense budget that mitigates the adverse effects of these five dysfunctions.

PROPOSALS FOR REFORM

There are three broad tasks the Congress must accomplish if it wishes to improve the quality of its treatment of defense matters. First, Congress must alter the structure of the Pentagon so that better results emerge from it. The better the quality of Pentagon proposals, the more effective and efficient can be Congress' oversight of them. Second, Congress must achieve timeliness in its budgeting procedures. The more timely Congress is in deliberating and passing its defense bills, the more effective will be its oversight of the Pentagon and the better will be the quality of Pentagon management of its own affairs. Third, Congress must enhance the quality of its policy oversight. The better the quality of its policy oversight, the more likely Congress will be to mitigate the dysfunctions that pervade the defense budgeting system.

Structural Change of the Pentagon

The most efficient place for Congress to begin is with the Defense Department. If Congress is serious about improving the quality of national defense, it must take the steps necessary to improve the quality of the products that come out of the defense establishment. Congress must not try to do what it is institutionally not well suited to do. We must distinguish between those measures that are organizationally necessary to *initiate* policy and those that are organizationally necessary to *judge* policy. The former is the task of the executive; the latter, of the Congress. The tasks of initiating and judging derive from the organizational differences between bureaucracies and legislatures. Congress' organizational structure is more nearly horizontal in nature; the executive branch's, more nearly hierarchical. As a decentralized institution, Congress can never achieve the degree of centralized control that is requisite to develop, coordinate, and reconcile competing policy positions—all of which are necessary steps for policy initiation. What Congress is uniquely positioned organizationally to do is to judge. It does so by reacting to, and hence overseeing, executive proposals. Its decentralized structure ensures that multiple perspectives and points of view will flourish and be brought to bear upon anything that comes before it. Centralization is necessary to produce the coherence that the initiation of policy proposals requires. Decentralization is aptly suited to the task of overseeing—to judging, amending, and ultimately legitimizing proposals that have originated elsewhere.

Congressman Les Aspin, a member of the House Armed Services Committee, has aptly summarized the institutional nature of the Congress and why it is best suited for oversight, not initiation:

A second role that Congress performs [the first being a conduit for constituent views and the third acting as guardian of the processes of government] is as general overseer of government policies and resource allocation. In this role it acts not unlike a board of trustees. With very few exceptions, Congress is not the place where policy is initiated. Most Congressional committees or subcommittees have no overall plan or policy which they would like to see implemented in the area of their concern. The Pay and Allowances Subcommittee of the House Armed Services Committee has, for example, no guiding policy about the structure of pay and allowances in the armed forces. They do not initiate legislation in this area, but simply modify, if necessary, and ultimately give their approval to what the Executive is proposing to do. In performing this role they have certain advantages. They have often had long years of experience, and they know what has been tried before. They have lines of communication open to various branches of the armed forces, which provide them with information that the Executive may not have; and they are very sensitive to the conflicting pressures that build up around any change in policy.

There are, of course, exceptions to the rule. Some committees or subcommittees try to take the lead or initiate new policy. . . . But any effort to do so is hampered by divergences in the views of individual committee members and wariness about taking issues to the floor, where, without Administration support, they are likely to be defeated. Most committees wait for the Administration to send over its proposals, and then they consider them from what might be described as a board-of-trustees perspective; this can be very useful, but it does not constitute leadership. Even this board-of-trustees function could be vastly improved—investigative work and legislative supervision are both activities that Congressional committees could and should do better and more extensively.[44]

Not only is Congress best suited for oversight, but its resources, even for this task, are limited. It must husband and use them efficiently. No matter how large its staffs become, it can never compete with the Pentagon in this respect. Influencing policy by its attempts to manage programs selectively is a poor way for Congress to deal with matters when compared to its ability to influence policy by getting better Pentagon management on all programs. In a task as large and complex as the formulation of the U.S. global defense posture, Congress can best influence policy by enabling (and requiring) the Pentagon to get things more nearly right before they come to Congress for consideration. Congress should take to heart the lesson it has applied to the task of federal budgeting in general: It does its task best when it gets the executive branch to do the bulk of the work for it. Structural reform of the Pentagon is, therefore, *the* fundamental step.

Viewed in broad perspective, then, the three attributes of the new congressional role in defense—budgeteering by the armed services committees, attempts at detailed management of the budget by the four defense actors, and slighting of policy oversight by all committee actors—are all pieces of the same whole. For they reflect the more general approach that Congress has taken toward defense matters since the end of World War II. After the end of the war, Congress created a type of defense structure that inevitably drew it deeply into defense matters. That was done because that was what the Congress wanted.

Since 1945, the Congress has favored a decentralized, pluralistic, and competitive defense establishment over one centrally run, highly hierarchical, and tightly controlled. It has favored pluralism and competition there so as to be better informed about what is happening and so as to be better positioned to arbitrate among the competitors. A decentralized defense establishment is the type of structure that enhances Congress' own power over it. One more centralized would risk a diminution in both its access to the information necessary to make decisions and its power to arbitrate and decide. As Huntington once put it: "Congress' constant concern with the danger of the 'Prussian General Staff System' reflected not so much a fear of enhanced military power as a fear of enhanced executive power."[45]

A secretary of defense truly powerful in his bailiwick would likely curtail the role that Congress would play in the more daily and mundane affairs of the Pentagon. If the secretary had the power to force decisions and make the sensible tradeoffs needed, there would be greater confidence in Congress about the state of affairs there, greater confidence in the quality of the products that reach it for consideration, less reason for it to second guess matters, and hence less need for it to attempt to manage defense affairs in such detail.[46] Similarly, if the nature and functioning of the Joint Chiefs of Staff were altered so as to produce better military advice for the secretary, his task—and that of the Congress—would be made easier. Just as the Congress can oversee and influence policy better if the Pentagon does better quality work, so too can the secretary of defense better oversee and influence military policy if the Joint Chiefs of Staff do better quality work.

Thus, the less confidence Congress has had in the Pentagon's management of its own affairs, the more deeply it has been drawn into them.[47] Congress' treatment of the defense budget suffers from too detailed a focus at the expense of the broader questions. The same has applied to the secretary's position vis-à-vis the military services. He has tried to do too much in military policy because the services have done too little. Lack of the proper defense structure has led to both congressional and secretarial micromanagement. Congress has thus accepted poor management within the Defense Department as the price to be paid for its deep and detailed intervention in military affairs.

The specific details of the changes that Congress must make in Pentagon organization need not concern us. What is essential, however, is that two alterations of a general nature be made: First, the quality of military advice and service use of resources must be improved; and, second, the secretary must be given the authority necessary to engage in an across-the-Pentagon oversight that will improve the degree of coordination and integration of military affairs. Pentagon reform must begin with a strengthening of the only two integrating bodies that exist in the Pentagon today—the Joints Chiefs of Staff and the secretary of defense.[48] Only by strengthening these two agents can there be hope of reducing duplication of missions, redundancy among weapons, and neglect of what are nontraditional, but urgently needed, service missions. Only by strengthening these two agents will the hands of those (the commanders of the unified and specified commands) who speak for readiness and sustainability be strengthened. Only a strengthened secretary of defense and his military counterparts can perceive the collective interest and construct it from the separate ones.

Timeliness in Budgeting

The second task Congress must accomplish is to authorize and appropriate the defense bills in a timely fashion. This has not happened consistently under the procedures of the 1974 Act, even though timeliness in passing appropriations bills was one of the purposes for which the new procedures were devised. For a period, the budget act forced Congress to get its act together, but that was a short lived phenomenon. The situation now is better than before, but only marginally. From fiscal years 1962–76, Congress passed 167 out of 174 appropriations bills after the start of the fiscal year. For fiscal years 1977–82, Congress passed 57 out of 84 late. The percentage of late bills in the first period was 96 percent; in the second, 68 percent.[49] More to the point, although matters were initially better under the act, they have become progressively worse. As the following table shows, since the act came into full force in 1977, the number of appropriations bills passed before the beginning of the fiscal year progressively decreased:[50]

Fiscal Year	No. of Bills Enacted by 10/1
1977	13
1978	9
1979	5
1980	3
1981	1
1982	0
1983	1
1984	4

In fiscal year 1985, which was an election year, the congressional budget process nearly collapsed because of political maneuverings between the Democratic House and the Republican presidency. Deadlines were not met and appropriations bills were late. Election years complicate the budget process when one party fails to control the presidency and both houses of Congress. But the point is that the process was in deep trouble before 1984. In the case of the defense appropriations bills, five out of seven of them from fiscal years 1977–82 were passed after the start of the fiscal year.

The defense budgeting process is affected by the procedures of the 1974 budget act. If timeliness in defense appropriations is to be achieved, some modifications in the budget act are required. Currently, the most carefully prepared approach is contained in the set of recommendations of the Beilenson Task Force of the House Rules Committee.[51] Its report represents two years of detailed study and consensus building within the House, where opposition to the budget act has been more vocal than in the Senate.

In making its recommendations, the task force adopted a guiding principle: Make a virtue out of necessity. It accepted the new budget procedures as a permanent feature of Congress, but suggested putting into law those informal practices, as they have evolved since 1974, which have modified the 1974 Act. The task force also accepted the fact that radical changes—such as biennial budgeting, abolition of the budget committees, or the consolidation of the appropriating and authorizing committees into program committees (committees that would both authorize and appropriate after being given budget authority allocations by the budget committee)—do not currently have sufficient political support within Congress to be adopted, although it did suggest that biennial budgeting be studied in order to determine its substantive as opposed to its political feasibility. In short, the approach of the Beilenson Task Force was to preserve the new budgeting process in the face of considerable opposition to it and to recommend incremental improvements in the process because they seemed more likely to be adopted.

Of relevance to our considerations are three major changes recommended by the task force. First, Congress can gain more time for the annual budgeting exercise by accelerating its timetable, thus starting work earlier. Second, Congress need pass only one binding budget resolution each year, which should come at the outset, not at the end, of the process. Third, Congress should develop a longer term perspective on budgeting by taking seriously three features of advanced budgeting: one-year-ahead-of-time authorizations, multi-year authorizations, and adoption in the single budget resolution of more binding planning numbers for two years beyond the current fiscal year under consideration.

Table 7–5 sets forth the accelerated timetable for Congress. Compared to the current budgetary timetable (refer to Table 7–3), Congress would begin its calendar year work about two weeks earlier than it now does. The task force recommends even greater acceleration in the specific steps of the budget process. It pushes up by one month the adoption of the single binding budget resolution to April 15 from May 15 and allows nearly one and one-half months for House-Senate conference work on their respective appropriations bills. It also requires monthly scheduling of authorizing and appropriations bills by the leadership of the House so that the traditional May-June floor logjam can be avoided. Finally,

Table 7–5. Congressional Budget Timetable Recommended by Beilenson Task Force.

January 3	Congress convenes and elects committees by seventh day after commencement of new Congress
First Monday after January 3	President submits his budget
	Congressional Budget Office submits a report listing authorizations expiring prior to the upcoming fiscal year
By February 15	Congressional Budget Office submits its annual report on fiscal policy to budget committees
By February 25	Standing committees submit views and estimates to budget committees
By April 15	Congress adopts its budget resolution
By June 10	House Appropriations Committee reports all general appropriations measures for upcoming fiscal year
By June 4 Recess	House completes consideration of all general appropriations measures and any reconciliation measures before considering a resolution for adjournment for the Independence Day District Work Period
By August 15	Senate completes consideration of all general appropriations measures
October 1	Fiscal year begins

Source: Committee on Rules, House of Representatives, 98th Congress, 2nd Session, *Report of the Task Force on the Budget Process* (Beilenson Task Force) (May 1984), pp. 18–25.

the task force has cannily tied the traditional July 4 House recess to the accelerated budget schedule: Complete passage of all appropriations bills and any reconciliation measures that may be necessary must occur before the House can take its July recess. In short, timely completion of the budget is to be achieved by starting earlier in the year and by working more efficiently during it.

Second, the task force has called for abandonment of the Second Concurrent Resolution and passage of only one resolution, which would come at the outset of the process and would be binding. This modification reflects a recognition that under current procedures, the First Resolution, because it sets only targets and not binding figures, has proved a political football and has wasted much time. Members could vote for the First Resolution because they knew it was not binding. Authorizing committees could ignore the targets because they affected only budget authority, not authorizing authority. Both the authorizing and appropriating committees could be cavalier about their March 15 recommendations, because they knew that the real battles would be with the appropriations bills and with any reconciliation measures that would be needed some four months hence. Recommendations were, therefore, inflated to allow freedom to maneuver later on. Passage of a single binding resolution at the outset considerably strengthens the process by forcing members and their committees to take their reviews of the president's requests and their recommendations for spending in the functional accounts more seriously. There is likely to be less slippage and game playing in the entire process if it "bites" earlier than it previously has. Finally, because the Congress has been politically unable to pass a Second Concurrent Resolution these last three years (having merely affirmed the First Resolution as the Second in September), the task force has recommended making de jure what has become de facto.

Third, the Beilenson Task Force has urged that Congress take seriously some of the advanced budgeting features suggested in the 1974 Act so as to mitigate the more unproductive aspects of annual budgeting. The 1974 Act asked that authorizing committees consider and recommend to the floor authorizing legislation one year in advance of the year in which appropriations would be made. Authorizations on the fiscal year 1985 budget, for example, should be completed in the 1983 calendar year. By reaffirming this recommendation, the task force has attempted to end the delays in budgeting caused by the lateness in the authorizing committees' work. By calling for more multi-year, and fewer annual, authorizations, it has attempted to achieve the same objective. Finally, by recommending that Congress take a three-year perspective in its budgeting, it has asked for the longer term view that could counteract the one-year-at-a-time focus of the present process.[52]

Moreover, if Congress took the outyear figures of its current resolutions more seriously, it could require the executive to submit budget requests that conformed to the outyear *outlay* figures contained in previous budget resolutions.[53] Requiring the administration to submit requests that conform to the outyear figures, but not making the outyear figures have the force of law, could get around the constitutional provision that makes appropriations for the army beyond two years unconstitutional. Congress would therefore not make the outyear figures binding upon itself, but would require the administration to use them as the starting point for its budget formulation. The administration would have the flexibility to depart from those figures, but the onus should be on it for explaining why there is the need to do so. If multi-year planning is to mean something, then steps must be taken to make the outyear figures a credible basis for planning *within* the Pentagon.

Through a combination of all these measures, the task force has tried to preserve the main features of the annual budgeting process, but at the same time build into it a multi-year perspective. If the features for timeliness and advanced budgeting work, they would help to mitigate several of the more perverse defense budgeting dysfunctions. If defense bills were passed before the onset of the fiscal year, the Defense Department's management task obviously would be made easier. Timeliness in budgeting would also improve the quality of congressional oversight. Too often the defense appropriations bills have been part of continuing resolutions that have lumped together several appropriations bills and that have been passed hurriedly to keep the government running. This is a poor way for Congress to deal with the defense budget, because such "lumped sum" resolutions are notoriously poorly scrutinized by each house as a whole. Ill-considered, hurriedly passed, omnibus appropriations bills are not conducive to quality oversight. The advanced budgeting features of the Beilenson bill could also help mitigate the one-year-at-a-time focus that pervades budgeting today. These features could reduce the ease of buying into programs, because the three-year costs would be known up front; and, by providing estimates for three years, they could make program funding more stable, which is a requirement for more efficient production rates. Were the Congress to realize timeliness and a multi-year perspective in annual budgeting, at least two of the five defense dysfunctions could be ameliorated.

Can the Congress achieve timeliness and a multi-year perspective with an *annual* budget process? No one has a definitive answer to this question. Only implementation of the above reforms will provide the evidence necessary to evaluate their success. There is some basis for optimism, however. The new budget process worked reasonably well initially, at least with regard to timeliness. Matters became especially bad during the first three Reagan years, a period of intense budgetary conflict between a Republican president and Senate on the one hand and a Democratic House on the other. Delay in the passage of appropriations bills was due as much to political disagreements and polarization as it was to anything inherent in the process itself. No procedure, no matter how good, can override intense and powerful political forces.

More to the point, it is not evident that another major alternative—biennial budgeting—considered but rejected for now by the Beilenson Task Force—would improve matters significantly. The purpose of biennial budgeting is to reduce the budgetary workload of Congress and at the same time enhance its oversight activity by giving the authorizing committees more time to do it. Rather than go through the time-consuming process each year, Congress would take two years to pass a budget that would last two years. During those two years, the first would be devoted to oversight and passage of legislation by the authorizing committees; the second, to passage of appropriations bills.

At first glance, the biennial budget looks quite attractive, but a closer look reveals several problems. First, it is not self-evident that a two-year budget would enhance the quality of policy oversight, at least in the defense area. Biennial budgeting per se will do little to enhance policy oversight as long as the armed services committees adhere to their budgeteering approach. Biennial budgeting could even work adversely to increase further their "trees-instead-of-the-forest approach." By giving the committees twelve instead of three months to review the president's budget, the biennial approach is permissive: more detailed line iteming can happen *if* that is the inclination of the authorizing committees. The biennial approach must depend upon factors extraneous to it if better quality policy oversight is to occur. Alone, neither biennial budgeting nor the Beilenson reforms can produce it. By giving Congress more time to budget, moreover, Congress may take more time to budget. Budgeting could expand to fill the time available, and the Congress could become more, not less, preoccupied with it. Finally, by calling for a budget to last two years in the face of often swiftly changing economic circumstances, biennial budgeting may in fact produce annual budgeting, but in another guise: frequent supplementals and revisions, which themselves could consume a great deal of Congress' time.

None of the above objections deals with the political saleability of biennial budgeting. Members complain about the time that annual budgeting takes, but they also know that it is one of their most powerful tools for controlling executive agencies. Two-year budgets would, of necessity, require that Congress grant more flexibility to the executive than it now does. Whether Congress is ready for such a grant is problematical. Most other democratic nations, even though some of them claim to do multi-year budgeting, in fact do not. What they do is multi-year *planning* within the framework of annual budgeting, exactly the approach envisioned by the Beilenson bill.

None of the above has to happen under biennial budgeting. Nor is it cast in stone that Congress would never give up annual budgeting. The points remain, however, that all of the above *could* happen and that Congress as yet is unlikely to adopt biennial budgeting. As the Beilenson Task Force recommends, biennial budgeting should be studied further. But until the potential pitfalls are thought through more carefully, the more modest but achievable approach of the Beilenson report should be pursued.[54]

Enhancement of Quality Policy Oversight

The third thing that Congress can do to improve defense budgeting is to engage in more policy oversight. As was pointed out above, however, this may be the most difficult to achieve. For all the reasons stated earlier, political incentives, as they are currently structured, work against it. As Warner Schilling sagely observed many years earlier: "At election time little reward will await the Congressmen who chose to become expert critics of the defense budget, and no punishment will befall their colleagues who did not."[55] If policy oversight is to occur, therefore, it must be grounded in concrete political incentives, not in specific procedural requirements.

Let me describe a few specific things that could be done to put some bounds on budgeteering by the armed services committees before wrestling with the more difficult question of how to create the political incentives to do more quality policy oversight. This seems reasonable because some limits must be put on budgeteering if there is to be more time and resources for policy oversight.

First, the armed services committees could move to multi-year authorizations of the defense budget. Defense appropriations would still be done annually, and, as a consequence, the armed services committees would be giving up some of their close control over programs. The effects of the loss of power in a multi-year authorization and annual appropriation combination, however, could be lessened for the committees if the reprogramming of defense funds were done on a more regular and systematic basis.[56] The armed services committees could authorize the defense budget for a three year period but be involved, along with the defense appropriations subcommittees, in approval of any Pentagon reprogramming of funds. If the Defense Department were required to come to the Congress regularly—say two or three times a year rather than haphazardly as is now the case—and bring before it the changes that must inevitably be made in programs, the committees could monitor significant program changes. The armed services committees would retain control over the approval of new programs (R&D) and of production buys (procurement), but would give up fine-tuning each program each year. Through these devices, they would be assured of being involved in any major program changes, such as cancellations or large alterations in production runs, and would confine the bulk of their efforts to initial approval and periodic review of programs.

A variant of this approach is one suggested by John J. Hamre of the Congressional Budget Office.[57] It calls for "milestone" authorizations, a specific form of multi-year authorizations, in lieu of annual authorizations. Congress could establish its own "milestone review process," modelled after the DSARC (Defense Systems Acquisition Review Council) process of the Pentagon. At each phase in a weapon systems life cycle—research and development, full scale engineering and development, initial award of procurement funds, further production buys—the

Congress would require from the Pentagon full documentation. Before each milestone decision is made, the armed services and appropriations committees would have to review, accept, modify, or cancel the Pentagon's proposed action. Congress would, therefore, review a given program intensively only during the critical decision points in its development.

This proposal would make sense, as Hamre argues, only in the framework of multi-year authorizations for both research and development and production. Its virtues are several: It retains for Congress the final say over any milestone decision; it forces the Pentagon to do the work by providing documentation in presentable form for congressional review; it pushes the committees out of detailed management; and it saves some scarce committee time for other matters. In short, it substitutes selective review for annual management but without loss of significant control. It has the final advantage of tying congressional oversight to a specific procedure, something that always works well for an institution that is itself poorly run and buffeted by short-term political winds.

Third, the armed services committees could take up the suggestion of Senator Pete Domenici and treat different aspects of the defense budget differently.[58] Research and development and procurement could be authorized on a multi-year basis; operations and maintenance and personnel on an annual basis. Multi-year authorizations make a great deal of sense for programs in development, just as they do for those in production. Operations and maintenance involve items where the connection between budget authority and outlays is quite close, as is the case also with personnel. Considering their clear and significant effect on readiness, it makes sense that they be annually authorized and protected from undue cutting by the appropriations committees.

These three devices have been presented merely for illustration. There is no dearth of ideas on how to get the armed services committees out of budgeteering and yet still enable them to retain significant control over the programs in the defense budget. The dilemma, however, is that the devices cannot substitute for the will to do so. If the will is there, the exact devices best suited for a more selective yet still influential programmatic control will quickly be found.

Exactly the same problem exists for policy oversight. The problem, then, is how to create the incentives for doing policy oversight. Only one comes to mind, and here we should take a lesson from the House Armed Services Committee. When it appeared that readiness was suffering because there was no constituency on the Hill to do it, the committee created one by constituting a subcommittee on readiness. Why can the same not be done for policy oversight? On the Senate Armed Services Committee in particular, there are members such as Sam Nunn, Gary Hart, and William Cohen, who are unhappy with the current budgeteering approach and whose instincts and outlook run to the more general questions that policy oversight involves. A subcommittee whose province it is to oversee policy generally—one, moreover, that consists of members whose interests and energy run in that direction—could create the agency necessary to begin systematically building policy oversight into the annual (or biennial) budgeting process. This type of subcommittee could combine a wide-ranging mandate with a group of self-styled policy entrepreneurs. That is, in fact, the way that Congress works best: It combines the individualistic and entrepreneurial nature of congressional initiative with the subcommittee structure of Congress. In short, it combines the personal and the institutional.

Over the long run, the Senate Armed Services Committee is the best place to create such an agency, not only because of the predilections of several of its younger members, but also because the Senate committee traditionally has taken the road of "high" policy.[59] Not every committee that deals with defense matters has to engage in policy oversight for such a task to be done; it is sufficient for one to do it. This is so because of the iron law of executive-legislative relations: Because the Congress reacts, the executive anticipates. If there is a clearly defined group within the Senate committee that will engage in more systematic oversight of general policy matters, the Pentagon will be required to do so also. What was the case for annual budgeteering can be the case for policy oversight. The overweening focus on the annual budget to the neglect of the longer term occurred in the Pentagon to a large extent because it happened previously in the Congress. The Pentagon had no choice but to focus primarily on the next fiscal year because Congress' actions required it to do so. In some fashion, the same should happen for policy oversight. If a Hill constituency does it, the Pentagon will be forced to do so out of self-defense.

This may seem a weak reed upon which to hang so momentous a task as policy oversight. Perhaps it is. But at least it is realistic. Members of Congress will do only what is in their interests. The creation of a Hill constituency for policy oversight, by whatever means, is the only way that such a review will in the long run be sustainable.

CONCLUSION

Taken together, these three reforms—structural change in the Pentagon, timeliness in budgeting, and more emphasis on policy oversight—could accomplish much. They could reverse some of the more negative aspects of Congress' treatment of defense by reviving the sensible distinction between the authorizing and appropriating committees. They could make Congress more selective, yet still influential, in its programmatic focus. And they could build policy oversight into whatever type of budgeting procedures the Congress ultimately ends up with. In the process, they could ameliorate, even if not eradicate, the defense budgetary dysfunctions that have for so long eluded our control.

In our expectations for improvement, however, we must be cautious. As has been argued, the dysfunctions in defense budgeting stem from powerful political forces built into the very structure of the defense policy process. Similarly, the programmatic/fiscal focus and the detailed congressional control over the defense budget stem from powerful political factors built into the current political system, both within Congress and between the Congress and the executive branch. Even with significant structural change of the Pentagon, the habits of nearly a quarter of a century will not easily wither. The best that we may hope for, short of a revival of partly discipline and Pentagon structural reform, may be only some more systematic policy oversight along with annual budgeteering. But even that is a significant improvement over what now obtains.

NOTES

1. Research support for this piece has been provided by the Arms Control Seminar of New York held at Columbia University, the Roosevelt Center for the Study of American Policy, the Ford Foundation, and the Defense Reorganization Project of the Georgetown Center for Strategic and International Studies. I am indebted to Warner R. Schilling for suggesting the subject to me and for providing the initial research support and to Warner, Barry Blechman, I.M. Destler, Richard Fenno, and Allen Schick for comments on earlier drafts of this piece. To the nearly one hundred staffers (to whom I promised confidentiality) and to the handful of members of Congress whom I have interviewed from 1979 through 1984, I also owe a great debt. I would also like to thank Ruth Elvin for her assistance in the preparation of the tables. This piece draws from my book in progress, *Legislating Defense: The "New" Congress and National Security.*

2. In the 96th Congress (1979–80), for example, junior members constituted 50 percent of the House; careerists (those serving ten or more terms), 13 percent. By comparison, in the 92nd Congress (1971–72), the proportion of members who had served six or fewer years was 34 percent; and the proportion who had served twenty or more years was 20 percent. In the Senate, the number of junior senators increased from twenty-seven in 1971 to forty-eight in 1979. See Thomas E. Mann, "Elections and Change in Congress," in Thomas E. Mann and Norman J. Ornstein, eds., *The New Congress* (Washington, D.C.: The American Enterprise Institute, 1981), pp. 36–37.

3. See Arthur Maass, *Congress and the Common Good* (New York: Basic Books, 1983), pp. 54–63 for a useful summary of the purposes and types of congressional reforms in the 1970s. For an excellent essay that relates changes within Congress to changes in the state of presidential-congressional relations, see Lawrence C. Dodd, "Congress and the Quest for Power," in Lawrence C. Dodd and Bruce I. Oppenheimer, eds., *Congress Reconsidered* (Washington, D.C.: Congressional Quarterly Press, 1977), pp. 269–307.

4. For a thoughtful analysis that argues that more staff does not mean better policy, see Michael J. Malbin, *Unelected Representatives: Congressional Staff and the Future of Representative Government* (New York: Basic Books, 1980).

5. The best book on the origins of the act and the early years of the new congressional budget process is Allen Schick's *Congress and Money: Budgeting, Spending and Taxing* (Washington, D.C.: The Urban Institute, 1980). Also useful are Schick, "The

Three-Ring Budget Process: The Appropriations, Tax, and Budget Committees in Congress," in Mann and Ornstein, eds., *The New Congress*; Schick, *The Congressional Budget Act of 1974: Legislative History and Analysis* (Washington, D.C.: Congressional Research Service, 26 February 1976); U.S. Congress, Joint Study Committee on Budget Control, *Recommendations for Improving Congressional Control over Budgetary Outlay and Receipt Totals*, 18 April 1973; John W. Ellwood and James A. Thurber, "The New Congressional Budget Process: the Hows and Why of Senate–House Differences," in Dodd and Oppenheimer, eds., *Congress Reconsidered*; Dennis S. Ippolito, *Congressional Spending* (Ithaca: Cornell University Press, 1981; Lance T. Leloup, *The Fiscal Congress* (Westport: Greenwood Press, 1980); and Joel Havemann, *Congress and the Budget* (Bloomington: Indiana University Press, 1978).

6.   My analysis of both the workings of the new budget process and the congressional treatment of the defense budget relies primarily on over one hundred interviews that I conducted with congressional staff and to whom I promised confidentiality. To avoid numerous footnotes, I cite an interview source (by committee or personal staff) only when directly quoting someone. Thus, all assertions about the budget process or the manner in which Congress deals with the defense budget are supported by at least three interviews. These were conducted with staff members of the defense subcommittees of the House and Senate Appropriations Committees, the House and Senate Armed Services Committees, the House and Senate Budget Committees, personal staff of representatives and senators who handle foreign, defense, and budget issues, other selected staff, and relevant individuals from the Congressional Budget Office. These interviews began in the summer of 1979 and were concluded in the spring of 1984. They lasted anywhere from 30 to 120 minutes and were open-ended. Through these interviews, I have thus tracked the new budget process through its first ten years.

   I have relied primarily on staff, because they, hard-pressed though they are, have more time than the representatives and senators for whom they work. They were easier to see and to see for longer periods than their bosses. There is a danger, however, in relying primarily on staff perceptions. What staffers see may not be what the members of Congress or the committees they serve perceive. I feel reasonably confident, however, that this is not the case. In the main, the data collected from these staff interviews cross-checked nicely with the views of those members of Congress whom I have interviewed (about ten) and with the quantitative data that I present below.

   There are, in addition, two other reasons for my trust in the staff data. First, members of Congress have become increasingly dependent on staff, not only for knowledge and expertise on issues, but also for dealing with other members of Congress. A staffer now plays a vital role both in educating his boss *and* in helping him deal with other bosses by working with their staffs. Second, members generally set the parameters of a staffer's job, both in terms of what he can do and how he can do it. I was explicit in asking a staffer how his member or committee operated and what guidance he was given. With some credibility, therefore, I can claim to have interviewed many members of Congress, even if only indirectly. A larger project, of which this piece is a part, will involve a large number of direct interviews with members of Congress.

7. There were also features designed to circumscribe the president's ability to impound funds, but I shall omit these, because they are not relevant to the defense area.
8. Through the device of "backdoor spending," the authorizing committees were able, in effect, to authorize and appropriate funds and thereby commit the appropriations committees to a set level of spending. Entitlement programs were one type of backdoor spending. A law entitled a category of citizens to certain funds. The appropriating committees had no choice but to approve the funds in order to meet the terms of the law. Had they not done so, the federal government would have been subject to class action suits.
9. I deal with each budget committee's manner of dealing with the defense budget over the years in detail in my forthcoming *Legislating Defense*.
10. *The Congressional Budget Act of 1974*, pp. 29 and 30–32. Prior to the 1974 budget act, the fiscal year began on July 1.
11. See Louis Fisher, "Annual Authorizations: Durable Roadblocks to Biennial Budgeting," *Public Budgeting and Finance* (Spring 1983):23–40; and Fisher, "The Authorization-Appropriation Process in Congress: Formal Rules and Informal Practices," *Catholic University Law Review* 19(1979):51–105.
12. The best treatments of the advent of annual authorizations by the Armed Services Committees are Edward A. Kolodziej, *The Uncommon Defense and Congress, 1945–1963* (Columbus: Ohio State University Press, 1966), pp. 364–82; Raymond H. Dawson, "Innovation and Intervention in Defense Policy," in Robert L. Peabody and Nelson W. Polsby, eds., *New Perspectives on the House of Representatives* (Chicago: Rand McNally, 1963), pp. 273–304; Bernard K. Gordon, "The Military Budget: Congressional Phase," *Journal of Politics* 23 (November 1961):689–724; and Herbert W. Stephens, "The Role of the Legislative Committees in the Appropriations Process: A Study Focused on the Armed Services Committees," *Western Political Quarterly* 24 (March 1971): 146–62.
13. See Harrison W. Fox, Jr., and Susan Webb Hammond, *Congressional Staffs: The Invisible Force in American Lawmaking* (New York: The Free Press, 1977), p. 169.
14. See his "Congressional Committees and the Defense Budget: By the Numbers," unpublished paper, Spring 1983, p. 3.
15. See Deborah M. Kyle, "Congress 'Meddled' With Over Half of DoD's FY 84 Budget Line Items," February 1984, p. 24. My review of the documents on which this article was based, commonly called the "FADS," which are internal DoD documents that track the changes Congress makes in Pentagon spending requests, shows that Congress changed items that ranged in importance from the Trident submarine (a $1.5 billion item) to the "Naval Air Station Oceana Aircraft Parking Apron in Virginia" (a $4 million item). See the DoD document, *Congressional Action on the FY 84 Authorization Request*, pp. 30 and 54.
16. See the table of contents of the FY 84 Memorandum.
17. Quoted in the *National Journal*, 31 March 1984, p. 614.
18. Quoted in *Budget Reform Act of 1982*, Hearings before the Senate Committee on Governmental Affairs, 19 August 1982, p. 1.
19. The last three quotes are taken from my interviews and must remain confidential.
20. See the discussion below for an attempt at such counting.
21. Warner R. Schilling, "The Politics of National Defense: Fiscal 50," in Schilling, Paul Y. Hammond, and Glenn H. Snyder, *Strategy, Politics, and Defense Budgets* (New York: Columbia University Press, 1962), p. 116.

22. Edward Kolodziej, *The Uncommon Defense and Congress*, p. 487.

23. Nancy J. Bearg and Edwin A. Deagle, Jr., "Congress and the Defense Budget," in John E. Endicott and Roy W. Stafford, Jr., eds., *American Defense Policy* (Baltimore: Johns Hopkins Press, 1977), p. 337.

24. Quoted from a report of the Senate Armed Services Committee in 1977; cited by Thomas A. Dine, "The Politics of the Purse," in Alan Platt and Lawrence Weiler, eds., *Congress and Arms Control* (Boulder: Westview Press, 1978), pp. 87–88.

25. Interview with a former staff member of the House Armed Services Committee.

26. See his "Congressional Committees and the Defense Budget," pp. 40–41 and the Appendix.

27. Norman Ornstein put the case this way: "Greater activity in legislating has thus been accompanied by even greater activity in oversight. But both the House and the Senate . . . have gotten caught between the Scylla of excessive attention to legislative-administrative detail and the Charybdis of inadequate focus on the foundations of broader policy directions." See Mann and Ornstein, eds., *The New Congress*, p. 381.

28. See Lawrence C. Dodd and Richard L. Schott, *Congress and the Administrative State* (New York: John Wiley and Sons, 1979), p. 171.

29. See Samuel P. Huntington, *The Soldier and the State* (Cambridge: Harvard University Press, 1958), p. 403.

30. Kolodziej, *The Uncommon Defense*, p. 440.

31. In analyzing why the Armed Services Committees did not take one elemental step that would improve their capabilities for policy oversight—the adoption of a mission budgeting format for analysis—a sophisticated observer in the Congressional Budget Office remarked to me: "If they adopted mission budgeting, they would lose control of what the Defense Department does. If Congress decided upon strategic missions, then they would delegate to the OSD control over weapons procurement and give the OSD much greater freedom to allocate among the services. For then the OSD could define what systems could be used for what missions and which services would perform them. This is the central reason—loss of control—why Armed Services will not do mission budgeting."

32. Scher, "Conditions for Legislative Control," *Journal of Politics* 25 (August 1963): 531. Scher's article remains the best single analysis of why oversight routinely does not occur and why periodically it does.

33. Malbin, *Unelected Representatives*, pp. 35–36.

34. This is the message of David Mayhew, *Congress: The Electoral Connection* (New Haven: Yale University Press, 1974). He argues that the safeness of an incumbent's seat is not a good measure of how hard he runs for reelection. The fact that his seat is safe can just as easily reflect how hard he runs while in office to discourage formidable competitors from taking him on rather than being attributable to any other factors.

35. Schilling, "The Politics of National Defense," pp. 248–49.

36. These two quotes are drawn from my interviews.

37. See J. Ronald Fox, *Arming America: How the U.S. Buys Weapons* (Boston: Harvard Graduate School of Business Administration, 1974), p. 138.

38. See Robert J. Art, "Restructuring the Military-Industrial Complex: Arms Control in Institutional Perspective," *Public Policy* 22 (Fall 1974):431.

39. A recent study by The Analytical Services Corporation (TASC) of Washington, D.C., for the air force concluded that funding instability was the prime cause both

of cost growth in weapons acquisition and of the decline in units produced. Based on studies of successful and not-so-successful programs, it concluded that on the average 20 percent savings on each program could be realized if production occurred at efficient rates. I am indebted to Jacques Gansler, Vice President of TASC, for providing me with a copy of this study.

40. There is some evidence that the Weinberger Pentagon has tried to take the planning phase of PPBS more seriously. It is too early to know the results. See John Bellinger, "Strategic Planning and Decision Making in the Defense Department," unpublished paper, June 1984. Also, there is some evidence that one of the services, the air force, has begun multi-year planning by use of a technique called "baselining." That requires accurate pricing of the entire costs of a weapon and the reserving (akin to encumbered accounting) of funds for the weapon in future budgets. If both practices are taken seriously, it will mean fewer starts on new systems.

41. For the best recent statement on these issues, see Morton and David Halperin, "The Key West Accord," *Foreign Policy* (Winter 1983–84):114–130.

42. See *Department of Defense Appropriations for 1985*. Hearings before a Subcommittee of the Committee on Appropriations, House, 98th Congress, 2nd Session, Part I, pp. 665, 801, and 902.

43. The recent report by the Pentagon on readiness is more optimistic than the House report. But even it notes some serious deficiencies. See *Improvements in U.S. Warfighting Capability, FY 1980–1984*, May 1984.

44. Les Aspin, "The Defense Budget and Foreign Policy: The Role of Congress," in Franklin A. Long and George W. Rathjens, eds., *Arms, Defense Policy, and Arms Control* (New York: W.W. Norton, 1976), p. 168.

   Aspin's view that Congress can do a better job of overseeing and legislating is not idiosyncratic. A House Commission on Administrative Review concluded the following in 1977 (as reported by Roger H. Davidson): "In the 1977 survey, 154 House members were asked to identify those activities that should be very important and those to which they actually devoted a great deal of time. The greatest gaps occurred in such activities as studying and legislative research; overseeing executive agencies, either personally or through formal subunits; debating and voting on legislation; negotiation with other members to build support for legislation; and working in committees to develop legislation. See Roger H. Davidson, "Subcommittee Government: New Channels for Policy Making," in Mann and Ornstein, eds., *The New Congress*.

45. Huntington, *The Soldier and the State*, p. 423.

46. For an analysis of how little real power the secretary of defense has over the Pentagon, see James Schlesinger, "The Role of the Secretary of Defense," in Robert J. Art, Vincent Davis, and Samuel P. Huntington, eds., *Reorganizing the Pentagon: Leadership in War and Peace* (New York: Pergamon, 1985).

47. Robert Pastor found that much the same pattern had occurred in foreign economic policy. The Congress delegated power to (or took it back from) the president in direct relation to the degree of trust (or distrust) it had in him. See his *Congress and the Politics of U.S. Foreign Economic Policy, 1929–1976* (Berkeley: University of California Press, 1980).

48. For a perceptive set of detailed suggestions for Pentagon reorganization, see Samuel P. Huntington, "Defense Organization and Military Strategy," *The Public Interest* (Spring 1984):20–47.

49. See *Proposed Improvements in the Congressional Budget Act of 1974*. Hearings before the Committee on the Budget, U.S. Senate, 97th Congress, 2nd Session, September 14, 16, 21, and 23, 1982, p. 305.

50. See *The Congressional Budget Process*. Hearings before the Task Force on the Budget Process of the Committee on Rules, U.S. House of Representatives, 98th Congress, 1st Session, 29 April 1983, p. 73; and *Report of the Task Force on the Budget Process of the Committee on Rules*, U.S. House of Representatives, May 1984, p. 331.

51. See the Report of the Task Force on the Budget Process of the Committee on Rules, House, 98th Congress, 2nd Session, May 1984. The formal title is *Recommendations to Improve the Congressional Budget Process*. It is commonly referred to as the Beilenson Report, after the chairman of the task force, Congressman Anthony C. Beilenson.

52. In this regard, the Beilenson Bill (H.R. 5247) has further recommended that the allocations made to the spending committees by the budget committee could be made effective for up to three years. That is, while the aggregate spending, revenue, and functional allocations in the budget resolution would hold only for a year at a time (with planning numbers for two additional years), the specific spending allocations to committees (what are known as the 302A allocations) could hold for up to three years.

53. Budget authority differs from outlays. Budget authority creates the legal right for an executive agency to obligate funds and have them paid from the federal treasury. The funds thereby obligated may or may not be spent in the given fiscal year for which they have been obligated. Outlays are those funds that are *actually* spent in a given fiscal year.

54. Some analysts, such as Jacques Gansler, have argued that biennial budgeting will work to provide more stability in defense program funding because funds will be allocated for more than one year, managers of weapons programs can therefore plan better and stretch-outs can thereby be avoided. This is another example of where biennial or multi-year appropriations per se will do little to solve a problem. The stretching out of programs occurs because there are too many programs chasing too few dollars. It has nothing to do with how many years the dollars are obligated for. Too few dollars obligated over three years instead of two are still too few dollars. With the shortage of funds, production runs for each program have to be reduced each year in order to stay within the overall budget. Multi-year appropriations will do little to prevent this. Only the stopping of the practice of starting more programs than the budget can sustain (buying in) will obviate the inefficient practice of stretch outs. For Gansler's analysis, see his "Reforming the Defense Budget Process," *The Public Interest* (Spring 1984):   •
62–76.

55. "The Politics of National Defense," p. 116.

56. I am indebted to former Secretary of Defense Melvin Laird for this suggestion, which was made when I presented several of my proposals for reform to the Steering Committee of the Defense Reorganization Project in February 1984.

57. See John Hamre's proposals in chapter 8 of this volume, "Potential New Patterns of Congressional Review of Defense Budget Requests."

58. See his testimony before the Senate Budget Committee, 21 September 1982, in *Proposed Improvements in the Congressional Budget Act of 1974*, p. 141.

59. Les Aspin, the new chairman of the House Armed Services Committee, has created a policy panel with such a purpose in mind. He refrained from establishing the panel as a regular subcommittee to avoid a battle over subcommittee chairmanships.

8 POTENTIAL NEW PATTERNS OF CONGRESSIONAL REVIEW OF DEFENSE BUDGET REQUESTS

by
John J. Hamre

Almost no one likes the current way the Congress reviews and approves the defense budget. The debate seems endless. The defense budget request draws the first critical comments of the annual budget cycle and is almost guaranteed to be the one appropriation left unfinished at the start of the fiscal year, requiring the Department of Defense (DoD) to spend at least part of the year under the authority of a continuing appropriation. The hearings are repetitive, and the decisions are subject to countless appeals and frequent compromises in other committees or the other chamber. Increasingly, participants with little substantive knowledge and even less institutional jurisdictional credibility disrupt the process. The Congress debates the same issues year after year after year. It is all very frustrating.

Many observers with widely differing substantive perspectives on defense issues share a common conviction that biennial budgeting offers a remedy for this situation. If the Congress would undertake the painful process of establishing budget priorities only half as often, the remainder of the time could be devoted to other substantive legislative matters. I am not convinced this is right. Biennial budgeting would be very difficult, if not impossible, to implement. More important, however, the problems with the way the Congress establishes defense priorities are not likely to be solved by adjusting timetables in the budget process. The budget process does not cause but rather highlights the underlying

---

This paper reflects the opinions of the author and not necessarily those of the Congressional Budget Office or any member or employee of the Congress.

weaknesses in the congressional defense debate. Before outlining those weaknesses, I should like first to review several biennial budgeting proposals in order to indicate the limits of this approach as a solution to the shortcomings of current procedures.

THE PREOCCUPATION WITH BIENNIAL BUDGETING

Numerous members of the House and the Senate have introduced or cosponsored legislation to establish a biennial budget process. Unfortunately, for all their detail, there is no consensus on how to proceed. Although all the solutions appear to be similar, their advocates lack agreement on the principles guiding their recommendations and on the goals they seek to achieve.

Four major proposals for biennial budgeting were introduced at the start of the 98th Congress. A glance at their principal features, as presented in Table 8–1, shows that their differences are essential and not superficial. The differences reflect fundamentally divergent assessments of the failings of the current system and what should be done to amend its flaws.

S. 12 is perhaps the least radical proposal. It would extend the current one-year process over a two-year period. In this respect it contrasts with the other three. Sponsors of H.R. 750 believe that the authorizing committees have lost too much power and substantive control under current procedures and seek to rectify that deficiency by reserving the entire first session for legislative oversight. All budgeting, authorizing, and appropriating activities would be confined to the second session. Virtually the opposite philosophy informs S. 20. Its proponents place emphasis on the need to establish broad spending priorities first, incorporating those priorities in an omnibus appropriations bill, all concluded in the first session. The second session would be reserved for legislative oversight activities and substantive changes to current law. Finally, advocates of S. 922 would pare back the budgeting functions, leaving largely unchanged the annual authorizing and appropriating activities. Such a reform would de-emphasize the debate over aggregate spending priorities while retaining the traditional power arrangements between legislative and appropriating committees.

Beyond these obvious differences in philosophy and goals, there are persistent technical problems that affect all schemes for biennial budgeting. How would the system adjust to significant changes in the economy without reopening the substantive debate over spending priorities? Should substantive priorities be isolated from economic developments? In which year should deliberations take place and the budget begin? If the debate occurred in odd-numbered years, members of Congress would be forced to run for reelection on the basis of budget compromises set more than a year before the election. The sharp economic swings of

Table 8-1. Principal Features of Alternative Biennial Budgeting Proposals.

	S. 12[a]	H.R. 750[b]	S. 20[c]	S. 922[d]
Mandated Floor Action On Budget Resolutions	Both sessions	Second session only	First session only	First session only
Authorization Legislation	First session only	Second session only	Second session only	Both sessions
Appropriation Bills	Second session only	Second session only	First session only	Both sessions
Session Reserved for Legislative Oversight	Second session	First session	Second session	Both sessions
Fiscal Year to Begin in Odd/Even Year	Even	Even	Even	Odd
Structure of Budget Resolution(s)	Retain current system	Drop second concurrent resolution	Adopt new resolution procedure	Drop second concurrent resolution

[a]Budget Procedures Improvement Act of 1983, introduced by Senator Ford on 26 January 1983, with numerous cosponsors.

[b]Biennial Budgeting Act of 1983, introduced by Representative Panetta on 25 January 1983, with numerous subsequent cosponsors.

[c]Budget Reform Act of 1983, introduced by Senator Roth on 26 January 1983.

[d]Two Year Budgetary Planning Act of 1983, introduced by Senator Cochran on 24 March 1983.

the past three years highlight the perils of that approach. Were the deliberations to take place in even-numbered years, however, newly elected presidents would have to wait nearly three years to implement new policy initiatives. Since both situations would be patently unacceptable, supplemental budgets would quickly evolve into an annual budget review.

In the absence of a clear consensus on goals and philosophy, and in light of these difficult technical problems, I foresee little prospect of creating a biennial budget process. Changing the current process, in any event, is not likely to solve the fundamental problems that make the defense budget debate so inefficient and difficult. These fundamental problems are only tangentially related to the timing of budgetary milestones. In my judgment, the real challenge lies in finding ways to ameliorate the effects of these underlying problems, not in proposing changes in a budget process that only reflects the problems.

FUNDAMENTAL CHARACTERISTICS OF THE
DEFENSE BUDGET DEBATE

The problem with the current system is not the length and redundancy of the defense debate but rather its quality. Congressional review of defense issues is increasingly dominated by factors secondary to national security requirements. Three problems underlie this trend, and they should be the focus of any procedural changes. The proposals outlined in the next section will not resolve these fundamental problems, but would lessen their adverse effects.

First, the defense debate is never limited to the substantive merits of proposals based on a reasoned assessment of defense requirements. Rather, the defense budget debate has increasingly become (and probably always has been) a political debate. Although the congressional budget process has accelerated this trend, changes in the budget process will not be able to reverse it.

The budget process is the only comprehensive act of policy integration that the Congress engages in. It is designed to highlight national spending priorities and establish their relative claims to limited national resources. Defense spending, as such, is but one of a number of priorities. The defense budget request is bound to engender controversy when we have such historically unprecedented deficits. Since this condition is likely to persist for some time, the defense budget is guaranteed to be the centerpiece of controversy. It ensures that the level of defense spending and the rate of change in spending over time will be political issues, not just issues of national security policy.

Second, proponents of other national priorities have always looked to cuts in the defense budget for resources to fund their own projects. This will be even more the case in the future because of the changes in tax policy that link tax rates to inflation, erasing the inflation dividend that has helped to finance expanding government services during the past two decades. In the future, absent revisions in the tax law, revenues will grow only as the economy grows. New or enlarged programs will have to be financed by reductions in other areas or by larger deficits.

This broadening participation in the defense debate exerts a subtle pressure on the defense committees of the Congress. To retain credibility in an increasingly competitive arena, the committees have to be ever more vigorous in examining and challenging the administration's proposals. In a climate where the Congress broadly agrees on plans to cut the administration's spending request, the defense committees can retain their institutional credibility only by leading the Congress in making cuts.

The cuts in defense spending requests these last two years, and certainly those expected in fiscal year 1985, testify to this new environment. Whether this condition is permanent is open to question. Congressional cuts have become larger in no small part because of the unprecedented increases sought by the Defense Department. If future administrations moderate their annual requests, the committees will be under less pressure to reduce them. Nevertheless, the massive deficits inherent in current spending and tax policies ensure that defense spending will continue to be under close scrutiny for years to come.

Third, an unfortunate outcome of annual budgetary review is the obstacles it raises to efficient long-term planning. The yearly nature of current review procedures gives military planners an incentive to postpone difficult decisions and instead to develop defendable budget detail only for the budget year (and, to a somewhat diminished degree, for the following year). The Congress has little time, and even less incentive, to scrutinize the outyear projections because they invariably change and have little bearing on decisions that must be reached in the budget year. This unfortunate situation is amplified when the Defense Guidance provides enormous outyear spending projections, frequently accompanied by over-optimistic forecasts of falling inflation (especially the case in the late 1970s). These conditions conspire to permit far more optimistic plans than can possibly be afforded once the outyears become the budget year.

This pattern distorts near-term decisionmaking. Far more programs proceed to engineering development than the Defense Department can afford to buy with the procurement funds likely, to be available. Systems and technologies of questionable promise are not challenged sufficiently early. With funding tight only in the budget year, there is no incentive to terminate marginal programs; instead, the incentive is to pare back a large number of programs modestly. As a consequence, annual purchases of individual weapons rarely achieve efficient production rates, systems judged to be technically obsolete are sometimes sustained, redundant efforts continue, and new program starts must accept a slower production buildup. In short, the preoccupation with only the current budget year, combined with unrealistic outyear projections, creates an excessive number of future claimants to the defense budget, all with economic and thus political interests at stake in the budget process.

The Congress currently lacks a means of tempering unrealistic five-year plans. Even more important, the Congress lacks a means of relating aggregate five-year spending levels to detailed acquisition and operations plans. For example, can we afford to buy both the C-5 and the C-17 transport aircraft if the defense budget grows only 3 percent annually in real terms over the next five years? If the added airlift capabilities are that necessary, what other priorities can be deferred in a 3 percent real growth budget? This absence of a credible means for reviewing five-year plans is the third—and perhaps most pernicious—problem confronting the Congress as it seeks ways to amend its current procedures for reviewing defense budgets.

SOME ALTERNATIVE PROCEDURES FOR REVIEWING DEFENSE BUDGET REQUESTS

The burden of reform rests with the two legislative committees, the House and Senate Armed Services Commitees. The current annual defense budget review process is really of their making. Anxious to limit what they considered undue interference by outsiders in the process, and particularly to delimit the power of the appropriations committees, the two armed services committees have pressed during the last twenty years for even greater control over the process. For better or worse, control evolved along the lines of annual authorizations of virtually all components of the defense budget. If the process has become burdensome, these two committees will have to take the lead in changing it.

There is little hope, in my judgment, that sweeping reform will solve the problems. Sweeping reforms generally entail removing procedural steps that were developed as instruments to gain and exercise power. Annual authorizations are just such instruments of power. If the armed services committees are to abandon annual authorizations, they will need other tools that will allow them to retain control while channeling the debate in more productive ways. That is the emphasis of the following recommendations.

Establish Explicit "Congressional DSARC" Milestones

For procurement of major new weapon systems, the Defense Department follows elaborate procedures explicitly outlined in DoD directives that collectively might be called major systems acquisition procedures. These outline a series of major milestones in the life-cycle development of a new major weapon system. Though the procedures change somewhat with the emphasis of each administration, the acquisition milestones identify key program development phases such as concept development, demonstration and evaluation, full-scale development, and production go-ahead decisions. At each phase a Defense Systems Acquisition Review Council (DSARC) meets to assay the promise of a system in meeting documented needs. Each DSARC phase represents a major decision point in the development cycle of a new weapon system.

The Congress has had no similar explicit review process. Informally, however, two events in congressional review serve as de facto milestone decision points—the decision to fund full-scale engineering development and the initial appropriation of procurement funds for a new weapon system. Often, the circumstances attending these two events are vague, with proponents and opponents arguing over the extent to which such congressional decisions constitute commitments. This tends to prolong the period of contention over the need for the new system, the appropriateness of the design approach taken by the Defense Department, and so forth. The lack of explicit milestone authorization also tends to encourage de facto appeal actions by unsuccessful contractors seeking to have the Congress entertain alternatives rejected earlier by the secretary of defense or the military services.

The Congress could choose to establish an explicit procedure to authorize milestone decisions in the weapons acquisition process, paralleling the current system of DSARC milestones used by the Defense Department. To establish the appropriate role for these new procedures, the Congress would have to establish in the law explicit reporting and documenting procedures for the department to follow in meeting these two milestones. Those documents should lay out optimal procurement patterns, life-cycle costs, key development and production milestones, inventory and force structure objectives, and test and performance parameters. The committees would, on their part, need to establish procedures for hearings, staff reports, and committee authorizations.

This new procedure would be designed to concentrate the debate in the appropriate forum—the authorizing committees—and to structure in that forum the appropriate bounds of review, revision, and dissent. The cognizant committees with jurisdiction and expertise in these matters would concentrate the review process and delimit the opportunities for compromise and dissent. The committees themselves would have to do more than rubber-stamp administration plans if the procedure were to be at all effective in concentrating debate in the right forum.

There is an implicit risk in establishing an authorization procedure of this nature. The current system of de facto milestones in Congress allows systems that are contentious to develop slowly, building empirical and political bases of support. It is doubtful, for example, that binary chemical munitions could ever emerge from such an overt and explicit procedure of milestone acquisition authorization, since the committees would fear that an explicit decision authorization might be rejected on the floor. Nonetheless, such a procedure could be instituted gradually (and not retroactively), in order to establish its utility. I suggest related strategies below that would help to implement this approach by providing greater stability, minimizing program turbulence, and limiting the number of times a program must be reviewed and reendorsed.

Establish Multi-year Research and Development Authorizations

As a natural extension of the foregoing change, the Congress could authorize multi-year research and development funding for all systems once they received a congressional milestone authorization. To date, multi-year actions have largely emphasized procurement and have had to meet a rigorous test of economic reward. Such could not be the case for multi-year research and development (R&D) authorizations. Nonetheless, multi-year R&D authorizations would be particularly helpful in giving program managers stable funding profiles that would extend for a number of years. Once a program was provided a multi-year

R&D authorization, the armed services committees could devote efforts in following years to oversight, rather than occupying the calendar with annual authorizations.

Multi-year appropriations always carry a risk that arises from the limitations of cost estimating. This would be particularly so for research and development, where cost estimates are generally based on crude cost-estimating relationships and not on the detailed engineering estimates that can underlie multi-year estimates for procurement. As such, multi-year R&D authorizations might need to make explicit use of authorization horizons (three years, for example). Further, they might need to have explicit procedures for budgeting for technical risks. The army has developed a method for forecasting and budgeting for technical risk in new programs that appears to offer a useful approach to the problem. This technique may require more explicit development so it could be applied to a broader range of projects.

Establish "Matrix" Authorizations for Procurement

Consistent with the multi-year approach to research and development, the Congress could choose to expand multi-year authorizations for procurement. Multi-year procurement has proved to be a relatively successful means of introducing greater stability in DoD purchases, but it will not become widely used in defense procurement until an underlying problem has been solved. The Congress has become particularly concerned that it is less able to make reductions in defense spending to meet lower spending targets because of the commitments it has assumed during the past three years. Multi-year procurement is increasingly seen as a loss of flexibility for the Congress, which of course it is. An even greater problem, however, is presented by the unrealistic outyear planning targets that have characterized defense budgeting and planning. For multi-year procurement to be extended successfully, the Congress needs to develop a method that relates specific weapons programs to aggregate levels of resources. A useful technique to do this is what I call "matrix" authorizations.

Matrix authorization is an adaptation of a contracting concept developed for procurement of the KC-10 advanced tanker. When the McDonnell-Douglas Corporation was awarded the contract for the advanced tanker, it proposed a unique arrangement offering very attractive price discounts for the tanker (a modified form of the DC-10 commercial transport) if the air force made its buys in an optimal pattern determined in advance by the contractor. The contractor was willing to offer attractive discounts because that optimal procurement pattern was tailored to match its anticipated commercial business. The contract specified a quantity/cost matrix by year, with agreements on price adjustments to allow for inflation. The Defense Department was permitted to buy any quantity of tankers from year to year (subject to several limitations), but if it followed a specified five-year "optimal" program it would obtain the largest number of aircraft for a fixed total price.

The Congress could adapt this quantity/cost matrix concept as a means of relating an individual weapon system to aggregate levels of spending over a five-year period. A hypothetical quantity/cost matrix for a single weapon system is shown in Figure 8-1. The contractor, in conjunction with the Defense Department, would develop the matrix and would be prepared to accept any path the government might choose on the matrix. (Note that it would be necessary to establish this unit cost matrix in constant dollars with mutually acceptable price adjustment arrangements to cover inflation, which was the case in the KC-10 contract.)

The Congress would then direct the Defense Department to submit two procurement profiles, one that represented its desired five-year plan consistent with the president's overall budget (spending path A), and an alternative procurement path representing a five-year plan consistent with a certain baseline rate of growth—for example, 5 percent, which was the congressional spending baseline adopted in the fiscal year 1984 budget (spending path B). The Congress then would have two alternative five-year plans, one that represented the desired path consistent with the president's projections, and on that represented a path acceptable to the Defense Department but also consistent with the Congress' funding intentions. The Congress would then authorize one of the two, or potentially

Figure 8-1. Hypothetical Matrix Authorization for a Weapon System.

Quantity (annual)		Unit Cost Matrix (per unit, in thousands of FY 1985 dollars)				
		FY 1985	FY 1986	FY 1987	FY 1988	FY 1989
60				25.3	25.0	24.7
55				25.3	25.1	24.7
50			26.0	25.4	25.1	24.8
45			26.1	25.4	25.1	24.8
40		27.7	26.2	25.5	25.2	24.8
35	*A*	28.0	26.3	25.5	25.2	24.8
30	*B*	28.2	26.4	25.6	25.2	24.8
25		29.2	26.5	25.7	25.2	24.9
20		30.1	26.7	25.8	25.3	24.9
15		32.2	26.8	25.9	25.3	25.0
10			26.9	26.0	25.3	25.0

Path A: Administration fiscal year 1985–1989 request.

Path B: Authorization request for fiscal year 1985–1989 consistent with 5 percent real growth budget.

a third path, specifying quantities and base-year prices for a five-year period. It would also specify a formula for price adjustments. The appropriations committee would review the annual price adjustments.

Obviously, the Defense Department could choose to disregard the congressional directive and insist on a single optimal path whatever the level of aggregate spending. Such a position, however, would not be inevitable; the Defense Department routinely adjusts its five-year procurement plans, usually downward, as a result of altered funding constraints. This approach would require a commitment by service programmers and budgeters to consider seriously in advance how they would amend an individual program to accommodate a somewhat more restrained aggregate spending path. It also would require service program managers to stabilize weapons designs, since price adjustments would be limited to inflation-induced changes.

In order to appraise the validity of the two spending paths, the Congress would need to examine the DoD request in terms of the aggregate balance of spending priorities within the Defense Department among alternative procurement programs and between procurement and operations. Ideally, the Congress could require the president to submit a budget consistent with the previous year's budget resolution or some alternative baseline, together with the programs that the president would fund with resources beyond those provided in the congressional baseline. Such a change in defense budgeting may be beyond the range of feasible political adjustments in the next few years. The purpose of this approach, however, is to move the annual procurement debate away from the issue of funding resources alone and more toward priorities within aggregate limits.

Extend SAR Reports to Include Operating and and Support (O&S) Costs

It is often said that organizations do well those things the boss checks. The Congress applies this dictum vigorously in the area of investment. In the area of operations, however, the difficulties of checking the work of the Defense Department are particularly great.

First, the Congress cannot cope with the mass of detail required to understand current operations and relate them to expenditures. The fact that the Defense Department has never developed believable methods for linking dollar inputs to readiness outcomes is indicative of the problem.

Second, decisions that have a substantial impact on long-term operating costs are often made years before the system is fielded and has a budgetary impact. Weapon developers may be confronted with a broad array of requirements for a system. The services may be committed to achieving certain performance specifications long before detailed assessments of maintainability are offered. During the development cycle system designs are modified to address deficiencies but rarely with any perspective as to the impact of the changes on long-term O&S costs. The M1 tank provides an apt, if unfortunate, example. I believe it is the most capable main battle tank in the world. It also will be without question a very expensive tank to maintain over the forty years it is likely to be in army inventories. Its transmission has over a thousand moving parts, some with tolerances so fine that dirt on the mechanic's hands could obstruct free movement. It will likely be enormously expensive to keep in running order. The transmission design was not a mistake. It was required in order to achieve performance specifications.

This is indicative of a pervasive problem: technical performance specifications and requirements are far more important considerations early in the weapons acquisition cycle than are long-term maintenance costs. The services are perfectly capable of procuring systems for which long-term maintenance is the primary selection criterion. A 1984 decision on the selection of jet engines for the air force's F-15s and F-16s is a fine example. That example was born of sorrow, however, caused by the initial endurance failings of the original "F100" engine and its dramatically high maintenance requirements.

The Congress is always deeply concerned over the long-term support requirements of new weapon systems but has little opportunity to correct problems once a system reaches Capitol Hill for procurement. The only effective remedy is to follow the dictum that organizations do well those things the boss checks. The best hope for improvement rests in changing the incentives given the Defense Department in the weapons acquisition process.

The Congress could similarly draw high-level attention to long-term support and maintenance issues by insisting that the Defense Department prepare an O&S annex for each Selected Acquisition Report (SAR). SARs are required for all major weapon systems the Defense Department is acquiring. Such an annex would identify a baseline for major operating and support cost elements, such as annual operating tempo, the concept and design goals for maintenance, projected annual stock-funded and procurement-funded spare parts requirements, projected annual depot maintenance requirements, and so forth. Design changes that affect projected operating and support costs should be reported, just as are changes that affect procurement costs. The baseline would be compared to the antecedent system the new weapon is designed to replace (e.g., the M1 would be compared to the M60A3). This approach would give the Congress an early benchmark for future operating costs and would give high-level managers in the Defense Department an incentive to pay close attention to those costs early in the design process.

Such an O&S annex would not solve the larger issue with which the Congress is currently preoccupied—that is, whether we are buying forces too numerous and expensive to own and operate in the future. It would provide a basis, however, for improving the procurement of the next generation of systems, so that the future size of our military forces will not be limited by peacetime operating costs.

180 TOWARD A MORE EFFECTIVE DEFENSE

CONCLUSION

Changing the way the United States budgets for defense spending is unlikely to solve the underlying problems that confound the efforts of the Congress in allocating resources to national security. The foregoing discussion outlined several steps to help improve the quality of review the Congress gives to the defense budget and to shift the focus away from near-term budget issues. The aim is to strengthen the hand of the legislative committees by developing tools that would concentrate their control of the review process. Those committees will always be subject to heavy budgetary pressures in their review of defense requests. Their charter, however, is to establish a cogent defense program in an increasingly contentious environment. I believe the suggestions I have outlined would be useful first steps in improving the process and directing the annual defense debate to more appropriate national security issues.

9 THE OFFICE OF THE SECRETARY OF DEFENSE WITH A STRENGTHENED JOINT STAFF SYSTEM

by

John G. Kester

The post–World War II period has seen the coalescence of the Department of Defense into a staff-heavy structure with an ineffective central military staff, a secretary of defense office that is weaker than it seems, and four military services (arranged in three military departments) that dominate according to their own bureaucratic imperatives. No substantial changes in the Defense Department's legal foundation have occurred since 1958 and none in its day-to-day realities since the centralized program and budgeting procedures established by Secretary of Defense Robert S. McNamara in the early 1960s.

What would happen to the overall equilibrium if, by virtue of reforms of the sort proposed by the CSIS Defense Organization Project, the central military staff were to become able to contribute significantly to defense decisions? How can the resulting readjustments be foreseen and shaped in a way that will profit from an enhanced joint military contribution, while at the same time ensuring a proper and adequate role for the civilian leaders chosen and appointed through the country's constitutional system? What are the obvious pitfalls to be avoided, and how can adjustments in the system be channeled in the most desirable directions? And, most specifically, how would a restructured Joint Staff relate to the staffs of the military departments and to the large staff that since 1947 has grown up around the secretary of defense?

The conclusion of this paper is that a strengthened Joint Staff system will not supplant, and indeed will enhance, the need for an effective staff of the secretary of defense; and that any shifts of influence in the defense organization toward a greater role for the Joint Staff should come from the three military departments and not at the expense of the secretary of defense and his staff.

BACKGROUND CONSIDERATIONS

In any pondering of how the defense establishment of the United States should be organized, two issues are perennial. The first, and the one that preoccupied the authors of the Constitution itself, is how to maintain civilian control of the organizations that are entrusted with military arms. The second (that more often receives insufficient attention from civilian policymakers) is how to conduct the military activities of the United States—whether deterrence or active combat—in a reasonably efficient and effective manner.

This paper focuses on one limited but sensitive arena of those concerns: the relations between the secretary of defense (and his staff, called the Office of the Secretary of Defense) and the chairman of the Joint Chiefs of Staff (with the staff organization that he or the Joint Chiefs collectively direct). It considers what would be the best structuring of both those organizations and of their interaction if the Joint Staff organization were reformed along the lines proposed by the Defense Organization Project.

This examination seeks not so much to examine detail as to frame the issues in light of the overriding concerns of civilian control and efficiency that are noted above. In addition, there are some recurrent themes in U.S. defense policy that set a context for organizational reforms of any kind, themes which are worth extended discussion in themselves but which can only be acknowledged here.

The first is that since World War II the permanent bureaucratic conflict in the Pentagon has not been between military and civilian staff members. Rather, it has been between, on the one hand, those staff elements that focus on issues without regard to service boundaries and, on the other hand, those powerful elements, centered in the service organisms themselves, that seek to preserve parochial service interests.

A second is the inevitable conflict between organizing for relative peacetime and organizing for war. Much that is reasonable and efficient in one context, with one set of overriding dangers and concerns, becomes unduly costly or inappropriate in terms of the objectives under the other set of circumstances. It is impossible to devise a single organization that optimizes for both of those two very different conditions.

Third is the two-hundred-year-old rivalry between the Congress and the executive over who shall run the country, including its armed forces.

Fourth is the tendency of both officials and institutions to overvalue the short run and ignore the long run, especially in an institution where top officials, both uniformed and civilian, change jobs as often as in the Department of Defense.

Finally, related to the short-run, long-run problem, is the endemic structural inability of the U.S. political system (like that of other democracies) to allocate sufficient resources to defense needs. Contrary to some mythology, defense interests except in wartime are not politically powerful, and there is no present reason to expect that they are likely to become so.

The foregoing context probably will not change much whatever is done (within limits) in organizing the defense staffs. This paper also assumes, however, that there are some improvements that better organization can promote and that substantial reorganization of one part of the staffs, as is proposed for the Joint Staff, may require at least some adjustments elsewhere. The following are suggested as organizational axioms:

1. To say that reorganization cannot solve all problems and that people are more important than organization is a correct but not very useful observation. Organizations can help or hinder the conduct of business; and it is worthwhile to design those that generally help.

2. Efficiency requires that defense organization should be kept flexible and in general should be prescribed at the lowest legal level possible—that is, an act of Congress should not be hammered into the statute books when an executive order by the president will suffice; an executive order should not be issued when a directive promulgated by the secretary of defense will do the job. The higher the level at which the organization is mandated, the more difficult it is to change —and certainly defense staff organization, however brilliantly conceived, will always have to adjust to a changing world. Nor should anyone expect a secretary of defense, if he is to be held responsible at all for results, to run the department through exactly the organization devised by a predecessor or by the Congress.

Unfortunately, the tendency of the Congress in recent years has been to clutter the defense charter with more and more bits of special or detailed legislation, some of these laws mandating positions in the defense organization that make no sense except to politicians. At some point, too, if statutes begin to instruct the president as to the manner and chain of command he shall use in commanding the military forces, they probably would violate his constitutional authority under Article II as commander in chief.

3. It is a good idea to avoid laws that try to prescribe who shall give advice. A public official is entitled to, and inevitably will, take his advice from whence he pleases—and he ought to, for it is he who is held responsible for his decisions. Laws that tell him to whom to listen are more likely to create bureaucratic confusion and formalism than to improve decisionmaking.

4. It should always be clear that, although the president of course has access to him, the chairman of the Joint Chiefs of Staff works for the secretary of defense and reports to him. In particular, the chairman should not have a staff separate from the secretary of defense's to deal with other government agencies or with foreign ministers of defense.

CIVILIAN CONTROL OF THE MILITARY

Civilian Control in the Executive Branch

Civilian control is an ambiguous, if revered, phrase, to which all pay homage while often interpreting it differently. It can mean any of at least four things. First, most rudimentary, it refers to the maintenance of a constitutional system in which the commander in chief of the armed forces, the president, is a civilian elected official, and in which political decisions are made by civilians. Second, it means the military staying out of politics (which of course does not prevent an officer from making political speeches or running for political office if he retires or resigns first). Third, civilian control means that civilian bodies like the National Security Council and secretary of defense's staff and State Department, rather than a military staff, play the key role in shaping national security priorities. Fourth, civilian control has meant the right of the president or his delegatee to direct the conduct of military operations—the wisdom of which exercise has been questioned in particular cases like the Iran rescue mission and recent military operations in Lebanon, but the legal authority for which is not in doubt.

A poorly organized and inefficient military staff system has been one of the traditional supports of civilian control of the military in the United States. With the services competing with each other and unable to act collectively, their influence and power are automatically lessened. There ought to be a less costly way to maintain civilian control. At the same time, it is only realistic to recognize that if the role and effectiveness of the military staff are enhanced, the balance may need new adjustments.

The first aspect of civilian control—Who's in charge?—is obviously the most important and is not controversial. It has not been since George Washington at Newburgh, New York, chastised his officers who urged him to take a crown. As long as the military forces have control of virtually all the weapons and therefore possess the physical power to take over the government, however, it is a concern that can never be forgotten. It is the least likely but most disastrous scenario. The fourth, and sometimes controversial, element of civilian control—civilian direction of operational details—is beyond the scope of this paper. The organizational concerns addressed hereafter focus mainly on the second and third aspects listed above—the respective civilian and military roles in politics and policymaking.

The issue of preserving ultimate civilian decisionmaking is not implicated greatly by the Defense Organization Project's proposal for joint military reform. The appropriate concern is less apocalyptic and more practical: it is simply whether a president and the tiny handful of civilian officials whom he is allowed to appoint, with whatever staff they are allowed, can effectively select and impose their choices of national security policy with the assurance that uniformed leaders will carry them out. That does not prevent broad delegation and deference to the advice of senior military officers, if such be the choice of the appointed civilians, as long as the judgment and habit of taking such advice does not become confused with the obligation to do so. It also presupposes a recognition by military officers that it is entirely appropriate for duly appointed civilian leaders to question and reject military advice, not because they are smarter than the advisers, but simply because it is the civilian appointees who are charged with the ultimate responsibility. As Justice Robert H. Jackson once explained the role of the Supreme Court, "we act in these matters not by authority of our competence but by force of our commissions." In the Department of Defense, it is the secretary (and those to whom he delegates) who holds the commission.

For most of this country's history, military dominance in the government has remained a purely theoretical, rather than a practical, concern. This has been due in part to the traditions and training of the officer corps and, probably even more important, to the weakness of the country's armed forces for most of our two centuries of civil government. Until World War II, except for the Civil War and the last year of World War I, our army was a small garrison force focused on coastal defense and skirmishing with Indians on the frontier; the navy, what there was of it, was at sea. In terms of planning, the two services scarcely communicated with each other.

The advent, to counter a permanent Soviet threat, of a large standing force—stabilized in the range of 2.1 to 2.5 million except during hostilities in Korea and Vietnam—permanently altered the role of military concerns in the government's budgeting and planning. During that time there was one direct if brief challenge to presidential authority by General Douglas MacArthur, though MacArthur's insubordination never took the form of a threat to civil government. In the end, like General George B. McClellan in the Civil War, MacArthur sought power unsuccessfully through the constitutionally prescribed process of running for president.

When the Departments of War and Navy, with the new Air Force, were brought together in 1947, and called the Department of Defense in 1949, there was some concern expressed on Capitol Hill at the prospect of creating a centralized military authority. Debate centered less on the need for unified planning (the army's traditional position) than on ensuring safeguards against centralized military authority or a "German general staff"—a shibboleth more often invoked than understood by the legislators. That concern is still seen in the statute books, which by law limit the number of officers on the Joint Staff and forbid their being organized "as a general staff"—whatever that meant to the authors of the law.

The post-war organization has succeeded exceptionally well in keeping a central uniformed military from exerting undue influence on defense planning and national security policy. It has done so by keeping the real power in the Pentagon buried beyond easy reach in the three military departments—which in theory are merely the suppliers, manners, and equippers of the forces that the unified and specified commanders deploy, but which in reality dominate and control the positions taken by the Joint Chiefs of Staff.

In other words, for the past forty years the American military establishment has been structured to ensure civilian control partly by means of a divided and ineffective military organization. The Defense Organization Project proposals generally offer a healthy start toward removing some of that ineffectiveness. The concern is to be sure that as the central uniformed military voice is allowed to become stronger, it does not disrupt the traditional military subordination to civilian direction and policymaking.

Civilian Control in Congressional Perspective

Adding to the ambiguity of the term civilian control is that it traditionally means something quite different to the Congress than to presidents. The Congress, particularly the armed services committees of each house, always has asserted the prerogative of questioning military officers, and sometimes of supporting or giving a public forum to officers who disagreed with the policy decisions of the commander in chief. The Congress has seen itself as a coequal, perhaps dominant, engine of civilian control, as if civilian control really meant simply congressional oversight. And members often do not hesitate to use congressional authority to undercut the authority of the president and the secretary of defense, as, for example, by forcing senior officials to explain themselves for not following the advice of subordinates who have congressional allies. Presidents have complained about this intentional blurring of the chain of command that extends to the president; President Eisenhower grumbled that the statute authorizing JCS members to speak their personal views to the Congress was simply "licensed insubordination." But such resentment has been ineffectual.

The congressional dislike of strong civilian authority in the executive branch is another factor to be weighed in framing institutional arrangements. For it is to be expected that efforts by civilians in the executive branch to keep a tight ship will regularly be threatened by congressional slashing at the rigging.

THE WEAKNESS OF THE SECRETARY OF DEFENSE

This leads to a central reality of the current defense organization that is seldom perceived: though by its trappings it appears powerful from the outside and has had some strong incumbents, the secretary of defense occupies a weak office in our government. He is not weak when compared to other members of a president's cabinet; but his personal authority is not great when measured in terms of the responsibilities of his office and the rival governmental power centers that hem him in.

By statute, the secretary enjoys "direction, authority and control" of all that goes on in the Defense Department. In reality, his authority is impinged upon from all sides—by the Congress, by other executive branch power centers, by the parochial subparts of the Department of Defense, and sometimes even by some of his own appointees who busily pursue their own agendas. The secretary, if he does his job, is likely to be embattled constantly, and even if he does very little he still is likely to feel that he is less heading a department than sitting atop a centrifuge. His real authority is not as great as it seems, and his vast responsibilities are not in reality matched by commensurate powers.

Three other aspects of the secretary of defense's position merit comment. One is that he, almost individually, is unique in the Department of Defense in that he sits at the confluence of the providers of military power (mainly the services) and its users (the field commanders in chief). Most of the Defense Department's organization, and nearly all of his own civilian staff, are concerned with providing military resources. In his responsibilities for operations, however, the defense organization gives him little support except from the Joint Staff in a staff role and the field commanders themselves.

Also essential to remember is that any secretary of defense unavoidably occupies a very political office. He takes few decisions that do not carry some political impact, either for domestic politics or in the international political-military sense, and often both. Much of the policymaking and budget setting that the secretary does involves judgments and decisions about balancing risks, degrees of acceptable risk, allocation of resources, setting of priorities—all of them questions that have no precise answers. The basic decisions of military policy are, unavoidably, political decisions with political consequences.

Finally, a secretary of defense can sit at his desk and issue orders, yet sometimes very little will happen if those orders conflict with the bureaucratic interests of those assigned to carry them out. He needs some organization to monitor that policy is being put into practice.

To function effectively a secretary of defense needs all the help and all the institutional propping that he can get. It follows that any restructuring of the Joint Chiefs organization would best be done in a manner that enhances, and certainly does not diminish, the secretary's role.

THE OFFICE OF THE SECRETARY OF DEFENSE

From the beginning of the Defense Department it was clear that the competing demands of the four services for resources could not be resolved through the Joint Chiefs of Staff organization. Instead, secretaries of defense began to build their personal staff to undertake that task and to assist also in strategic planning, to the extent there has been such. That staff has grown from a grand total of four personal assistants under James V. Forrestal in 1947 to an Office of the Secretary of Defense (OSD) of nearly 2,000 today. (There is some slipperiness in the numbers, depending on what staff sections are included and on who is doing the counting.) The basic OSD staff consists of a deputy, two under secretaries, four-teen officials with the rank of assistant secretary of defense (up, unwisely, from only eight in the previous administration), plus their respective staffs. Partly through additions by the Reagan administration and partly through additions by the Congress, it has become even more top-heavy.

The OSD staff can be conveniently grouped into four categories: (1) the secretary's personal and political cadre (military assistants, general counsel, Public Affairs, Legislative Affairs); (2) the program and budget group (Program Analysis and Evaluation, comptroller); (3) the strategic, political-military and international relations group (under secretary for policy, international security affairs, international security policy, intelligence policy); (4) resource areas (under secretary for research and engineering; command, control, communications, and intelligence; manpower and logistics; health affairs; reserve affairs). Most of the OSD offices have counterpart (and to varying degrees duplicative) offices in the secretariats of the three military departments and also in the four service military staffs.

The current manning of OSD probably is too large, and too many sections of it (particularly in manpower and in research and engineering) engage in program supervision rather than policy direction. (Some of what is denounced as OSD micromanagement, of course, is follow-through necessary to assure that the secretary's decisions are in fact carried out by the services, but too often subdivisions of the OSD staff simply keep themselves busy on parochial concerns of little relevance to the secretary's program.) Thus there already exists adequate basis for a trimming down of OSD, though the present administration and the Congress instead have profligately added assistant secretaries and moved in the opposite direction.

The OSD staff relates to the Joint Staff in these separate areas:

1. Planning and strategy (mainly with the under secretary for policy).
2. Program and budget (mainly with the Office of Program Analysis and Evaluation and the Comptroller, and also those OSD offices involved in the respective particular programs).
3. Relations with allies (mainly with the assistant secretaries for International Security Affairs and for International Security Policy).
4. Operations and execution of military orders (if at all, with the under secretary for policy).

In the first and third areas listed, the OSD staff dominates, but the Joint Staff makes a contribution. In the second, the Joint Staff, because of interservice rivalries that prevent addressing tough choices, has had virtually no role at all. In the fourth, the Joint Staff has dominated, subject to careful supervision by the services of their respective interests, while the OSD staff has had little to say.

In addition to all the above, the OSD staff has another vital function: to ensure that the secretary's decisions are carried out. That is no small task, as anyone familiar with bureaucracy will suspect, and anyone experienced with the power the service bureaucracies exert in the Pentagon will recognize.

The portions of OSD that traditionally have worked the most closely with the Joint Staff organization are the Office of International Security Affairs, which is the Pentagon's "little State Department," and its hierarchical supervisor, the under secretary for policy. Indeed, the new and potentially powerful position of under secretary for policy was established in 1978 at the request of then Secretary of Defense Harold Brown in order not just to pull together the various offices contributing to strategic policy, but also to assist the secretary in supervising and directing the activities of the Joint Staff and to assist him in his role as deputy commander in chief in monitoring or directing military operations.

EFFECTS OF A RESTRUCTURED JOINT STAFF SYSTEM ON OSD

Would OSD as currently constituted benefit from restructuring? Almost surely it would. Would institution of a more effective Joint Staff organization necessitate additional restructuring of OSD? Probably not.

A reconstituted Joint Staff should complement, rather than supplant, the OSD organization and functions. To be most useful to the secretary and other decisionmakers, the Joint Staff should provide analysis and recommendations from a supra-service military perspective, to complement advice generated from the less military-oriented offices of OSD. Such a duality will not only ensure that professional military voices contribute to the decisional process but also will likely improve the quality of decisions by giving the secretary more ideas to choose among. The rational underlying reform of the JCS is not that military advice to the secretary will necessarily be better than that he already obtains from the offices of OSD. Rather, it is that currently military advice from a cross-service perspective is missing, and that such advice would be useful to have. For the most part, the contemplated reformed Joint Staff would not be doing work different from what the Joint Staff does today (with the important exception that it would recommend how to allocate resources among the services). It would simply be doing that work better.

If the Joint Staff is restructured and rejuvenated so that it is able to provide effective planning and advice for the secretary of defense, does it follow that great changes should result in the structure of OSD? It has often been observed that some of the key activities of OSD—for example, the program tradeoff alternatives prepared by OSD's Office of Program Analysis and Evaluation—came to OSD in part by default, because of the inability of the JCS to recommend choices among competing service programs. If the joint military apparatus can become able to deal with such issues, does it follow that the activity of the corresponding OSD civilian offices can be terminated? Was the OSD staff merely a stopgap arrangement until a true Joint Staff system could get on its feet, a stopgap that no longer serves a function? Can the Joint Staff now truly become the secretary's staff, and its chairman the secretary's chief of staff, so that much of OSD would be superfluous?

The answer to all those questions is no.

It certainly is true that the growth of OSD from Forrestal's four assistants to its present size was caused in some measure by JCS unresponsiveness to secretarial needs. As secretaries sought to exert some central managerial control over the sprawling defense organization, they found they could not do it alone and that the Joint Chiefs, being heads of the rival service bureaucracies, were themselves part of the problem, not the solution. It is also true that some observers have argued that the secretaries of the army, navy, and air force should rely more on their military staffs and do away with a large number of positions in their respective civilian secretariats. The arguments for maintaining substantial civilian secretariats are far less compelling in the case of the three service secretariats than in the case of OSD.

It does not follow, however, that a secretary of defense who enjoys an effective JCS organization can get along with little else. The secretary of defense is a senior officer of the president's cabinet and the National Security Council and often a personal adviser to the president. His office quite properly is steeped in political considerations, both in the international and in the domestic sense. His position among other tasks must reconcile civilian and military thought, to the extent such a distinction can be discerned, and to function usefully he must be broad and flexible enough in his perceptions to take account of concerns, variables, and risks that do not sort themselves out neatly or even in some cases explicitly. The secretary sees few purely military issues; he acts on many politicomilitary ones, and he needs help in discerning elements of both sorts. No matter how sophisticated it is (and even if we start now we are many years from having a Joint Staff of adequate training and sophistication), a military staff by its background will not be able to illuminate all aspects of such questions to the same degree as can a staff that is differently composed. And to the extent that a purely military staff ventured too far in proposing national policies, it would begin to trench beyond its traditional and proper role.

If the secretary of defense seeks truly to steer events in the Department of Defense and in national security policy in an intelligent way (not all secretaries have tried), he needs not just an effective military staff but an effective civilian one—recognizing of course that the assistant secretaries of defense have always made good use of the invaluable talents of capable military officers seconded to them and allowed to advise outside the formal constraints of a military organization. What we have had up to now is the secretary of defense forced to take politicomilitary decisions with much help from the political and little help from the experienced military side of the house. It would not be an improvement for him to take such decisions with only uniformed military assistance. And simply as a matter of assuring meaningful civilian oversight of military activities, the secretary of defense needs a nonmilitary staff with adequate personnel and capabilities to help him keep track of what is going on, and what ought to be going on, in his department.

Three examples, involving different secretarial activities, illustrate the point.

Program Analysis and Evaluation

In 1961, Secretary of Defense Robert S. McNamara and his comptroller, Charles J. Hitch, undertook to capture control of the Pentagon program and budget process. Until then each secretary of defense had essentially distributed an allocation of money to each service and allowed it to be spent as the service staff saw fit. In 1965, a new position of assistant secretary of defense (Systems Analysis) was split off from the comptroller office. Its function was to analyze the entire budget and service programs and to advise the secretary on how to allocate funds among them along functional rather than purely service lines. From the time of its first incumbent, Alain C. Enthoven, right down to the present under its bowdlerized redesignation as the Office of Program Analysis and Evaluation (demoted by the present administration in 1981 from assistant-secretary level), the secretary's systems analysts have been controversial and widely resented. They, especially, were the "whiz kids" accused of taking key decisions away from the military advisers.

Given that their function has been to advise the secretary independently on how to ration limited resources insufficient to meet the services' demand, it is inevitable that this OSD staff office should be unpopular. But it has also been inevitable that, to the extent that secretaries since McNamara have tried to guide the department's programs and budget, the office has continued to exist in one form or another. The secretary has had nowhere else to turn for detailed independent advice in such matters.

Does the systems analysis function belong in a reconstituted Joint Staff? Surely it does. Inability and unwillingness to recommend choices among programs has been a striking failure of the present JCS system. No more than the secretary would the chiefs be able to come up with detailed and intelligent tradeoffs on their own, without staff support.

Does it follow that the program analysis function can and should be eliminated from OSD? Surely not. This is a subject matter in which an OSD office, adjunct to the secretary and clearly free of influence from one or another portion of the defense bureaucracy, will still be essential even if the Joint Staff develops a parallel capability. Moreover, on his crucial decisions of resource allocation, the secretary of defense cannot afford to depend totally on the recommendations of the military staff, as he would be without adequate analytical capability in OSD.

The staff of the OSD program analysis activity always has been small and talented. Its existence is not costly. And in this instance, where matters of judgment and opinion as well as of measurement are involved, the existence of more than one source of advice is a help rather than a burden to a secretary of defense. There is no reason to believe that a secretary would always favor one office's analysis over the other's. There is, however, reason to hope that the competition and diverse backgrounds of two such small organizations could lead to better analysis by each. Moreover, although judging the relative capabilities and interaction of weapons and people in battle is a matter in which the uniformed military may be assumed more expert, it is also true that a civilian-directed office will have expertise of its own. An office unhampered by current military dogma (even dogma not associated with a single service) probably can develop some insights that such an office in the Joint Staff cannot dependably be expected to—just as the military systems analysis office might uncover truths that a nonmilitary office will miss, as many civilian analysts are the first to concede. In addition, the systems analysis office is one of the few parts of the secretary's OSD staff that is not responsible for particular programs, and hence is less likely to develop vested interests in them.

In short, systems analysis capability is not costly, and this is an area in which, as in intelligence (for example, the Central Intelligence Agency, the Defense Intelligence Agency, State's Bureau of Intelligence and Research), having more than one analysis is often illuminating. Although civilians as such have no particular expertise to offer concerning battlefield conditions and force structure, there certainly are able civilian defense analysts who can and do contribute unique insights that might be lost in a Joint Staff environment. Indeed, if there is to be a single program analysis office it belongs where it is in OSD, where it has a level of independence nowhere else available. But it is preferable, if the Joint Staff is to be able to speak the secretary's language, that it also develop capability to analyze and propose in these terms.

The Under Secretary for Policy

In 1977, Secretary of Defense Harold Brown obtained authorization for abolishing the superfluous second deputy secretary of defense that had been set up in the early 1970s and filled only once, and somewhat in exchange establishing the new position of under secretary of defense for policy. One objective of the job was to pull together under a senior civilian just below the secretary all the politico-military and related responsibilities of the OSD staff—international security affairs, intelligence policy, arms limitations, and so forth.

An equally important, but less advertised, purpose of the new and opaquely named position was to assist the secretary of defense in his role as deputy commander in chief, responsible for planning and conduct of military operations and the relation of military plans to national security policy. No one in OSD below the level of the secretary himself had really been involved consistently in such matters; planning and operations except for occasional ad hoc interventions were purely in the bailiwick of the Joint Chiefs of Staff. The prescribed duties of the new under secretary reflected a judgment by the secretary that such matters required more oversight than he personally had time to give, from someone reporting to him but outside the JCS system. For example, with JCS acquiescence, Secretary Brown authorized then Under Secretary Robert W. Komer to review JCS contingency plans for consistency with policy (a practice that Komer's successor abandoned).

If the Joint Staff is revitalized, can some of the under secretary for policy's staff and role be cut back? Not for that reason. No doubt there can be a streamlining and consolidation of offices in that part of OSD (the present trend unfortunately has been to multiply titles and move in the opposite direction). However, it is not appropriate to remove large chunks of the International Security Affairs office (which deals with the State Department and National Security Council staff and with foreign defense ministries) into the Joint Staff. A revitalized Joint Staff can provide more useful contributions to the formulation and negotiation of departmental positions on such matters. But in this area of essential politico-military policy, the principal point of contact belongs on the secretary's staff if civilians are truly to contribute to and ultimately set U.S. national security policy.

Similarly, there is no reason to abandon civilian review of such sensitive JCS military functions as, for example, contingency plans. If such matters are important enough to devote time and staff work to in the JCS, they are important enough for the secretary of defense too to wish to monitor; and given the other demands on his time, it is entirely appropriate for him to seek a second opinion from the OSD staff (which, of course, includes not only civilians but also uniformed officers assigned outside their services to OSD). Indeed, to the extent a more capable Joint Staff might raise any fears of overweening military influence in national security policy, it is all the more appropriate that civilian review and oversight of essential Joint Staff activities be institutionalized. The logical focus of such review—which would not entail large numbers of people—is in the office of the under secretary for Policy. The under secretary's reviewing role is more necessary than ever in an organization with a strengthened Joint Staff.

Manpower and Logistics

The impact of a revitalized Joint Staff on the department's manpower and logistics office may be different. (Included for analysis in this grouping should be the staff of the assistant secretaries of defense for health affairs and for reserve affairs, both unnecessary offices that Congress imposed on the Department of Defense.) The manpower and logistics portion of the OSD staff is substantial, and some of its activities are of a program management rather than policy guidance character. Some of the former functions could be restored to the service staffs or, to the extent that they are multiservice in nature, might in part be addressed in the Joint Staff.

Properly, however, the Joint Staff should be engaged in planning, analysis, and coordinating operations rather than in program management. So again, although OSD staff cuts may well be appropriate in some offices in the manpower and logistics area, those shifts more appropriately would take place between OSD and the service staffs than between OSD and the Joint Staff.

Summary

Whatever is done to improve the functioning and capabilities of the Joint Staff, civilian control of defense policy as well as balance in that policy still will require that the secretary of defense maintain a substantial secretariat—OSD—that is answerable directly to him and is staffed to assist him in his defense planning and oversight responsibilities. Some OSD offices can be reduced and some of their functions transferred elsewhere in the department, but, to the extent any such need exists, it exists independently of Joint Staff reform. No doubt a great deal can be done to make the Joint Staff the secretary's military staff in a way it has not been up to now. But it defies belief to assume that the Joint Staff ever would respond unreservedly to a civilian secretary without regard to the wishes of a chairman or JCS members. The secretary will always need a substantial secretariat.

The OSD staff came into being by default of an adequate military staff, but only partly. The advent of an effective military staff can strengthen the secretary and create a useful decisionmaking dialogue, but it cannot take the place of, or even significantly supplant, OSD. The secretary of defense's business is not, for the most part, simply military business. To shift functions from OSD to the Joint Staff would move the secretary of defense back toward the position of Forrestal and his four assistants: unable to manage, and at the mercy of the decisions negotiated among themselves by competing Pentagon bureaucracies.

ORGANIZATION AND PROCEDURES TO ACCOMMODATE A RESTRUCTURED JOINT STAFF SYSTEM

The law of unintended consequences asserts that when government institutes reform, the unanticipated results often exceed the intended ones. That is no less true with respect to organizational reform, which can have a disruptive effect like adding a weight to one arm of a delicately balanced mobile. That is not a sufficient reason to shrink from reform, however. Adjustment must be constant in human affairs. It is a caution to try to anticipate and deal in advance with collateral consequences that might be undesirable.

This overall goal, in the context of the Defense Organization Project proposals for a stronger chairman and Joint Staff, should be to ensure that strengthening of those power centers comes at the expense of the four individual services, which are already too strong, and not at the expense of the secretary of defense, who is already too weak in proportion to his duties and who also represents the interest of central and integrated military planning beyond service boundaries. Several techniques can support this goal.

1. Do Not Attempt by Statute to Prescribe the Chain of Command

The current chain of military command runs from the president to the secretary of defense to the nine unified and specified commanders, and from them to their subordinate commands. There have been criticisms from time to time, including the case of the recent marine deployment to Lebanon, that the chain is too long and unwieldy. That may well be so, but the unwieldiness, if any, comes from the length and the bulges in the middle and not from the crucial arrangements at the top. Any inefficiency down the line is correctable by orders from the president, the secretary of defense, or subordinate military commanders, and does not require legislation to implement. If the extended chain is not sensibly arranged, criticism is properly directed at the president and the secretary of defense.

For the Congress to enact statutes prescribing command relationships, however, puts the Congress into an area where its skills and insight are at their least and risks adding confusion to command relationships in the executive branch. Just as importantly, even if a congressionally mandated command arrangement turned out to be wise and effective on one occasion in one environment, there is no assurance that it would serve well in other circumstances. A virtue of the present command arrangements is that the president can alter and adjust them at the stroke of a pen, to meet immediate needs. The Congress can never act that quickly, and for Congress to prescribe one set of arrangements might raise unnecessary legal disputes if the president were to choose to employ a different one. That potential conflict illustrates that for the Congress to prescribe operational command arrangements almost surely would violate the powers of the president as commander in chief under Article II of the Constitution.

2. Ensure Sufficient Access by the OSD Staff to Joint Staff Deliberations

An adequate balance must be struck to allow OSD staff offices to be generally abreast of the deliberative process in the Joint Staff and for dialogue to proceed at several levels. The chairman of a reformed JCS organization should not view the role of his organization as advising exclusively the secretary of defense, with the OSD staff reduced to learning what they can find out from the secretary. Institutional pressures have at times led to such "stovepipe" organizations in the military departments, with uniformed service staffs insulated from civilian input except at the very top. Work has proceeded more effectively when members of the secretariat and members of the uniformed military staff, headed by a chief of staff, have recognized that they both serve a single civilian secretary. Maintaining that kind of healthy lateral dialogue (while also holding off eager civilian staffers who would try unduly to influence JCS decisions) is possible if it receives the benign attention of both secretary and chairman from time to time. Some precatory language in a secretarial directive might also be helpful.

3. Limit Access by Non-DoD Staff to Working-level JCS Activities

Conversely, if the secretary of defense is to remain truly in charge of the department, there will have to be some limits on the contacts and accompanying demands imposed on the Joint Staff from outside. Such demands are most often received from congressional staffs, from the White House and Office of Management and Budget, from the National Security Council staff, and from the State Department. Because it is impossible to cut off all requests for information, and some are quite legitimate, the solution is to channel and filter each group of such requests through a single point or limited points of contact, highly enough placed in the secretary's office to be able to refuse demands that are unduly burdensome and also to keep track of what is going on. Again, it is helpful, perhaps essential, to establish the points of contact clearly and to make clear to officers of the Joint Staff that they are not to respond to requests from outside the department except when authorized by the secretary's delegatee to do so.

4. Consider Cuts in the OSD Staff

It does not follow that a more efficient Joint Staff needs a larger OSD staff to watch it. The contrary may be true: A better job of joint planning by the JCS organization might make unnecessary some few OSD positions that perhaps now exist by default because no one in the JCS organization effectively does the job. There are parts of the OSD staff that have grown by accretion over the years and probably could well be cut and some of their functions shifted to the service staffs. Candidates here include the staffs in public affairs, manpower and logistics, research and engineering, and the comptroller.

5. Cut Service Staffs

If the Joint Staff is reconstituted to do more meaningful work, there ought to be less to do in the operations sections of the four service military staffs that currently dominate the Joint Staff but too often work primarily to promote the bureaucratic and budget interests of their particular services. In addition, there is considerable duplication in the secretariat staffs of the three military departments that is overdue for trimming, quite apart from JCS reform.

The enhancement of the Joint Staff itself should be more substantive than numerical and should also lead to reductions in the other eight central staffs of the Pentagon.

CONCLUSION

The current respective roles of the Office of the Secretary of Defense and the Joint Staff result partly from default, from not having an effective military staff organization. But the current structure is not the result of the civilian-headed staff usurping duties that more properly are purely military.

The department's processes might be thought of as a piano score set for two hands. The OSD staff has not elbowed the Joint Staff away from the keyboard and tried to play both parts. Rather, OSD has been playing the treble part—and because the Joint Staff has been crippled and unable to play, no one has been playing the bass at all. A tune is there, but it is not very rich.

If the Joint Staff were vitalized, that does not mean that the piano should be turned over entirely to the military artists. What the secretary of defense needs is to hear from both hands, even if (indeed, perhaps especially when) they do not always harmonize. As in intelligence analysis, national security policymaking often can be sharpened by exposure to varying opinions from thoughtful but differing sources, profiting both in more careful thinking and in richer availability of alternatives. The civilians and the uniformed military in the Defense Department need each other, and so do the civilian and military organizations.

There is no good reason why an effective Joint Staff should put any significant part of OSD out of business or engender any wholesale shift of responsibility. Savings in organizational structure and personnel should come from the service staffs, all of which now devote considerable resources to keeping the Joint Staff from functioning effectively. And in terms of maintaining a strong and effective civilian role in formulating national security policy, the development of a capable Joint Staff presents all the more reason and need for effective organs of civilian direction and review. A continued strong office of secretary of defense requires a continued strong Office of the Secretary of Defense.

10 ACCOUNTING AND BUDGETING SYSTEMS IN THE DEPARTMENT OF DEFENSE

by
Robert C. Moot

Accounting and budgeting functions are the hub of any resource management system. The overall system is aimed at assuring that resources are obtained and used efficiently and effectively to accomplish planned goals. This paper examines the resource management process of the U.S. Department of Defense (DoD) and suggests areas for improvement in the system. While the focus of the paper is on the accounting and budgeting functions, some perception of the integrated process is necessary for an understanding of the components. Therefore, this examination includes an oversimplified outline of the sequential steps in the process as, in concept, it is designed to work.

By almost any measure, the Defense Department is the largest and most complex nonprofit organization in the West. Nonprofit organizations, without a profit spur or bottom line measure, must look for other management techniques to control resources. They need to measure the input of resources against the output of services, and they need to measure the effectiveness of the output in contributing to the objectives of the organization.

But even in the different management environment of nonprofit organizations the Defense Department is unique. In peacetime, its forces serve as a deterrent and its services are required only in an actual or threatened emergency. Long periods of time can elapse without any significant demand for military action or show of force. Consequently, for DoD managers to be sure that resources are used efficiently and effectively in peacetime, the resource management system must provide the following information:

- How well can the active and available forces meet the given goals, objectives, and plans under emergency conditions?
- What is the amount, timing, and type of any resource shortfall? What is the risk involved in the shortfall?
- Are resources justified and accounted for on the basis of current, complete, and actual costs?
- Are resources used efficiently in accordance with program justification and established performance standards?
- Are resources used effectively to attain readiness and capability standards?
- Are managers provided with accurate, complete, and timely reports on the status of forces?
- Is the process of resource management validated periodically by internal and external audit reviews to assure continued integrity?

Any appraisal of the DoD resource management process should determine how well it provides these types of information and assurances. This appraisal starts with a brief outline of the process as it is designed conceptually. Then, with a focus on the accounting and budgeting operations, existing problems are identified and corrective actions proposed.

KEY ELEMENTS OF THE RESOURCE MANAGEMENT SYSTEM

Resource management encompasses all of the functions of planning, programming, budgeting, accounting, reporting, and auditing that are necessary to assure that resources are efficiently and effectively utilized in the accomplishment of clearly stated national objectives. In the DoD the resource management system is made more complex because of the dual lines of civilian and military authority. The phases of the resource management system must provide for a clearly articulated overview of U.S. defense priorities; for evaluated force and program alternatives over a multi-year cycle; for program pricing within established fiscal targets and for control procedures to monitor program execution.

National Security Policy

The allocation of resources within the DoD must be preceded by the setting of military priorities. In order to make the subsequent tough choices on force structure and spending objectively, these priorities should be set by the secretary of defense. In the setting of military priorities it is essential that the input of external agencies be included in the decision process. Such external input should cover current foreign policy and its relationship to the required military posture, the use of foreign territory for U.S. forces, overflight rights, the level of assistance to be expected from treaty allies, and forecasts of energy and scarce materials availability. The president, with the staff assistance of the National Security Council and the Office of Management and Budget, should set broad objectives and fiscal targets for the DoD.

Planning to Support National Security Policy

Once military priorities are set for the multi-year cycle, the planning process evaluates and recommends alternative approaches to achieve the stated policy objectives. Each area of military interest worldwide is reviewed within the Office of the Secretary of Defense. Data for this review are received from the intelligence agencies and from the commanders-in-chief of the combat commands. Using given priorities, estimates of threats and capabilities are made and realistic alternative policies are developed to counter assessed threats. With consideration given to the capabilities of coalition forces, the Joint Chiefs of Staff (JCS) determine the balanced force structure best suited to carry out the selected alternatives. The JCS separately develop contingency plans to guide area operations in the event of required military action. The secretary of defense, faced with the impossibility of assuring military capabilities to match threats in every area, makes decisions as to the acceptability of risk, area by area. Within given resource limitations, the JCS can then develop an alternative force structure best suited to meet the threats at an acceptable level of risk.

Defense Guidance

The output of the planning process is given to the military departments that are charged with supporting the combat forces. The defense guidance includes a description and assessment of the military threats, program objectives, and the planning force developed by the JCS within resource limitations. The military departments are given fiscal targets within the overall resource limitation of the DoD. The guidance charges the military departments with developing quantitative and qualitative measures to track performance and utilization of resources.

Programming

The military departments recruit and train the manpower and develop the weapon systems and field facility structure to support the planned forces. The five-year program provides an analytic framework for evaluating the benefits and costs of recommended weapon systems and supporting establishment. The military departments submit their recommended programs, which are reviewed by the Office of the Secretary of Defense (OSD) for consistency with policy and by the JCS to assure optimum force capability.

Budget Justification

The operating and capital requirements of the first year of the OSD approved five-year program are priced in detail. The fiscal impact of the outyear programs is provided in broad terms. The budget format is designed to identify, for each appropriation, what program results should be realized after utilization of the requested resources. The budgeted program results are related directly to the national defense objectives they are designed to help achieve. Budget pricing is based on costs developed from the accounting records as modified by the fiscal projections of the Office of Management and Budget (OMB) covering inflation rates, future pay raises, and so forth. Budget submissions are reviewed by the OSD and OMB, final presidential approval is secured, and congressional justifications are prepared.

Budget Execution

After completion of congressional action the military departments prepare program/budget execution plans, which are submitted to the OSD for approval. The plans are reviewed by the OSD for consistency with guidance, the adequacy of their content, and compliance with prior congressional directions. Resources are allocated down command channels paralleling the delegation of responsibility and authority. The results of the operating and investment programs during the budget execution period are tracked against these plans.

Accounting

Military department accounting systems are designed to record costs and performance on a detailed program element basis. Integration of budgeting and accounting provides a common set of rules by which managers can make valid comparisons between planned and actual results. Timely variance detection allows for prompt corrective action.

In addition to obligational accounting to meet fiduciary requirements, the accounting system design calls for accrual accounting to match the delivery of service or product with its related cost. Because obligation-based accounting systems do not record costs as the service or material is used, the program utilization of resources (program input) is not comparable to program accomplishment (program output). Obligation-based input/output comparisons are misleading and distort program evaluation.

Data processing systems provide timely reports, matching program/budget plans with actual costs and performance. Costs, performance, readiness, and capability status are all recorded at the force unit and field installation level. Fiduciary and management accounting procedures are complementary and reconcilable.

Reporting

Managers at all levels within the DoD receive regular cost/performance reports scaled to the appropriate management level. Program costs are related to program output and the reports allow for comparison of results between time periods and operating units. Actual costs and performance are measured against program/budget plans and variances are explained. Corrective action, as required, is taken on a timely basis. Analysis of the way costs vary in relationship to output is used in future program planning.

Audit Validation

The resource management system is fully documented, and the detailed system procedures are maintained on a current basis. Uniformity in the application of procedures and interpretation of definitions is essential to the objective management of resources. Organizational units in each of the military departments are dedicated to the writing and updating of system procedures under the guidance of the OSD. Internal and external audit organizations use the procedural documentation of the system as a benchmark for audit review. The validity, completeness, and timeliness of the cost and performance data are verified. The DoD managers' use of the system reports is reviewed and periodic evaluations of the process are submitted.

CURRENT PROBLEMS OF THE RESOURCE MANAGEMENT SYSTEM

Effective and efficient use of resources requires disciplined control of the resource management system, which is a series of interlocking functions, the output of one forming the input of the next. The system is circular with accounting and performance data from the current year flowing to the earlier phases as the planning base for the next year's cycle. Faults may occur at each phase of the cycle.

National Security Policy

From the viewpoint of the DoD, resources are never enough to minimize the military risk in every potential problem area of the world. Without priority guidance from the White House, there is a natural tendency for the department to overplan, overprogram, and overbudget. Alternatively, when confined by fiscal limitations, the department tends to allocate on the basis of compromise and previously determined priorities. If the sequence is reversed and the DoD budget developed before fiscal restrictions are imposed, the subsequent pressures to raise the final resource level made available is enormous, as the OMB has discovered in recent years.

Sound budgets require that guidance or priorities be directly related to national goals and objectives. Without policy guidance on worldwide levels of military interest, expressed in terms of relative national importance, the DoD is on its own in developing priorities. Therein lies a problem. The current system is not designed to establish national goals or to set priorities among objectives competing for limited resources. Given national guidance, the system can develop cost-beneficial alternatives. In its absence, compromise and special interests will dominate. The DoD has great difficulty resolving internal conflicts of interest and thus usually provides something for everyone, resulting in compounded resource requirements.

Guidance to the Pentagon on priorities in the past seems either to have been lacking or so broad as to be of little assistance in planning. Robert Komer, for one, has identified this problem pointedly.

> Especially in the non-nuclear area, we need more systematic inter-agency review of grand strategy, relating our interests to the options open to us. If the ends we seek are beyond the resources likely to be available, then the Pentagon is entitled to get from the President (and Congress) broad priority guidance as to which needs come first. . . . Indeed, one of the biggest problems is that the President, his Assistant for National Security, SecState, and SecDef have not posed the broad issues and insisted they be addressed.[1]

A recent DoD/General Accounting Office (GAO) study found that the secretary of defense has wide discretion and receives little specific guidance.

> Under a cabinet form of government as practiced by the current administration, the Secretary of Defense exercises wide discretion in achieving national security goals, within policy and fiscal guidance from the National Security Council and OMB. Program initiative therefore does not entail an elaborate mechanism for conveying specific instructions for translation of the national goals into plans and programs for the Defense Department.[2]

OSD/JCS Planning

The output of DoD's planning phases, when integrated to form program guidance, is the key to assuring a high qualitative content of programs and budgets.

Given priority areas of military interest and fiscal constraints, the secretary, with the Joint Chiefs of Staff, can provide tailored force planning guidance through risk management analysis. The secretary must control the planning functions centrally if quality programs and budgets are to be assured. In the absence of centralized control, each service will set its own priorities, offer its own new smorgasbord of weapon systems, short-change readiness in order to expand the size of forces, and concentrate resources on its unique, rather than cross-service, missions. There are gaps, disconnects, and deficiencies in the planning guidance now being provided to the services. Robert Komer says:

> There is no long term policy or strategic planning, except in technology. . . . Bureaucratic politics has greater influence on Pentagon planning than systematic thinking. . . . As a result, there is an enormous disconnect between US strategy and posture.[3]

The joint DoD/GAO study cites mismatches between resources and requirements for airlift and sealift as examples of gaps in program guidance.[4] In a separate report, the GAO cites three key problems:

> The planning phase is poorly linked to programming, and plans are ambiguous and imprecise as a guide to program design.

> The program and budgeting phases predominant focus on the first year of the 5-year defense program obscures the future costs and affordability of today's program and budget decisions.

> Funds are budgeted (as well as executed) in terms quite different from those in which they are programmed, and no clear link between the two exists. (Programming emphasizes missions, or outputs, whereas budgets are formulated in terms of inputs . . . personnel, procurement, and operating expenses.)[5]

The current system does not provide the services with force planning data that take account of risks and are sized within fiscal limitations. The joint DoD/GAO study reports:

> That issue is focused on the differences between a Planning Force (as defined in the JSPD) which is significantly greater than any current or programmed resources can achieve, and the force levels, toward which the DoD topline is aimed.[6]

While it may be sound practice for the services to propose their choices of force postures to meet given objectives under a decentralized or participatory management philosophy, it is certainly the job of the secretary of defense to state clearly what those forces are expected to achieve. And it is the function of risk management to delimit each area of potential military involvement in terms of the objectives sought and the resources available. This function cannot be decentralized.

Programming

Unless the output of the planning phase is converted to program guidance in clear, precise, and uniform terms, the multiple program submissions by the individual services can never be aggregated to measure readiness, sustainability, or capability to meet program objectives. Poor or inconsistent programs make for poor or inconsistent budgets. The joint study group finds:

> There appears to be inconsistent application within and across DoD organizations of the readiness concept or definition(s), which lessens the comparability of different analysis.[7]

In discussing military capabilities and the importance of the four pillars of force structure, readiness, sustainability, and modernization, the GAO reports:

> Although DoD has planned for and described accomplishments within the framework of the four pillars, the services do not fully agree on a definition of the pillars, nor are these output categories clearly linked to the funding sources (appropriation amounts) that support them. Opinions differ on how to distribute budget resources among the pillars and how increases in funding affect accomplishments.[8]

It is obvious that congressional committees, as well as OSD, might have trouble comparing and analyzing service budgets if the services cannot agree on how to classify the resources being requested. The joint study group agrees that congressional understanding of the budget is complicated when both common definitions and guidelines are deficient.

> The budget justifications contain a wealth of information and detail on program needs through the operating accounts, but lack a consolidated summary showing how the past, current, and proposed resources levels affect readiness and sustainability. . . . Further work in establishing common or more explicit guidelines could ease this impediment to better analyses.[9]

The promulgation of precise, common definitions and guidelines for the formulation of programs and budget, and for the recording of accounting data, is the responsibility of the secretary of defense. Budget shortfalls and overfunding, which lead to the need for reallocation, are difficult to eliminate when resources are classified under differing definitions.

Budgeting

The budget is actually the first year of the five-year program, priced in detail. The cost of personnel, services, equipment, and supplies is related directly to associated programs, and performance measures quantify the program output being funded. The proposed efficiency of operations (resources needed per unit of output) and effectiveness of operations (contribution of output to objectives) are stated in quantitative terms. Budget reviewers must thus be able to relate results sought with resources requested.

The DoD has made changes recently in the congressional budget justification process. Unnecessary detail has been eliminated and the format simplified. The joint study group, however, finds no change in the concept of the justifications. The concerns of the group are:

The appropriations orientation of the justifications do not make it readily possible to track items in the budget requests to mission capabilities.

The justification documents are not designed to shed much light on future program levels so it is difficult to determine the effects of one year's budget level on future requirements.[10]

The GAO, as earlier stated, finds that funds are budgeted (as well as executed) in terms quite different from those in which they are programmed, and no clear link between the two exists.[11]

In testifying before the House Committee on Rules, Comptroller General Charles A. Bowsher put the problem this way:

The current Defense budget system needs to be improved; it is virtually silent on what was accomplished with the funds provided. In addition, defense needs to (a) better justify its requests, (b) develop a strategy for carrying out the programs, (c) clearly state their objectives and develop a measure to gauge performance, (d) report their accomplishments in relation to their established criteria, and (e) build into subsequent budget requests, feedback on actual performance.[12]

All observers agree that improvements are needed in the way that program objectives are tracked through the budget justification and execution phases.

PROPOSED CORRECTIVE ACTIONS

The purpose of the defense resource management system is to provide a structured process that integrates planning, programming, budgeting, accounting, and evaluation in order to make rational decisions on the allocation and utilization of resources. The resource management system must provide the mechanism to assure that resources are being efficiently and effectively employed in the accomplishment of clearly stated national objectives.

Within the Department of Defense, risk assessment and the setting of priorities must be retained as functions of the secretary of defense. These functions cannot be delegated to or passed by default to the military services. Given the priority determinations of the secretary of defense as well as his fiscal targets, the Joint Chiefs of Staff must develop a resource constrained planning force as guidance to the combat commanders and the military services. For the several phases of the resource management system to be integrated, the Department of Defense must develop a common management language and a uniform chart of accounts to assure that plans, programs, budgets, accounts, and reports are all on the same basis.

The problem with the current operation of the defense resource management system is that it does not satisfy the specifications as set forth here. There is little policy and priority input from the White House; planning is decentralized, confused, and poorly linked to programs; budgets are in terms different from those used in programs, and pricing is focused on the first year of the five-year program; accounting is on a fiduciary rather than on a management basis, and evaluation of budget execution is almost nonexistent.

A Revised Program/Budget Format

Integration of the programming, budgeting, and accounting phases of the resource management system, absent in the current operation of the system, can be accomplished. A framework can be designed to match programs with budgets, and both with objectives. The congressional need for input resource control and DoD's need for output management control require a budget that identifies both simultaneously.

Under a revised budget format, each appropriation justification would include matching program and resource data for:

1. The national goals and OSD program objectives being supported (in terms of priority worldwide areas of interest).
2. The force units and activities being funded relative to the goals and objectives.
3. The performance measures used to track progress toward program objectives (effectiveness).
4. The planned accomplishment in terms of quantitative performance measures and resources to be consumed (efficiency).
5. Interservice support required by others and interservice support being provided to others.
6. The outyear extension of requirements by goal and objective.
7. Current and past year comparative data reflecting actual progress in terms of performance and resources consumed.
8. A summary of resources used and requested in normal appropriation terms.

This justification framework is oversimplified, but the intent is to develop program and budget requirements up through command channels so that the integration starts at the operational field level and the data remain integrated throughout the process. Such is not uniformly the case today. The basic principle of management that responsibility, authority, and resources should flow through the same channel is not always followed. Military operational command flows from the president through the secretary of defense for transmittal through the Joint Chiefs of Staff to the unified and specified commanders. The commanders have the responsibility for direction of operations in the field. Resources, on the other hand, flow through the military services to the field component commanders, not to the unified commanders. Changing the format of appropriations to focus on objectives, performance, and resource requirements at the field operational level would allow (although not demand) resources to follow command channels for both requirements and execution.

To ensure that the program/budget marriage is consummated and the process simplified, the two phases should be merged. In effect, the reformed format would be a first-year program/budget request. There are obvious differences between programs and budgets—in the level and scope of detail—but the advantages of the combined form outweigh any disadvantage. In fact, the job of matching resources to program outputs to objectives must be done to assure that missions are directly and visibly linked to budgets.

Accounting and Budget Execution

Much of the value of budget reform would be lost without a parallel and integrated improvement in the accounting system. An improved accounting system should record the use of resources in the same manner as they are planned, programmed, and budgeted. And the reported status of the program/budget in the execution phase should provide the cost and performance basis for the new planning cycle.

Current DoD accounting systems, although adequate from a fiduciary control standpoint, are deficient in many management respects. The comptroller general sees it this way:

> The Secretary and the Congress need better visibility over the way funds are used in the operations and maintenance areas. Currently the reporting to higher levels is primarily through the financial controls, such as obligation rates, rather than through reporting on what was accomplished with the funds in relation to the plan.[13]

There are multiple references throughout GAO studies and reports of recent years to the need in the DoD for better cost accounting for major missions. One report says:

> Such data would be essential in determining (1) whether sufficient funds are being directed to the critical missions and (2) how much these missions are really costing. This would allow managers to make the necessary trade-off decisions.[14]

In recent reports, the GAO has found that the final unit costs of weapon systems have been sharply higher than initially forecast in the five-year program. These cost increases have been greater than the sum of the costs of unanticipated inflation, technical or schedule changes, and development difficulties. And it makes little difference whether the original forecasts were based on contractor estimates, service estimates, or independent OSD cost estimates. None of these estimating methods use total actual costs, recorded on an accrual basis, as a cost benchmark in forecasting. In a report prepared for the Pentagon, Gene H. Fisher made this cogent statement:

> There is one way to minimize costs that we should not allow the decision-maker or the cost analyst. We should not allow either of them to minimize costs by *overlooking* them![15]

The GAO terms what is needed as integrated cost-based management. Cost-based management requires that budgets be based on costs that are related to performance (output) for the same period as the costs are incurred rather than being based on obligations that may be related to entirely different time periods. Costs include salaries and related fringe benefits, rents and utilities, supplies and ordnance, and services. Orders or payment for resources do not always occur in the same period in which those resources are used. Salaries are paid basically in the same period that the services are performed, but the retirement benefits earned during that period are paid years later. Stockpiled parts and supplies may be ordered and paid for many periods prior to when they are actually used. Contractual services are seldom paid for in the same period they are provided. To better understand the relationship between performance and its cost, the cost of material or service must be recorded in the same period that the material or service is used or provided.

The use of accounting principles that are accrual based is already a matter of law. Accrual accounting allows managers and policymakers to compare results of operations across periods, to compare similar operations performed by multiple organizations, and to make better informed cost/benefit evaluations.

THE CONGRESSIONAL MANDATE

For decades, the Congress has exerted pressure on the executive branch to stimulate budget and accounting reforms. The Budget and Accounting Procedures Act of 1950, amended through the years, the Budget and Impoundment Control Act of 1974, the Federal Managers' Financial Integrity Act of 1982 were all directed toward improving budget and accounting procedures throughout the federal government.

The cumulative legislation and its associated financial management program call for the following key actions in the executive branch:

- Establish accrual accounting.
- Develop cost-based budgets and financial reports.
- Establish responsibility-oriented accounting and operating budget systems.
- Develop consistent classifications.
- Integrate programming, budgeting, accounting, and reporting systems.
- Ensure that programs reflect total costs.
- Establish suitable internal control practices.

The legislation places responsibility for developing adequate financial management systems on the heads of each executive agency. It directs that the systems conform to the accounting principles, standards, and related requirements prescribed by the comptroller general. Agencies are directed to submit accounting systems to the comptroller general for approval.

Over the years, improvements in financial management systems have been spotty and slow in coming. The PPBS innovation of Secretary of Defense Robert McNamara and the cost-based budgets of the Atomic Energy Commission are isolated examples. And, as we have seen, even the sophisticated DoD system does not, in fact, integrate its component parts; the accounting system is less than a full partner in the management process.

Progress has been slow for many reasons. Agency heads tend to remain in office only a short time. The development of an accounting system takes a relatively long time. Accounting is not glamorous; programs are more likely to get public attention. Resources are limited, and accounting system improvements can be expensive. Limited data processing capabilities have been used for higher priority projects.

Above all, the comptroller general has had little leverage in seeking to induce the agencies to comply with his principles, standards, and related requirements. Less than one-half of the federal funds expended each year are accounted for in GAO-approved systems, and most of these systems have been modified significantly since they were approved initially.

The recently passed Federal Managers' Financial Integrity Act (FIA), however, provides what may be the leverage needed to initiate action. The FIA requires each agency head to submit an annual statement to the president and the Congress that the agency's systems fully comply with the comptroller general's internal control standards, or, in the event they do not comply, to explain why not and what is being done to correct identified weaknesses. A separate annual report in the same channels is required to state whether the agency's accounting system conforms to the principles, standards, and related requirements prescribed by the comptroller general. It can be assumed that the interest to be displayed by the legislative and appropriation committees in these reports will result in continuous pressure for reform.

The comptroller general has issued new standards for internal control systems. The OMB has issued guidelines for the evaluation of and reporting on internal control systems. The comptroller general has reorganized his defense review and audit organization. The new organization will apply over 1,000 man-years of effort to the review of defense programs and defense management. Emphasis is being placed on resource management systems and compliance with the FIA.

The comptroller general's conceptual framework embraces the key elements that have been legislated over the years and thus provides a baseline for an integrated DoD accounting system. The stage is now set to improve accounting systems and, with that improvement, to secure a general upgrading of the entire resource management system in the DoD. Guidance is now being provided by the GAO and the OMB; leverage will have to come from the Congress. The problem of soaring federal budget deficits demands that resources be used as efficiently and effectively as possible.

The secretary of defense also must be convinced that a change is needed. If the secretary wants a reliable, consistent, integrated budget and accounting system with all it can provide, the secretary must exert dynamic leadership and seek full and integrated participation by all of the military services. The secretary must guide and coordinate development of the system, constantly validating the integrity of the common approach.

The underpinning of the revised accounting system, its chart of accounts, must include an updated and revised program element structure. The new structure should include the full scope of input resources, program outputs, and performance measures. Each element or account should be defined precisely and included in an authoritative chart of accounts issued by the OSD for use throughout the resource management process.

Together with the revised program element structure, an updated and authoritative dictionary of military terms is needed for mandatory use throughout the DoD. All military terms such as readiness, sustainability, and modernization used in planning, programming, budgeting, and accounting need to be defined commonly and consistently applied within and across all DoD appropriations.

The system must account for, and report on, quantitative and qualitative measures of output as well as financial resources. Planned program performance must be tracked and evaluated.

Accrual accounting is long overdue and a matter of law. The cost of material, equipment, and services must be recorded in the same time period in which it is used. True costs can then be compared with program/budget costs and used in planning for the future. Unit costs derived from the system can provide a solid basis for cost estimating.

The system will continue to account for commitments, obligations, and outlays. Accounting for commitments to make future payments is required fiduciary control and necessary appropriation accounting.

The accounting system should consider the needs of planners, system analysts, budgeteers, and managers. The accounting cycle should be timed to assure a responsive flow of data to users. Feedback reports should compare planned with actual data and should be designed to meet the needs of each category of user.

A companion system of internal controls must be designed with GAO and OMB guidance to assure that objectives are accomplished.

After the system has been designed and approved by the GAO, the OSD should publish complete documentation of not only the accounting system but, rather, the entire, integrated resource management system.

IMPLEMENTING THE CHANGE

The comptroller general has been designated the focal point for financial management improvement in the federal government. He is responsible for approving agency accounting and internal control systems, and he has taken the lead in developing a conceptual framework for improved financial management. It is logical for the DoD to use this guidance in rebuilding its resource management system.

Using the comptroller general's and the Office of Management and Budget's guidance, the secretary of defense should prepare a Department of Defense concept document, upgrading the current system, adding improvements, and correcting the disconnects, mismatches, omissions, and the like. After completion and after GAO approval, step by step specifications should be written for the reformed system. While GAO approval is needed only for the accounting and internal control phases, a review by the GAO and the OMB of the entire, redesigned process would certainly prove beneficial. The completed specifications would be given to the military services as controlling guidance for their individual but integrated system designs.

DoD automated resource management systems are in a constant state of flux. Upon receipt of the new specifications, all system modifications should be in conformance thereafter, and, under OSD leadership, consistent improvements should be initiated as programmed resources become available.

Within OSD, the comptroller's office is the logical organization to assume project leadership. Because the comptroller's primary emphasis has been on the obtaining of resources, his organization for management and accounting needs strengthening. Further, there is a disconnect between the OSD comptroller's office and the counterpart offices in the military departments. Department offices should likewise be strengthened and clear communication channels established with the OSD comptroller.

SUMMARY OF RECOMMENDATIONS

The following recommendations are limited to those that affect the budgeting and accounting systems. Certain recommendations are directed to other phases of the resource management process but are included because they relate directly to the data input of the budgeting and accounting functions.

- National security policy provided to the DoD should include priority guidance as to areas of military interest throughout the world. A target range of fiscal guidance should be provided and the secretary of defense asked to report back on the degree of risk involved in matching priority guidance with fiscal guidance.
- National security policy guidance should include an outyear assessment of the part our treaty allies can be expected to play in offsetting U.S. military requirements. Such assistance can be evaluated in the risk assessment report.

- • To eliminate the disconnect between planning and programming, the secretary of defense should, on the basis of risk assessments, require the Joint Chiefs of Staff to prepare an alternative planning force which is within fiscal guidance.
- • The secretary of defense should update or revise all terms and military definitions used throughout the resource management system. An authoritative dictionary with precise definitions should be issued and made mandatory for use.
- • In consultation with the OMB and with appropriate congressional committees, the secretary of defense should revise the DoD appropriation format and combine the budget with the first program year as is suggested herein.
- • As command channels are clarified and strengthened, the flow of resources should be matched with responsibility and authority, and the budget justification and execution process modified in accordance.
- • For cost estimating and parametric pricing of outyear procurement, analysts should start with complete, actual costs provided by the accounting system.
- • The secretary of defense should initiate an accounting system improvement project embracing the key elements outlined herein and following the general implementation schedule proposed.

NOTES

1. Robert Komer, *Maritime Strategy or Coalition Defense?* (Cambridge, Mass.: Abt Books, 1983).
2. Joint DoD/GAO Working Group, *DoD's Planning, Program & Budgeting System* (September 1983):37.
3. Robert Komer, op. cit., p. 24.
4. Joint DoD/GAO Working Group, op. cit.:40.
5. GAO, *Defense Budget Increases: How Well Are They Planned And Spent?* (1982), p. 57.
6. Joint DoD/GAO Working Group, op. cit.:41.
7. Joint DoD/GAO Working Group, op. cit.:96.
8. GAO, *Defense Spending and its Relationship to the Federal Budget* (1983), p. 17.
9. Joint DoD/GAO Working Group, op. cit.:96.
10. Joint DoD/GAO Working Group, op. cit.:65–68.
11. GAO, op. cit., p. 57.
12. Charles A. Bowsher, *Testimony Before the Task Force on the Budget Process*, Committee on Rules (September, 1982).
13. Charles A. Bowsher, op. cit., p. 34.
14. GAO, op cit., p. vii.
15. Gene H. Fisher, *Cost Considerations in Systems Analysis* (1970), p. 40.

11 JOINT MILITARY ADVICE AND THE DOD PLANNING, PROGRAMMING, AND BUDGETING SYSTEM

by

Russell Murray II

BACKGROUND

Prior to 1961, the Pentagon had been managed primarily on a service-by-service basis. Even the Department of Defense (DoD) budget was described solely in terms of service-oriented categories (Military Personnel Air Force, Procurement of Equipment and Missiles Army, Ship Construction Navy, and so forth). Nowhere was there any comprehensive way of describing the budget in functional terms; there was no tally of what was being devoted in the aggregate, regardless of service, to (for example) strategic nuclear forces, or to intercontinental mobility, or to conventional forces. Much less was there any coherent program beyond the immediate budget year.

All of that changed, apparently permanently, with the 1961 introduction of the Defense Department's Planning, Programming, and Budgeting System (PPBS) by Secretary Robert S. McNamara and his comptroller, Charles J. Hitch, who had fathered the idea in his former position as head of the economics department at the Rand Corporation. With that change came a new emphasis on planning on a department-wide basis, centering on the functions to be performed rather than on how the budget would be split among the various services.

That sea change brought with it another that was to be a source of great and enduring controversy—the invasion by the staff of the Office of the Secretary of Defense (OSD) of an area long considered the exclusive province of the military: specifying the military forces and selecting the weapons to achieve national objectives. McNamara's famous—or infamous—"whiz kids" on the OSD staff took

215

a major role in shaping the new defense program through control of the PPBS and use of then-novel systems analysis techniques.

In the years that followed, the influence of the OSD staff rose and fell with changes in adminstration and managerial styles. But never, even at its lowest ebb, has it reverted to anything approaching the statu₋ ₋uo ante 1961, nor is it likely to.

That shift in the traditional relations between the military and the civilians was undoubtedly due in part—but only in part—to a natural, human tendency on the part of the civilians to seize an opportunity for new power and influence. As one of those civilians, I think it is fair (and I hope not too self-serving) to say that our motivation was not primarily a mean grasping for power per se, but rather an opportunity to contribute in a significant way to an immensely important undertaking: managing the nation's defenses. What we did was very much in keeping with the new vigor and sense of dedication that John Kennedy inspired in so many of us who worked in his administration.

But that was not at all the way that the change was viewed by a great many in the services. In some officers, particularly the more senior ones, there arose deep feelings of resentment and frustration. The military positions of prestige and authority, which they had finally attained after an entire career of preparation, suddenly seemed to have become meaningless. They felt shouldered aside by arrogant young civilians who had muscled their way into managing the DoD as a sort of temporary diversion or hobby.

Although the aggressiveness of the young civilians was the most obvious explanation for the shift in power and influence, that was not all there was to it. Indeed, though part of what happened in the 1960s might be attributed to the aggressive personalities of the young civilians and the unprecedentedly tough management style of Secretary McNamara, the fact that their eventual departure did not lead to a return to the status quo ante shows that there must have been another reason for the shift in influence—a reason that must persist today.

That other and more enduring reason was the change in the center of attention—away from the individual services and toward a more comprehensive view of the Department of Defense—which had come with the introduction of the PPBS. But when the secretary of defense turned to the Joint Chiefs of Staff for advice on joint matters (their statutory responsibility), he found that they could not give it, at least not in a way that was of much use to him. The Joint Chiefs simply could not cope with matters involving the interservice allocation of resources other than to agree among themselves that all four services needed more. Thus the secretary turned to his civilian staff, not because they were young and aggressive, but because they were his only source of advice on joint matters that was reasonably free of service parochialism. The civilians filled the vacuum of advice, and they still do.

Civilian advice on joint matters was and is greatly needed. Civilians bring special talents and insights to such issues, but they cannot substitute for professional military advisers, who have their own special talents and insights. The issue, then, is how to introduce and institutionalize joint military advice into the PPBS. This paper turns next to three alternatives to accomplish that—one that was suggested to the author and two that the author suggests, the second only as a "fall-back" in the event of congressional opposition to the first.

ALTERNATIVE I

The suggested alternative is described as "replacing the present service POMs with a unified POM prepared by the Joint Staff with service inputs" with the objective of permitting "a joint military input to the programming/budgeting process, which would be both fiscally constrained and would permit the horizontal integration of service programs by the professional military themselves."

For those unfamiliar with the annual PPBS cycle, a word of explanation: POM stands for Program Objective Memorandum, though the unsuspecting reader should be aware that these "memorandums" are at least a foot thick. The POMs are drafted in the format of the department's five-year defense plan (FYDP), and specify the service secretaries' recommendations for their services' budgets and five-year programs. The army POM, for example, specifies for the next five years how many tanks and trucks and missiles and helicopters and rifles he proposes to buy and what they will cost, how many divisions and brigades of which types he proposes to maintain, how many people (military and civilians at all levels) that will require and what they will cost, what military bases he proposes to operate and what new installations he intends to build, what he intends to spend on training and on building supplies of ammunition, and, indeed, precisely how he proposes to spend the entire army budget, in detail, over the next five years.

The POMs are immensely comprehensive and involve a vast effort of preparation. Presumably, they respond to the Defense Guidance issued each year by the secretary of defense. (Though the services' adherence to the specified funding levels is by and large rigorous, some scholars of the process question whether the usual loose writing in the rest of the secretary's Defense Guidance has any discernible effect on the POMs.) The secretaries of the three military departments submit their annual POMs to the secretary of defense for his review, modification if necessary, and approval for incorporation in the new FYDP. The influence of the OSD civilians is felt both during the preparation of the secretary's Defense Guidance and during the secretary's subsequent review of the service POMs.

The essence of the suggested alternative to the current practice is to eliminate the three separate POMs prepared by the military departments (and, presumably, those from the independent defense agencies as well), and replace them all with a single POM in which the allocation of resources between the services has already been rationalized by professional military officers on the Joint Staff before it reaches the secretary of defense. I believe there are a number of serious objections to such a proposal relating both to political feasibility and to efficacy.

• I do not believe that this proposal meets the criterion of political feasibility. Admittedly, most service secretaries (with some exceptions such as the current secretary of the navy) have had little influence on the content of the POMs, the vast bulk of which is almost inevitably the product of the military side of the service bureaucracies. Nonetheless, the POMs are submitted to the secretary of defense not by the military service chiefs, but by the civilian service secretaries who are by law their superiors [Sec. 3012 (a) of Title 10, United States Code, for example, states that "There is a Secretary of the Army, who is head of the Department of the Army."]

But whether a mere legal formality or a serious undertaking, the responsibility for the POM is perhaps the principal evidence of a service secretary's authority. Stripping him of that responsibility would strip him of whatever power of the purse he can now claim and, with it, any ability to manage his service. And that is what this proposal would do.

Even if a service secretary were to continue to prepare the POM, he would have to submit it to the JCS rather than directly to the secretary of defense. That, in turn, would make the civilian service secretary a de facto subordinate to his military chief of staff who, as a member of the JCS, could (and doubtless would) revise his secretary's POM to suit his own preferences—a complete reversal of roles and an abandonment of civilian control within the services. In fact, one wonders what would be left for the service secretaries to do.

The idea of eliminating the service secretaries has been seriously considered many times in the past, and there are good arguments both for and against it. I believe that, on balance, they serve a useful purpose and should be retained. But more to the point in this context is that any proposal to eliminate them would doubtless be highly controversial, widely perceived as a further concentration of power in OSD, and viewed as the first step toward eventual unification of the services. In my opinion, such a proposal would meet with strong resistance both within the Pentagon and on Capitol Hill. In short, I doubt that it could attract a critical mass of military, bureaucratic, political, and public support.

Even if the proposal were to clear such high political hurdles, I doubt its efficacy in the absence of fundamental changes in the JCS system. First, consider the mass of detailed input to each of the POMs. Literally thousands of individuals down to every nook and cranny and up to the highest pinnacle of authority in each service are involved in building the foot-thick pile of paper known as a POM. The exercise is by no means limited to some smoke-filled room in the Pentagon; it is a nationwide and, indeed, worldwide operation. There is no conceivable way that the Joint Staff, as we know it today, could take that over. They would have to rely heavily on the services.

The question then arises as to how the responsibilities would be split between the Joint Staff and the service staffs. Because it would swamp the Joint Staff, the detailed preparation of the POMs would clearly have to be left to the services.

The broad outlines and major decisions inherent in the POMs are, presumably, what would become the province of the JCS and the Joint Staff.

The JCS and the Joint Staff would have two ways of imposing those broad outlines and major decisions on the service POMs. The first would be to issue mandatory guidance to the services before they began to draft their POMs. The other would be for the JCS and the Joint Staff to review the finished drafts of the service POMs and direct such revisions as they might think advisable before forwarding them to the secretary of defense. The process could be set up to impose either or both of those forms of joint control over the services. Both, however, seem to me to be inadvisable.

The issuance of guidance by the secretary of defense for the drafting of the service POMs is consistent with and important for the principle of civilian control over the department. But if that guidance were to be diverted on its way to the services and made subject first to interpretation and revision by the JCS and the Joint Staff, civilian control could be seriously undermined.

The obvious answer to such a concern would be for the JCS and the Joint Staff to consult with the secretary on the guidance before it is issued, rather than after. That would assure that the guidance remained the secretary's and not the military's. But that would be a very long way from the concept of a "unified POM prepared by the Joint Staff." In fact, it would be nothing more than what is supposed to happen now. The reasons why such consultations as do occur now have so little effect in promoting "jointness" in the POMs are deeply rooted in our current system. And without fundamental changes in that system, such consultations will continue to be fruitless in reconciling the individual service POMs into a sensibly unified budget and program.

As for the other way of imposing JCS and Joint Staff control over the service POMs—directing revisions in initial drafts by the services—a major objection would be the imposition of yet another layer of review in the already lengthy annual PPBS process and the real possibility that many of the changes imposed by the JCS and Joint Staff could be revised or even reversed after the unified POM was forwarded to the secretary for another round of review.

The obvious answer to such concerns would be to combine the two reviews—the one by the JCS and the Joint Staff with the one by the secretary and the OSD staff. But again, that would be a very long way from the concept of a "unified POM prepared by the Joint Staff" and nothing more than what is supposed to happen now. The reasons why JCS and Joint Staff participation in the POM review process is of such little use to the secretary are also rooted deeply in our current system and will persist until that system is changed.

In summary, I doubt that this is a desirable alternative.

- Stripping the service secretaries of such a large part of their authority would be seen as a move toward unification of the services and thus is likely to be politically infeasible.

- No Joint Staff—as we understand that term—could possibly cope with the details of building even the POM of a single service, much less a unified POM. Building a unified POM the way that the services now build their individual POMs would require a de facto, if not de jure, unification of the services.
- The JCS and the Joint Staff would have to restrict their participation in the POM-building process to broad outlines and major decisions and leave most of the detailed work to the service staffs. But imposing those outlines and decisions via mandatory guidance prior to the services' drafting of the POMs could jeopardize civilian control of the department. Imposition via a review after the POMs were drafted would be wasteful and time-consuming. Finding a practical mechanism for joint control of the service POMs, if possible at all, would be a major problem.

But even if such a mechanism could be found and all the other objections overcome, none of these procedural changes would come close to achieving the desired objective as long as the fundamental weakness in the current JCS system persists: It is incapable of dealing with interservice allocations or reallocations of resources, a prime prerequisite for building a unified POM. Correction of that fundamental weakness must be the first order of business and a principal criterion for any alternative to the current system.

ALTERNATIVE II

This alternative would introduce fundamental changes, not in the organization of the military departments or the procedures of the PPBS system, but in the organization of the joint system and in its participation in the PPBS process. It would introduce badly needed comprehensive, well-staffed, disinterested, professional military advice on joint matters for the first time. Such advice has not been and is not now available to the secretary of defense.

Nominally, such advice does exist: The JCS make recommendations to the secretary on a flood of issues, they meet regularly with him and occasionally with the president, and they publish an annual Joint Strategic Planning Document (JSPD) covering their recommendations for the entire defense program. The JCS chairman normally maintains a close working relationship with the secretary and shares his professional views with him. But that advice, even in the aggregate, falls far short of what the secretary needs. To date, his most useful advice on joint matters has come not from the JCS, but from the civilians in OSD.

The service chiefs can furnish useful professional military advice, but only when service interests are not at stake (and in many joint matters, service interests *are* at stake in one way or another). Some observers attribute the service chiefs' inability to give useful advice on interservice matters to simple parochialism. They tend to view the service chiefs as hopelessly biased in favor of their own services and mentally incapable of other views.

Though simple, narrow parochialism may be part of the problem in some cases, in my experience the issue is more complex, and the reasons for the chiefs' behavior not always so deplorable. First, any chief who is seen not to fight for his service will soon lose his ability to lead it. For example, some air force chief of staff just might believe, in his most private heart of hearts, that the cruise missile would be a better choice than the B-1. That is, after all, an entirely respectable opinion, shared by many whose views on defense are held in high regard (including, for example, the last secretary of defense and former secretary of the air force). But could an air force chief, no matter what he secretly believed, abandon support for the traditional manned bomber in the joint arena? Since the days of General Douhet, the manned bomber has been the visceral heart and soul of the doctrine of airpower. Any air force chief who cut that sacred link with tradition would also cut his link to the air force. He simply could not do it and continue to command the respect and loyalty of his service. Nor could an army chief who failed to support Ranger battalions, nor a marine commandant who failed to support amphibious assault, nor a navy chief who failed to support aircraft carriers. (In fact, Admiral Denfield's inability to carry on as CNO following his decision—at the exhortation of Secretary Louis Johnson—not to press for the first supercarrier in 1949, and the resulting "Revolt of the Admirals," is a case in point.) So what may sometimes seem to be narrow service parochialism may, in fact, be only the price of leadership.

There are other reasons why service chiefs are not well-suited to advising on joint matters. One is that they are already fully occupied in managing their own services and do not have the time (and possibly the inclination) to do justice to joint matters. It has long been recognized that the double burden that a service chief bears—being the military head of his own service as well as a member of the JCS—is a heavy one. President Eisenhower's views on the subject were clear in his message to the Congress on April 3, 1958:

> I have long been aware that the Joint Chiefs' burdens are so heavy that they find it very difficult to spend adequate time on their duties as members of the Joint Chiefs of Staff. This situation is produced by their having the dual responsibilities of chiefs of the military services and members of the Joint Chiefs of Staff. The problem is not new but has not yielded to past efforts to solve it. We need to solve it now, especially in view of the new strategic planning and operational burdens I have previously mentioned.

> I therefore propose that the present law be changed to make it clear that each chief of a military service may delegate major portions of his service responsibilities to his vice chief. Once this change is made, the Secretary of Defense will require the chiefs to use their power of delegation to enable them to make their Joint Chiefs of Staff duties their principal duties.

That message led, four months later, to the Department of Defense Reorganization Act of 1958, in which the service chiefs' power of delegation was made clear. In a passage that was paralleled in the case of the other services, the new legislation said with respect to the army:

> The Vice Chief of Staff has such authorities and duties . . . as the Chief of Staff . . . may delegate to or prescribe for him. Orders issued by the Vice Chief of Staff in performing such duties have the same effect as those issued by the Chief of Staff.

A quarter-century later, however, the problem that President Eisenhower tried to rectify still persists. Although the service chiefs clearly have the power to delegate the running of their services to their vice chiefs, they have been reluctant to do it. The current assistant secretary of defense for manpower, Lawrence J. Korb, suggested why in his book, *The Joint Chiefs of Staff*:

> The problem of the service chief is that he cannot divest himself of his service duties. The real problem is he does not want to. The man who spends nearly forty years as a follower in his service sees his appointment to the JCS as the opportunity to remake his service in his own image. He does not view it as an opportunity to serve as a principal military adviser to the President and the Secretary of Defense. Recently retired CNO Admiral Zumwalt was so engrossed in reshaping the Navy and so little concerned with his JCS responsibilities that he sometimes skipped JCS meetings. He felt that the Chairman, Admiral Moorer, would safeguard the Navy position in the joint arena. Given a choice between the chairmanship of the JCS and the position of service chief, most military officers would opt for the latter. Admiral Radford was keenly disappointed when President Eisenhower selected him to be Chairman rather than CNO and spent much of his time as chairman trying to run the Navy.

But regardless of which of his two jobs a chief might prefer, there can be no doubt that the burden of carrying both simultaneously is very great. For example, the time they must spend away from Washington in connection with their service responsibilities makes it difficult to schedule JCS meetings. Less than a quarter were attended by all five principals between 1977 and 1981, and fully 40 percent were held with no more than three of the five present.

Another reason inhibiting expert advice from the chiefs on joint matters is that few are expert in the affairs of their sister services. Indeed, a chief has a hard enough time comprehending all of his own service. The navy, for example, is often described in terms of its three "unions": air, surface, and submarine. But even within the unions there are subunions; within the air union are the land-based and the carrier-based aircraft subunions, and within the carrier-based sub-union are the fighter community, the attack community, and other even more specialized communities.

The same applies to one degree or another to the other services. The air force comprises separate communities dedicated to strategic manned bombers, military airlift (both tactical and strategic), tactical fighters, ICBMs, and, now, ground-launched nuclear cruise missiles. With most military officers spending the bulk of their careers within only one of those communities, it is not too difficult to envision the problem of an air force chief with a SAC background, for example, trying to render a competent professional judgment on the relative allocation of funds between the navy's antisubmarine warfare programs and the army's anti-tank missiles.

The chairman of the JCS, on the other hand, being at least nominally free of the inhibitions and service responsibilities that plague the chiefs and with more time and opportunity to become familiar with the other services, should at least be in a much better position to render independent, professional military advice to the secretary. As the senior active military officer in the armed forces of the United States and the only military witness who testifies before the Congress on a joint basis, his opinions on joint matters are and should be accorded a weight and attention that none of the service chiefs can command.

But the potential for the chairman to advise on joint matters is nonetheless seriously inhibited. To some degree, it is inhibited by his relationship with the service chiefs. By law, the principal military advisers to the secretary, the NSC, and the president are the chiefs as a body—not the chairman by himself. The chairman cannot take it upon himself to speak independently for the other members and must be scrupulously careful in the way he represents their views.

But more of an inhibition in practice is the chairman's lack of a dedicated staff. The Joint Staff, though under the nominal control of the chairman, serves the chiefs as a body and not the chairman per se. The chairman's staff resources (other than administrative) consist of three colonels and a navy captain, plus one three-star assistant.

The task of trying to rationalize the allocation of the defense budget in the most logical way, independent of narrow service interests, is immensely complex. Broad generalizations are easy; getting down to the detail necessary to shape a budget and program is very much harder. Budgets are made not from adjectives but from explicit numerical decisions on divisions and squadrons and fleets, on procurement and research and personnel and bases, and on dollars and dates and schedules. No five-man staff, no matter how brilliant, can really play in that game. The independent advice that the chairman can render in the PPBS cycle comes close to being limited to the experience he carries around in his head and what he and his tiny staff can figure out "on the back of an envelope."

The major points of the alternative I recommend are:

1. Empower the chairman to decide in which issues he wants the chiefs' participation.
2. Allow the service chiefs continued access to the secretary of defense.
3. Make the chairman, rather than the chiefs as a body, the principal military adviser to the secretary of defense (but only to the secretary and not directly to the NSC or the president).
4. Add a four-star deputy chairman (from a different service) to act for the chairman when he is unavailable.

5. Assign the Joint Staff to support only the chairman.
6. Allow officers at roughly the 0–4 level (major/lt. cdr.) to volunteer for a new career specialty of multilateral staff officer; familiarize them with the operations of their sister services; give them specialized training in multilateral staff operations; have them serve primarily (and thus become experts) on the Joint Staff and the CinCs staffs, with occasional field tours in their own and other services; and have the chairman protect them and their careers from any possible coercion on the part of their parent services.
7. In advising the secretary on the allocation of resources, make the chairman the principal spokesman for the CinCs with the responsibility for helping to reconcile their competing geographical claims, just as he would help the secretary to reconcile competing interservice claims.

Point 1

A major reason for the ineffectiveness of JCS advice is the general, if unspoken, rule that it must not adversely affect the interests of any of the services. In the lengthy JCS process of hammering out recommendations—where the criterion is not so much agreement as lack of disagreement and not so much advice that would most help the secretary as advice that would least harm service interests—the tough issues tend to be sidestepped and the recommendations watered down to the least common denominator.

If joint advice is to be useful, service interests must give way to higher national interests. Given that a service chief cannot both defend and reject the interests of the service he leads, the only answer is to relieve him from the responsibility of rendering joint advice on interservice matters.

Therefore, the chairman should be empowered to decide when the chiefs should be excused from an issue on grounds of probable conflict of interest. An example of such an issue within the context of this paper would be the recommending of revisions for the secretary of defense to make in the service POMs (which are largely the product of the service chiefs in the first place). But the chairman would not exclude the chiefs from all participation in joint matters. For example, their expertise is important in an issue with far less potential for conflict of interest: evaluating our current military capabilities.

Point 2

To assure continued professional military advice on service (as opposed to interservice) matters and particularly to guard against abuses of the chairman's new and very considerable powers, the service chiefs' access to the secretary of defense would be preserved. If any or all of them should feel that the chairman had unjustifiably barred them from participation in any issue, they could appeal the chairman's action to the secretary.

Point 3

The chairman, who would have cognizance of the full range of joint matters, should replace the JCS as a body in the role of principal military adviser. There is, however, an associated issue that should be attended to at the same time: adviser to whom?

Title 10, USC 141(b) says that the JCS are the "principal military advisers to *the President, the National Security Council,* and the Secretary of Defense" (emphasis added). This legislative authority to end-run the secretary of defense and go directly to his boss, the president, has been described accurately as a license for insubordination. The chairman, therefore, should be the statutory military adviser only to the secretary of defense and not, as a matter of law, to the NSC or the president.

On the other hand, the secretary of defense should normally have the chairman accompany him to meetings with the NSC and the president, but by invitation rather than by law. The arrangement would parallel the secretary's practice of transmitting orders to the CinCs through the chiefs, but as a matter of custom rather than law.

Such a change can stand on its own merits and, in this author's opinion, is long overdue. But it is particularly desirable with this alternative as an additional precaution against too much independent power in the hands of a chairman with such an expanded charter.

Point 4

When the chairman is not available, his functions are now taken over on a temporary basis by one of the chiefs in rotation. But with the many burdens that a chief faces in running his own service, little time is left for staying current on joint matters. As a result, few chiefs are well-versed in the breadth of issues that the chairman must face and well-prepared to act for the chairman in his absence.

In a recent attempt to ameliorate the problem, the rotation has been changed from the former practice of a different chief stepping in each time the chairman is away. Now the chiefs are appointed in rotation to three-month stand-by assignments as acting chairman. Although this no doubt helps the potential acting chief to become better-versed on current joint issues, it by no means solves the problem of competing demands on his time.

Appointing a full-time deputy chairman, with the authority to act for the chairman in his absence, would assure the presence of someone with the time to stay current on all joint matters. Not only would this result in better informed joint advice, but it would free the chairman for trips away from Washington more often.

Though a deputy chairman would be desirable even with the current joint system, he would be a practical necessity for this alternative because the chiefs would have been barred from participation in many joint matters. To avoid any conflict of interest, the deputy would not be permitted to return to an assignment with his service, though he could subsequently be appointed either a CinC or the chairman. And to avoid any appearance of inequity, he would have to be from a service other than that of the chairman. Indeed, it could be argued that if one came from either the army or the air force, the other should come from one of the maritime services (navy or marines).

Point 5

If the chairman is to play such an important role in advising the secretary, he must have an adequate staff to support him. That staff should be the Joint Staff, which should be reassigned to support him alone—the service chiefs already have all the staff support they can use.

How big a Joint Staff the chairman would need would not be determined primarily by what it would take to support him in these advisory functions. Fifty to a hundred officers, if well-qualified, could support that part of his responsibilities in a style to which he is now quite unaccustomed. Far more demanding of manpower are the functions associated with the planning and execution of military operations. Though those responsibilities are beyond the scope of this paper, suffice it to say that the changes covered next in Point 6 would be at least as beneficial for professional military planning and execution as for rendering professional military advice.

Point 6

In the military profession, as in the business world, line jobs tend to be viewed as the first-class assignments, and staff jobs looked down on as less desirable and less important. Yet, few will go so far as to claim that staff work is so unimportant that competence does not really matter. In fact, the difference between success and disaster can turn on the competence of the Joint Staff.

Unfortunately, the Joint Staff, though far from incompetent, still falls far short of what it might and should be. The weakness is not in the character, intelligence, or dedication of its officers. It is in the system that mans the nation's most important and complex multiservice staff with officers that are, by and large, untrained and inexperienced in joint matters, totally unfamiliar with many of the major sectors in the defense establishment and subject to at least tacit coercion.

Although the officers serving on the Joint Staff are experienced in the particular sector of their own service, few have any training for or experience in handling interservice matters. As of 1 July 1981, fully 71 percent of the officers on the Joint Staff were on their first tours of duty on any sort of joint or multilateral staff, much less the Joint Staff itself. That, coupled with the relatively short tours of duty on the Joint Staff (averaging less than 2½ years as of 1980) and severe legal restrictions on repeat tours, means that few officers are the kind of "old hands"—experienced in interservice issues on more than a single-service basis—that are essential if we are to have a first-rate Joint Staff. If I may be excused for citing myself:

> The sad fact of the matter is that, while we would not dream of letting an officer fly an F-15 without years of highly specialized and immensely expensive training, we are perfectly willing to let him, without a trace of preparation, tackle matters demanding the most complex, professional military skills.[1]

The obvious first requirement in building a first-rate Joint Staff is first-rate officers. Past attempts in that regard have tended to rely on coercion, such as making joint service a prerequisite for appointment to flag or general officer rank. But, as it has been in that case, coercion is unlikely to be effective in the long run. What is required to attract first-rate officers to the Joint Staff is the perception that its work is interesting, important, and influential. Though it is not viewed that way now, it could be in the future with the return to credibility that this alternative promises and with military advice on joint matters no longer being dismissed as hopelessly faction-ridden.

A second requirement is proper training in joint staff operations and familiarization with the operations of the other services. The Armed Forces Staff College was created precisely to prepare officers for joint duty, but in the past there was no assurance that its graduates would ever see joint duty. The National Defense University, though preparing more senior officers for added responsibilities, did not prepare them specifically for joint duty. And training within the Joint Staff itself was strictly on-the-job. Fortunately, some steps are being taken to correct that situation, and they should be encouraged and expanded.

A third requirement is experience. The current legal restrictions on repeat tours are vastly wasteful of the experience so dearly gained in joint service. Those restrictions should be eliminated. In their place should be an option for a military career specialty in joint staff work. Officers at roughly the O-4 level should, upon evidence of a desire and talent for such work, be allowed to specialize in it. After thorough initial training and familiarization, most of their subsequent assignments would be on the Joint Staff and the CinC staffs. But to avoid isolation from reality, they would also serve occasional field tours with their own or, to broaden their professional expertise, another service.

A fourth requirement is that their careers be guided along the most productive channels and protected from any possible coercion on the part of their parent services. Inevitably, that would require that their assignments and promotions be heavily influenced, if not absolutely controlled, by the chairman. Many ways of assuring that are possible, though some intrusion on the services' virtually absolute control over their officers' careers and promotions would be unavoidable.

Some might argue that such a staff would end up locked in an ivory tower and totally out of touch with the practical realities of the armed forces in the field. That would indeed be a risk and is the reason for the occasional field assignments proposed for Joint Staff officers. On the other hand, that possible risk must be weighed against today's certain risk in having a Joint Staff with such shortcomings in knowledge, training, and experience. The current system values competence in the field above everything else. The alternative would also recognize the importance of competence in staff work and that it, as much as competence in the field, also requires training and experience. Novices belong neither in the field nor on the staff.

Point 7

The views of the CinCs should play a major role in shaping the defense program. The shape of the program, however, is determined largely by those stationed in Washington. That orientation may be responsible for what many view as too much emphasis on the long term (R&D and procurement to build forces for the future) and too little on the near term (operations and maintenance funds for readiness right now).

In an effort to have the CinCs play a more important role in the management of the department, Secretary Brown instituted a series of regular reports from them directly to him, with face-to-face meetings whenever possible. The current administration has added appearances by the CinCs at the deliberations of the Defense Resources Board.

Each CinC's views and recommendations are, however, necessarily conditioned by his responsibility for a particular geographic area, just as a chief's views and recommendations are necessarily conditioned by his responsibility for a particular service. The secretary, therefore, needs help in reconciling the competing geographical claims and allocating resources among them.

There is no reason why the secretary's help in inter-CinC matters should come from only his civilian staff; disinterested professional military advice is at least as important. Its source, obviously, should be the chairman, backed by an expert and dedicated Joint Staff. The views of the individual CinCs should continue to be solicited, but by the chairman rather than by the JCS as a body.

With the help of his staff, the chairman should consider their various merits and priorities from a military point of view and advise the secretary on what he believes to be the best worldwide allocation of resources. Direct contact between the CinCs and the secretary should, of course, continue; the CinCs report to the

the secretary as a matter of law. The difference would be in the availability of an integrated professional military view of relative needs and priorities on a world-wide basis, rather than a series of unreconciled recommendations from the individual CinCs.

Prospects for Implementation

The seven points outlined above would constitute a major change in the organization of the joint system. Two of the seven (establishing the staff career specialty and having the chairman reconcile and represent the views of the CinCs) could probably be effected by directive. But legislation would be required to achieve the following:

1. Make the chairman the sole principal military adviser.
2. Allow the chairman to exclude the service chiefs from consideration of joint matters in which he believes a conflict of interest to be likely.
3. Have the principal military adviser report by law only to the secretary of defense, and not also to the NSC and the president.
4. Establish the position of deputy chairman.
5. Assign the Joint Staff solely to the support of the Joint Staff.

Obviously, it would be better if no new legislation were required. A third, fallback, alternative requiring less is discussed briefly below. The most fundamental reason for the scarcity of disinterested, professional military advice on joint matters, however, lies in the existing law establishing the responsibilities of the JCS. That law should be changed, not just to make that kind of advice available, but at least as much to improve the planning and execution of military operations through a better trained and more experienced staff.

The difficulty that such new legislation would encounter is a matter of speculation. Clearly a strong endorsement by the administration would be important. But the traditional fears of a "man on a white horse" should be mitigated by the provision to abolish the chairman's current authority to end-run the secretary of defense and by assuring the service chiefs the right of reclama.

PPBS under Alternative II

The first and most important step in the annual PPBS cycle is, or should be, the deliberations of the president and the NSC on what the national security policy should be. To decide, the president needs to know, among other things, what military forces it would take to achieve alternative national objectives and what the associated risks would be (also how much it would cost and what the likely resulting effects on the economy and other national objectives would be). The chairman, backed by an expert and dedicated staff, should be a highly competent authority—the nation's best—on those military force requirements and risks. Alternative II would put him in that position. The resulting beneficial effects on the realism and practicality of our national security policy could be unprecedented.

The second step in the annual PPBS cycle is the drafting of the secretary's guidance to the services for the preparation of their POMs. If that key document is to cover all that it should from the most fundamental objectives of our national security policy to the secretary's desired allocation of resources to achieve them, if it is to be well-integrated and internally consistent, and if it is to be short enough for busy senior officials to actually read for themselves, it should be drafted for the secretary by one office. Disparate contributions from diverse players with their own special interests and views of the world, stapled together, simply will not do as the secretary's guidance to his services.

The criteria for selection of the office to do the drafting should be (1) a selfless dedication to the interests of the secretary of defense, untainted by any special interests or line authority over any specific part of the defense program, (2) a solid understanding of the entire defense program, and (3) a first-class talent for writing in simple English. On those grounds, the actual drafting of the secretary's guidance should continue to be an OSD responsibility.

Nonetheless, the chairman, supported by his reformed Joint Staff, should play a major role in helping the secretary with his guidance. As with his other traditional advisers, the secretary should solicit the chairman's views on what the guidance should be before the first word of it is drafted, and the chairman's reactions to the secretary's draft should be most seriously entertained. Of course, that is what is supposed to happen now. The difference under Alternative II would be that (1) the chairman could give his best professional judgment free of parochial service interests, and (2) he would have a proper staff to help him. For the first time, the secretary might actually get credible, detailed, professional military advice on matters ultimately and vitally affecting individual service interests.

The third major part of the PPBS cycle for the chairman's participation would be the review of the service POMs. The chairman, or perhaps his senior representative, should serve as a regular, full-fledged member of the Defense Resources Board. He should suggest issues for the DRB to consider, draft (with the help of the reformed Joint Staff) the issue papers for matters in which professional military judgment is paramount, and participate in the DRB's deliberations on an equal footing with the civilian members. To be sure, the Joint Staff already participates in the DRB process, but it is inhibited to the point of near-uselessness by having to cater to individual service interests.

The chairman's participation in the final phase of the PPBS cycle—the preparation of the detailed budget—could be extremely important. Many cuts are often made at the last minute to meet a budgetary target. Their consequences can be hard for civilians to judge, particularly in the last minute rush. Unfortunately, all too often they have pernicious effects on the objectives that the DRB thought it was endorsing. Readiness is an area that traditionally suffers from such final slashes, but the chairman, backed by a competent staff and representing the CinCs who understand best what such cuts mean, should be able to revert these unintended disasters and suggest less damaging alternatives.

Though the mechanics of the PPBS system and its annual cycle would be little affected by this alternative, its product—the FYDP—and indeed the national security policy it supports, should be greatly improved. The change would be that the secretary would now have, in addition to the advice of his civilian staff on interservice matters, disinterested, professional military advice available in all the phases of the annual cycle—when basic national security policy is debated, when he drafts his initial guidance, when he reviews the POMs, and when he prepares his annual budget. That is what is missing now from the PPBS and what is needed if future FYDPs are to reflect the best of both military and civilian thinking.

ALTERNATIVE III

This alternative is a fall-back from Alternative II that would require a minimum of new legislation. Its exact nature would depend on the degree of congressional opposition to Alternative II. To the extent necessary, it would sacrifice many of the provisions of Alternative II in order to preserve some improvement in military advice to the secretary of defense. If necessary, it would forgo the chairman's designation as the principal military adviser and his authority to relieve the chiefs from participation in specific joint issues; it would be prepared to abandon the concept of a deputy chairman; and it might not end the legal authority of the chiefs to end-run the secretary to the NSC and the president.

What it would preserve would be some provision for dedicated staff support for the chairman. If the Congress refused to assign the entire Joint Staff solely to supporting the chairman, the first fall-back would be to assign at least a portion of it to his exclusive use. That portion would then operate under the concept of the career staff specialty proposed for Alternative II, implemented by directive.

Should that also fail congressional approval, a final fall-back position would be to create a new staff specifically assigned to the chairman, also operating under the career staff concept.

None of the many possible versions of Alternative III would be preferable to Alternative II. They would, to one degree or another, improve the chairman's ability to provide dispassionate advice. But without the authority to end interservice haggling over words and delay in actions, it would leave him enmeshed in clumsy joint bureaucracy.

A far more serious failing, particularly if the career provision for the Joint Staff were not implemented, would be the continuing shortfalls in skill, professionalism, and responsiveness for planning and executing military operations. Though that subject is beyond the scope of this paper, it is surely no less important than providing professional military advice on joint matters.

Alternative III, particularly in its more modest versions, would be an expedient, minimal step in the direction of supplementing civilian advice with professional military advice. But it would fail to correct the fundamental weakness that has existed in the joint system since its creation: a body hobbled by inherent conflicts of interest and supported by a staff largely untrained, inexperienced, and at least tacitly subject to coercion; a body unable to cope with the hard choices it is charged with making.

NOTE

1.   Russell, Murray II, "Policies, Prices, and Presidents: The Need to Enlighten the Great Choices in National Security," *Armed Forces Journal* (June 1982).

INDEX

Accounting systems, 29–31, 63, 82–83, 84, 85, 202–203, 209–210, 211, 212
Accrual-based data. *See* Accounting systems
Aerospace Defense Commands, 47
Air Force. *See also* Air support; Airlift capability
  B-1 bomber, 35, 88
  baselining, 35, 96
  C-5, 120, 173
  chief of staff, 221, 222–223
  F-15 fighter, 92–93, 96, 179
  Key West agreement, 114, 116
  readiness/sustainability, 149
  specified commands, 47
Air support, 59, 114, 148
Aircraft carriers, 221
Airlift capability, 50, 59, 114, 148, 205
Antisatellite weapons, 143
Armed Forces Journal International, 138
Armed forces Staff College, 227
Army
  chief of staff, 221
  Delta unit, 117
  Key West agreement, 114, 116
  Rangers, 117, 118
  readiness/sustainability, 149
  unified commands, 47
Army-Air Force agreement (1984), 50
Art, Robert J., 105

Aspin, Les, 151, 166 n.44, 167 n.59
Atlantic Command, 47
Atomic Energy Commission, 211
Audit validation, 203
Augustine, Norm, 89

B-1 bomber, 35, 88
"Backdoor spending," 127–128
Baselining, 35–36
Bearg, Nancy J., and Edwin A. Deagler, Jr., 141 (quoted)
Beilenson Task Force, 154–158
Bledsoe, Robert, 138, 142–143
Blue Ribbon Defense Panel (1970), 113
Bowsher, Charles A., 207, 209 (quoted)
Brown, Harold, 67, 189, 192, 193, 228
Budget and Accounting Procedures Act (1950), 210
Budget and Impoundment Control Act (1974), 109, 126, 127–132, 143, 150, 154, 156, 210
Budgetary reserves, 34
"Buying into" programs, 37, 146–147

C-5, 120, 173
Capital investment plan, 31
Carlucci initiatives, 179
Carter administration, 67, 74, 149
Central Command, 47
Central Intelligence Agency, 192

Chain of command, 13, 52, 54–55, 65, 113–123 *passim*
Chief of staff to the commander-in-chief, 43, 44
Civilian control of the military, 14, 53, 63, 67, 99, 182, 184–186, 215–216
Cohen, William, 160
Combatant commands. *See* Unified and specified commands
Command, control, and communications, 50, 59
Command units, names of, 47
Competition for defense contracts, 36, 37, 95
Comptroller-general, 31, 207, 211, 212–213
Congress
    accounting reforms, 210–212
    authorization/appropriation committees, 24, 25, 104, 105, 109, 127–146 *passim*, 151, 159, 173–174
    "backdoor spending," 127–128
    Beilenson Task Force, 154–158
    biennial budgeting, 24–25, 104, 109–110, 157–158, 169–171
    Budget and Impoundment Control Act, 126, 127–132, 143, 150, 154, 156, 210
    budget timetable, 130–131, 153–158
    and civilian control of military, 186
    and defense budget, 104–111, 125–167, 169–180
    H.R. 750, 170
    matrix authorizations, 176–178
    "milestone" authorizations, 110–111, 159–160, 174–175
    national defense function, 128–129
    operating and support costs, 178–180
    policy oversight, 21–25, 106–107, 132, 139–146, 159–161
    and the president, 80, 81, 126, 195
    procurement authorizations, 134–135, 159–160, 176–178
    redundancy, 22, 105–106, 132–135
    research and development authorizations, 134, 135, 159–160, 175–176
    review activity, volume of, 136–138
    S. 12/S. 20/S. 922, 170
    Selected Acquisition Reports, 178–180
    short-term vs. long-term focus, 22–23, 106
    staff size, 21, 135–136
    and weapons acquisition, 99, 106
    work overload, 22, 105
Cost criterion, 37, 38, 97, 203, 209–210
Cost projections, 33–34, 82–83, 85

Cost savings reinvestment, 37, 38, 96
Costs
    operating and support costs, 178–180
    quantity/cost matrix authorizations, 176–178
Counterterrorist units, 117, 122

Defense Advanced Research Projects Agency, 97
Defense budget, 65, 150–161, 172–180, 206–207
    annual authorizations, growth in scope of, 132–135, 145–146
    Beilenson Task Force, 154–158
    biennial, 24–25, 35, 63, 93, 104, 109–110, 148, 157–158, 169–171
    budget justification/execution, 202
    and Command CinCs, 58
    and Congress, 24–25, 80, 81, 104–111, 125–167, 169–180
    dysfunctions, 146–150
    fiscal gaps, 79–80
    matrix authorizations, 176–178
    operating and support costs, 178–180
    operations and maintenance, 134–135
    and the president, 80, 81, 126
    procurement, 134–135, 159–160
    research and development, 134, 135, 159–160
    Selected Acquisition Reports, 178–180
    timetable, 130–131, 153–158
Defense contracts. *See* Weapons acquisition process
Defense Guidance, 70, 201, 217, 230
Defense industrial base, 90, 91, 97–98
Defense Intelligence Agency, 192
Defense Reorganization Act (1958), 44–47, 221–222
Defense Reorganization Plan (1953), 44
Defense Resource Management Study (1979), 26, 67
Defense Resources Board (DRB), 11, 67, 81, 230–231
Defense spending, discretionary, 129
Defense Systems Acquisition Review Council (DSARC), 159, 174
Delta force, 117
Denfeld, Admiral, 221
Department of Defense. *See also* Office of the Secretary of Defense; Secretary of Defense
    accounting and budgeting systems, 199–214
Defense Systems Acquisition Review Council, 159, 174
    established, 64, 185
    organization of, 4

Planning, Programming, and Budgeting System, 3, 26–31
reform proposals, 2, 150–153
weapons acquisition process, 25, 31–38
Department of Defense Report on the National Military Command Structure. See "Steadman Report"
Department of State's Bureau of Intelligence and Research, 192
Department of the Air Force, 64, 185
Department of the Army, 64
Department of the Navy, 64, 185
Department of War, 185
Domenici, Pete, 160
Douhet, General, 221
Draft Presidential Memoranda (DPM), 66

Eisenhower, Dwight D., 2, 42, 44–47, 50, 64–65, 113, 115, 186, 221–222, 225
Enthoven, Alain C., 191
European Command, 47
Evaluation, 29–31, 63, 82–85

F-15 fighter, 92–93, 96, 179
Federal Managers Financial Integrity Act (1982), 210, 211
Fiscal gaps, 79–80
Fisher, Gene H., 209
Five-Year Defense Program (FYDP), 26, 27, 62, 66, 79, 231
Force development. See Planning, Programming, and Budgeting System
Force structure. See Military command structure
Ford administration, 67
Forrestal, James, 43, 114
Fox, Ronald, 147

GAO, 209, 210, 211, 213
Grenada operation (1983), 91, 118, 121

Hamre, John J., 105, 159–160
Hart, Gary, 160
Helicopters, 116–117, 148
Hitch, Charles J., 191, 215
Holloway, James L., III, 117
Hoover Commission Report (1949), 43–44, 85
Hoover Commission Report (1955), 85
Huntington, Samuel P., 144, 152

Inflation, 172, 173
Intelligence systems, 192
"Internal contracts," 35
International Security Affairs Office, 193
Iran hostage rescue mission, 51, 117, 121, 122, 184

Jackson, Robert H., 185
Johnson, Louis, 221
Joint Chiefs of Staff (JCS). See also Joint Chiefs of Staff, chairman of; Joint Chiefs of Staff, deputy chairman of; Service chiefs
advisory function, 6, 45, 48–49, 201, 216, 221–222
established, 42–43
and Joint Strategic Planning Document, 220
and Office of the Secretary of Defense, 190, 204–205
and Program Objective Memoranda, 218–220
recognized by National Security Act, 64, 115
and Secretary of Defense, 152, 153
and strategic planning, 67, 69, 72–73
and unified operational commands, 43, 115–116
Vice Chief of Staff, 221–222
and weapons acquisition, 90, 92
Joint Chiefs of Staff (Korb), 222
Joint Chiefs of Staff, chairman of
advisory function, 7, 53, 54, 62, 70, 223
and chain of command, 13, 54–55
and Command CinCs, 228–229
and Defense Resources Board, 230–231
Eisenhower proposals for, 2, 44–45, 64
established, 44, 64
and Joint Staff, 8, 55, 223, 231
and "readiness budgets," 58, 77
and Secretary of Defense, 183, 225, 230
and service chiefs, 56–57, 224
and strategic planning, 9, 27, 49–50, 55, 73
and weapons acquisition process, 91–92, 98
Joint Chiefs of Staff, deputy chairman of, 9, 55, 225–226
Joint Staff, 55–56, 181–182
advisory function, 49, 70
career specialty/selection and training, 8, 46, 55–56, 226–228, 231–232
and chairman of JCS, 8, 55, 223
and Command CinCs' staff, 58–59
committee system, 45
and Defense Resources Board, 230
director, 9, 55
Eisenhower reforms, 45–46, 64
established, 42

Joint Staff (cont.)
    and Office of the Secretary of Defense, 188–190, 193–194, 195–196, 197
    and Program Objective Memoranda, 218–220
    readiness program and budget, 77
    size of, 64, 185
    and strategic planning, 50, 73
    and weapons acquisition, 92, 98
Joint Staff papers, 56
Joint Strategic Planning Document (JSPD), 10, 69, 72, 220
Jones, David, 117

KC-10 tanker, 176, 177
Kennedy administration, 120, 216
Key West Agreement (1948), 59, 113, 114–115, 116, 119
Kolodziej, Edward, 141 (quoted), 144
Komer, Robert W., 193, 204, 205
Korb, Lawrence J., 222
Korean War, 68

Laird, Melvin, 66, 67, 167 n.56
Lebanon, presence mission in, 52, 117–118, 121, 184, 195
Lift capability, strategic/tactical. See Airlift capability; Sealift capability
Long, Robert L.J., 52, 118

M1 tank, 179
MacArthur, Douglas, 185
McClellan, George B., 185
McDonnell-Douglas Corporation, 176
McElroy, Neil, 116
McNamara, Robert S., 66, 120, 181, 191, 211, 215–216
Malbin, Michael, 145
Management information systems, 30, 31, 83, 84, 85
Manpower and logistics office, 193–194
Marine Corps
    deployment in Lebanon, 52, 117–118, 195
    Rapid Deployment Force, 47
Market incentives, 36–38
Matrix authorizations, 76–178
Mayaguez rescue operation, 121
Mayhew, David, 165 n.34
"Milestone" authorizations/review, 110–111, 159–160, 174–175
Military advise, 3, 5–9, 48–49
    chairman of JCS, 7, 53, 54, 70
    cross-service, 69–70
    Joint Staff, 49, 70

service chiefs/JCS, 6, 7–8, 48–49, 57, 69, 70
Military Airlift Command, 47
Military command structure, 2, 5–14, 43, 46, 47, 63, 65, 67–68, 73, 76, 113–123, 140, 205
Military missions, 17, 18, 59, 70, 71, 148
Military operations
    limited, 121–123
    planning and conducting, 5, 10–13, 50–53
Military service staffs. See also Service chiefs
    and Program Objective Memoranda, 218–220
    size of, 21, 197
Moorer, Admiral, 222
Murray, Russell, II, 227 (quoted)
MX missile, 88, 106, 115, 129, 138

National Defense University, 227
National Security Act (1947)
    and Command CinCs, 11, 13, 51, 57–58
    and JCS, 43, 64, 115
    and Joint Staff, 43
    and Secretary of Defense, 63
National Security Council (NSC), 68
National security policy, 200–201, 204
    policy oversight, 21–25, 106–107, 132, 139–146, 159–161
NATO, 143
Navy, 47, 50, 114, 149, 221, 222. See also Sealift capability
Nixon administration, 67
North Atlantic and European defense, 17, 18, 70, 71
Nuclear deterrence, 17, 18, 59, 70, 71
Nunn, Sam, 138, 143, 160
Nunn-McCurdy Amendment, 179

Obligation-based data. See Accounting systems
Office of Management and Budget (OMB), 80, 202, 213
Office of the Secretary of Defense (OSD), 14–21, 64, 67, 187–189, 215–216. See also Secretary of Defense
    asst. secy. for acquisitions and logistics, 20, 77, 78
    asst. secy. for health affairs, 19, 20, 77, 78, 193
    asst. secy. for international security affairs, 74, 188, 189
    asst. secy. for international security policy, 74, 188

asst. secy. for manpower, reserve affairs, and logistics, 19, 20, 77
asst. secy. for NATO and European defense (proposed), 18, 62, 72, 73, 74
asst. secy. for nuclear deterrence (proposed), 18, 62, 72, 73, 74
asst. secy. for regional defense (proposed), 18, 62, 72, 73, 74
asst. secy. for reserve affairs, 19, 20, 77, 78, 193
asst. secy. for systems analysis, 191–192
comptroller, 138, 188, 213
deputy secretary of defense, 121
and JCS, 190, 204–205
and Joint Staff, 188–190, 193–194, 195–196, 197
mission orientation, 17–19, 62, 73–75
organization and size of, 3, 4, 14–21 73–75, 187–188, 196
readiness and sustainability, oversight of, 19–20
and strategic planning, 70–71
under secretary for manpower and readiness (proposed), 20, 63, 78
under secretary for policy, 17, 18, 27, 62, 70, 72, 188, 189, 192–193
under secretary for research and engineering, 74
and weapons acquisition, 91, 92, 99
Operating and support costs (O&S), 178
Operational commands. See Unified and specified commands
Operations and Maintenance (O&M), 134–135
Organization and Function of the JCS (1982), 56
Ornstein, Norman, 165 n.27

Pacific Command, 47
Parametric pricing system, 82–83, 85
Pastor, Robert, 166 n.47
Planning, Programming, and Budgeting System (PPBS), 3, 25, 26–31, 148, 211, 215. See also Resource allocation process; Strategic planning
and chairman of JCS, 55
evaluation, 29–31, 63, 82–85
planning, 26–27, 66, 68–75
programming and budgeting, 27–29, 62, 66, 75–82
"Planning wedges," 34
Polaris program, 115
President, the, 68. See also individual presidential administrations
as commander-in-chief, 184, 185
and Congress, 80, 81, 126, 195

Price elasticity, 96
Procurement authorizations, 134–135, 159–160, 176–178
Profit margin, 36, 37–38, 95–96
Program Analysis and Evaluation Office, 66, 70, 74, 188, 189, 191–192
Program Objective Memoranda (POMs), 11, 66, 76, 217–220, 230

Quantity/cost matrix, 176–178

Radford, Admiral, 222
Rapid Deployment Force, 47
Rangers, 117, 118
Readiness
budgets, 12–13, 58, 76–77
measures of, 30, 83–84
oversight, 19–20, 76, 77–79, 143, 149
Readiness Command, 47, 119
Reagan administration, 67, 74, 157, 188
Regional defense, 17, 18, 70, 71
"Requirements creep," 35
Research and development (R&D), 134, 135, 159–160, 175–176
Resource allocation process, 3, 65, 66, 26–31, 200–213. See also Planning, Programming, and Budgeting System; Strategic planning
and Command CinCs, 11–12, 50–51, 75–77
and NATO allies, 71, 75
and service chiefs/JCS, 9, 204–205
Rice, Donald B., 67
Roosevelt, Franklin D., 42
Roth, William, 138–139
Russell, Richard, 145

SALT II, 143
Scher, Seymour, 144
Schick, Allen, 131
Schilling, Warner R., 141 (quoted), 145, 159
Schlesinger, James R., 96
Sealift capability, 50, 59, 114, 148, 205
Secretary of Defense, 67, 190–191. See also Office of the Secretary of Defense
and budget/accounting system, 212
and chairman of JCS, 183, 225, 230
and Congress, 152
and Defense Guidance, 70, 201, 217, 230
and deputy secretary, 121
and Eisenhower's proposals, 2, 64
established, 63
and service chiefs/JCS, 152, 153, 224–225

Secretary of Defense (cont.)
  weakness of, 186–187
  and weapons acquisition, 91
Selected Acquisition Reports (SARs),
    178–180
Service chiefs. *See also* Joint Chiefs of
    Staff
  advisory function, 6, 7–8, 48–49,
    57, 70, 220–223
  and chairman of JCS, 56–57, 224
  and Defense Resources Board, 67
  dual-role conflict, 45, 48–49, 221, 22?
  and OSD/PPBS, 215–216
  and resource allocation process, 9,
    72–73
  right of dissent, 57, 120, 229
  and the Secretary of Defense, 224–22
Service secretaries
  and Program Objective Memoranda,
    217–220
Sole-source contract, 36, 37. *See also*
    "Buying into" programs
Southern Command, 47
Special operations, 59
"Steadman Report" (1978), 9, 30, 49
Stennis, John, 135
Strategic Air Command, 47
Strategic planning, 9–10, 49–50, 68–75.
    See also Planning, Programming,
    and Budgeting System; Resource
    allocation process
  costs of planning weaknesses, 71–72
  cross-service planning, 72–73
  and JCS/service chiefs, 9, 49, 69,
    72–73
  and JCS chairman, 9, 49–50, 70
  and Joint Staff, 50, 70
  and OSD, 70–71
  and the president/NSC, 68
Strategic Planning and Resource Analy-
    sis Agency (SPRAA), 9, 50
Submarines, nuclear-armed, 115
Systems Analysis Office, 66

Tax policy, 172, 173
Tower, John, 139, 146
Truman, Harry S, 43, 44

Unified and specified commanders-in-
    chief (CinCs), 42. *See also* Unified
    and specified commands

authority of, 2, 13, 47, 52–53, 57–
    58, 68, 113, 115, 116
  and chairman of JCS, 228–229
  and Joint Staff, 58–59
  and resource allocation process, 11–
    12, 50–51, 62, 67, 68, 75–77
  and weapons acquisition process, 91,
    92, 98

Unified and specified commands, 2, 11,
    12, 46, 52–53, 57–59, 65. *See also*
    Unified and specified commanders-
    in-chief
  association of each command with an
    individual service, 47
  established, 43
Unified Command Plan, 48

Vice Chief of Staff, 221–222
Vietnam, 116

Washington Headquarters Service, 21
Weapons acquisition process, 3, 25, 31–
    38, 88–101
  acquisition management, 37, 38, 95
  baselining, 35–36, 96
  biennial budgeting, 35, 93
  and chairman of JCS, 91–92, 98
  and Command CinCs, 91, 92, 98
  competition, 36, 37, 95
  Congress' role, 99, 106
  cost-savings plans, 33–34, 37, 38,
    88–89, 93–97
  and JCS reform, 90, 91
  and Joint Staff, 92, 98
  market incentives, 36–38, 90, 91,
    97–98
  milestone system, 110–111
  and military services, 99
  and OSD, 91, 92, 99
  planning and selection process, 31–
    34, 88, 91–92
  production stretch-outs, 89, 92
  profit margins, 36, 37–38, 95–96
  program and budget reforms, 34–36,
    90, 92–94
  subsystem demonstrations, 96–97
Weinberger, Caspar, 166 n.40
World War II, 42, 63

Zumwalt, Admiral, 222

LIST OF PARTICIPANTS

Robert J. Art is the Christian A. Herter Professor of International Relations at Brandeis University, and is research associate at the Center for International Affairs at Harvard University. He is coeditor with Samuel Huntington and Vincent Davis of *Reorganizing the Pentagon: Leadership in War and Peace* (Pergamon, 1985).

Les Aspin, newly elected chairman of the House Armed Services Committee, has represented southeast Wisconsin since 1970. He attended Yale, Oxford, and MIT, where he earned a Ph.D. in economics. Prior to his congressional service, Aspin worked in the Department of Defense.

Norman R. Augustine is vice-president of Martin Marietta Aerospace. He has served as president of the American Institute of Aeronautics and Astronautics, president of the Association of the United States Army, and chairman of the Defense Science Board. He has held several positions in the Department of Defense, including assistant secretary of the army (research and development) and under secretary of the army.

Archie D. Barrett, a retired air force officer, is a member of the professional staff of the House Armed Services Committee. Before retiring, Barrett served as military assistant to the Executive Secretary of the Defense Organization Study (1977–80). He is the author of *Reappraising Defense Organization* (National Defense University Press, 1983).

Anthony C. Beilenson represents West Los Angeles in the U.S. House of Representatives. He is presently a member of the Rules Committee and the Permanent Select Committee on Intelligence.

Ed Bethune represented the second district of Arkansas in the U.S. House of Representatives from 1979–84. He served on Budget Committee and the Banking, Finance, and Urban Affairs Committee.

William K. Brehm has served in several positions in the Department of Defense, including assistant secretary of defense for manpower and reserve affairs and assistant secretary of defense for legislative affairs. He is currently president and chairman of the board of the SRA Corporation in Arlington, Virginia.

Antonia Handler Chayes is a partner with the law firm of Csaplar & Bok and a director of United Technologies Corporation. During 1984–85, she was a fellow at the Center for International Affairs at Harvard University. She has served as assistant secretary (1977–79) and under secretary (1979–81) of the air force. Earlier, she was Dean of Jackson College, Tufts University.

Dale W. Church is a partner at Seyfarth, Shaw, Fairweather & Geraldson. He has served as deputy under secretary of defense for research and engineering and has had a wide range of government and private experience in the field of contract policy.

William S. Cohen has represented Maine in the U.S. Senate since 1977. He is currently a member of the Armed Services and Governmental Affairs Committees and chairs the Subcommittee on Seapower and Force Projection. Senator Cohen recently received the Non-Commissioned Officers' Association's L. Mendel Rivers Award for service to military personnel.

John M. Collins served in the U.S. Army for 30 years, retiring with the rank of colonel. Since his retirement, he has been a senior specialist in national defense at the Library of Congress. He is the author of several books on military strategy and the military balance.

Eugene J. D'Ambrosio retired from the U.S. Army after 37 years with the rank of major general. He is currently with Day & Zimmerman, Inc. General D'Ambrosio is a member of both the U.S. Army Infantry and Ordinance Halls of Fame.

Vincent Davis is director and Patterson Chair Professor of the Patterson School of Diplomacy and International Commerce at the University of Kentucky. His most recent publications as coauthor are, with Stephen J. Cimbala in *The Reagan*

Defense Program: The First Four Years (Wilmington, 1985), and with Robert J. Art and Samuel P. Huntington in *Reorganizing the Pentagon: Leadership in War and Peace* (Pergamon, 1985).

Edwin A. Deagle, a former army officer, is currently director of international relations at the Rockefeller Foundation. Deagle's positions in the public sector include service at the Congressional Budget Office and on the National Security Council staff.

Butler C. Derrick has represented the third district of South Carolina in the U.S. House of Representatives since 1975. He serves on the Rules and Budget Committees.

Norman D. Dicks has represented the Sixth District of the State of Washington in the U.S. House of Representatives since 1977. Dicks serves on the Appropriations Subcommittees for Defense, Interior and Military Construction. He is a founding member of the Military Reform Caucus.

Robert F. Ellsworth has had a distinguished career in government including service as deputy secretary of defense (1975–77), assistant secretary of defense (1934–74), U.S. Ambassador to NATO (1969–71), and assistant to the president (1969). He represented the 3rd district of Kansas in the U.S. Congress from 1961 through 1967.

James J. Exon represents Nebraska in the U.S. Senate. He is a former two-term governor of Nebraska. Exon serves on the Armed Services, Budget, and Commerce Committees.

John J. Ford is vice-president of government affairs of Avco Corporation. Formerly a journalist with the Army Times Publishing Company, he joined the staff of the House Armed Services Committee in 1965 and served as its staff director from 1977 to 1985.

J. Ronald Fox is Professor of Business Administration and Chairman of the General Management Area at the Harvard Business School. Previously he has served as assistant secretary of the army and as deputy assistant secretary of the air force. He is the author of *Arming America: How the U.S. Buys Weapons* (Harvard University Press, 1974).

Rowland G. Freeman III retired from the U.S. Navy with the rank of rear admiral after 37 years of service. Since retirement, Admiral Freeman served as Administrator of General Services Administration from 1979 to 1981 and is currently Staff Vice-President, Strategic Planning & Energy Systems Ventures for McDonnell Douglas Corporation.

Jacques S. Gansler is vice-president and director of The Analytic Sciences Corporation. He has held executive positions both in government and in the private sector, including deputy assistant secretary of defense for materiel acquisition. Gansler is the author of *The Defense Industry* (MIT Press, 1982).

Newt Gingrich represents west-central Georgia in the U.S. House of Representatives and is a member of the military reform caucus. He serves on the House Administration Committee and the Public Works and Transportation Committee.

Andrew J. Goodpaster is currently president of the Institute for Defense Analyses. His distinguished career includes service as defense liaison officer and staff secretary to President Dwight D. Eisenhower; assistant to the chairman of the Joint Chiefs of Staff; director of the Joint Staff; Supreme Allied Commander, Europe; and superintendent of the U.S. Military Academy. General Goodpaster's awards include the U.S. Medal of Freedom and numerous military decorations.

Bill Gradison represents the Second District of Ohio in the U.S. House of Representatives. He is a member of the House Ways and Means and Budget Committees. Gradison served as assistant to the under secretary of the treasury (1953–55) and as assistant to the secretary of health, education and welfare (1955–57).

David Halperin graduated from Yale College in 1984. He has worked at the Arms Control Association and the Physicians for Social Responsibility.

Morton H. Halperin is a former deputy assistant secretary of defense and member of the staff of the National Security Council. He is the author of *Bureaucratic Politics and Foreign Policy* (Brookings, 1974).

Paul Y. Hammond is currently Distinguished Service Professor of Public and International Affairs, University of Pittsburgh. Author of several books and many articles and reports in the national security area, he most recently coauthored *The Reluctant Supplier*.

John J. Hamre is a member of the professional staff of the Senate Armed Services Committee. Previously, he has served as deputy assistant director for national security of the Congressional Budget Office.

Thor Hanson, a retired naval officer, is president and chief executive officer of the National Multiple Sclerosis Society. Prior to his retirement from the Navy, Vice Admiral Hanson served as Director of the Joint Staff and as military assistant to Secretary of Defense Harold Brown.

Samuel P. Huntington is Eaton Professor of the Science of Government and director of the Center for International Affairs at Harvard University. A founder of the quarterly journal *Foreign Policy*, he served as its coeditor until 1977. He has worked in the government on the National Security Council staff.

David C. Jones was a member of the Joint Chiefs of Staff for eight years, serving under four presidents. General Jones served as chief of staff of the air force from 1974 to 1978 and chairman of the Joint Chiefs of Staff from 1978 to 1982.

Nancy Landon Kassebaum was elected to the U.S. Senate from Kansas in 1978. She serves on the Foreign Relations, Budget, and Commerce Committees, chairs Subcommittees on Aviation and African Affairs, and has been Senate chair of the military reform caucus.

John G. Kester, an attorney in Washington, was deputy assistant secretary of the army from 1969 to 1972 and the special assistant to the secretary and deputy secretary of defense during 1977 and 1978.

Robert W. Komer is currently a consultant with The RAND Corporation. He has served the government in various positions including deputy special assistant to the president, ambassador to Turkey, and under secretary of defense for policy. He is the author of *Maritime Strategy or Coalition Defense* (Abt Books, 1984).

Melvin R. Laird represented a Wisconsin district in the U.S. House of Representatives from 1953 to 1969. In the House, he served on the Appropriations Committee and as the ranking Republican member of its defense subcommittee. He served as secretary of defense from 1969 to 1973 and as counselor to the President for domestic affairs during 1973 and 1974. He is currently senior counselor for national and international affairs for the Reader's Digest Association, Inc.

Jan M. Lodal is currently president of INFOCEL. He has served as deputy director for program analysis, National Security Council, and in the office of the secretary of defense. He has published numerous articles on defense policy and arms control issues.

Edward N. Luttwak is a senior fellow at CSIS. He has served as a consultant to the Departments of Defense and State as well as at the NSC and for the U.S. Army. He is the author of several books, including *The Pentagon and the Art of War* (Simon and Schuster, 1985).

Dave McCurdy represents the fourth congressional district of central and southwest Oklahoma in the U.S. House of Representatives. He serves on the

House Armed Services Committee, the Science and Technology Committee, and the Permanent Select Committee on Intelligence.

William P. Mako is a senior consultant with the Washington office of Price Waterhouse. Earlier, while on the foreign policy staff of the Brookings Institution, he authored *U.S. Ground Forces and the Defense of Central Europe* and defense budget portions of *Setting National Priorities*.

Edward C. Meyer retired from the U.S. Army in June 1983 after serving for four years as its chief of staff. General Meyer's army service included several positions on the Joint Staff and with Supreme Headquarters, Allied Powers, Europe. General Meyer also served as a commander during the Korean and Vietnam Wars, leading all combat elements from platoon to division.

Norman Y. Mineta has represented the 13th district of California in the U.S. House of Representatives since 1975. He serves on the Science and Technology Committee and the Public Works and Transportation Committee. He is also a deputy majority whip.

Robert C. Moot retired from the Department of Defense after 25 years service. He served as administrator to the small business administration from 1966 to 1968, and as assistant secretary of defense (comptroller) from 1968 to 1973. Subsequently, he held the position of vice president for finance of AMTRAK.

Russell Murray, II is special counsel to the House Armed Services Committee. Formerly, he was principal to the SRA Corporation in Arlington, Virginia. He served as assistant secretary of defense for program analysis and evaluation from 1977 to 1981.

Janne E. Nolan is the foreign affairs and national security adviser to Senator Gary Hart and serves as Senator Hart's designee to the Senate Armed Services Committee. She is the author of *Military Industry in Taiwan and South Korea* (Macmillan Press, 1985).

Sam Nunn is the ranking Democrat on the Senate Armed Services Committee. He also serves on the Intelligence Committee, the Permanent Subcommittee on Investigations of the Government Affairs Committee, and the Small Business Committee. In 1984, Senator Nunn was elected to represent Georgia for a third term.

Philip A. Odeen is regional managing partner of Coopers & Lybrand's Management Consulting Group in the mid-Atlantic area. Mr. Odeen has had extensive experience in the government, including service on the National Security Council staff under Henry A. Kissinger, and in the Department of Defense, where he served as principal deputy assistant secretary for systems analysis. Mr. Odeen is a former vice-president of the Wilson Sporting Goods Company.

Leon E. Panetta has represented the sixteenth district of California in the U.S. House of Representatives since 1977. He is a deputy majority whip and serves on the Agriculture and House Administration Committees. He is also the author of *Bring Us Together* (Lippincott, 1971).

William J. Perry is managing partner of H&Q Technology Partners. Prior to that he was executive vice president of Hambrecht & Quist Inc. Dr. Perry served as under secretary of defense for research and engineering from 1977 to 1981.

Robert B. Pirie, a retired naval officer, is currently assistant vice-president at the Institute for Defense Analyses. Pirie has served in the government as deputy assistant director (national security) of the Congressional Budget Office and as assistant secretary of defense for manpower, reserve affairs and logistics.

Barry R. Posen is Assistant Professor of Politics and International Affairs at Princeton University. He has recently been a Fellow of the Council on Foreign Relations and of the Rockefeller Foundation. He is the author of *The Sources of Military Doctrine* (Cornell University Press, 1985).

Joel Pritchard represented the first district of Washington in the U.S. House of Representatives from 1973 to 1984. He served as the ranking minority member on the Merchant Marine and Fisheries Committee. He also served on the executive committee of the House Wednesday Group.

John S. Pustay retired from the Air Force after 29 years with the rank of Lieutenant General and is currently with The Analytic Sciences Corporation. He was president of the National Defense University (1981–83) and has wide experience in strategic planning. He is the author of *Counter Insurgency Warfare* (Macmillan, 1965).

Donald B. Rice has been president of the Rand Corporation since April 1972. Dr. Rice has had an active career in the public and private sector, including service as assistant director of the U.S. Office of Management and Budget.

Alice N. Rivlin is an economist and director of the economic studies program at the Brookings Institution. Prior to rejoining Brookings in 1983, Dr. Rivlin served for eight years as the first director of the Congressional Budget Office. She has written extensively on the U.S. economy, the budget, and public decision making, is a MacArthur Foundation fellow, and was Harvard's Godkin lecturer in 1984.

Thomas B. Ross is senior vice president for corporate affairs of the RCA Corporation. He served as assistant secretary of defense for public affairs from 1977 to 1981. A newspaperman for more than 20 years, Mr. Ross was bureau chief of the Chicago Sun-Times from 1970 to 1977.

Joseph F. Shea is the Senior Vice President, Engineering, at the Raytheon Company in Lexington, Massachusetts. He holds B.S., M.S. and Ph.D. degrees from the University of Michigan.

Walter B. Slocombe is a partner in the law firm of Caplin & Drysdale. He has served previously as deputy undersecretary of defense for policy (1979–1981), and as principal deputy undersecretary of defense for international security affairs (1977–1979). Slocombe also served as a member of the program analysis staff of the National Security Council from 1969 to 1970.

William Y. Smith served in the U.S. Air Force for 35 years before retiring in 1984. General Smith's service includes positions with the office of the Joint Chiefs of Staff and the office of the secretary of defense; he also served as deputy commander of the U.S. European Command.

Lewis Sorley is a Washington-based public policy consultant. A graduate of the U.S. Military Academy at West Point, Sorley has served in the U.S. Army and later as a civilian intelligence officer with the Central Intelligence Agency. He holds a Ph.D. from the Johns Hopkins University.

Marvin Stern is a private management consultant. He has consulted for the office of the secretary of defense, the Defense Science Board, and the Central Intelligence Agency. He served in the Department of Defense as the deputy director, weapon systems, defense research and engineering (1960–62).

Samuel S. Stratton is a senior member of the House Armed Services Committee and chairman of its Procurement and Military Nuclear Systems Subcommittee. A member of Congress since 1950, Congressman Stratton is recognized as a leading congressional expert on defense matters. He served in the U.S. Navy during World War II.

George H. Sylvester retired from the U.S. Air Force in 1981 with the rank of Lieutenant General. Since that time he has been an independent defense analyst for the U.S. Air Force and a number of government agencies and private industry.

Harry S. Train is executive vice-president of Future of Hampton Roads, Inc. A graduate of the U.S. Naval Academy, Admiral Train served for four years as commander-in-chief of the United States Atlantic Command, as NATO's Supreme

Allied Commander-Atlantic, and as commander-in-chief of the United States Atlantic Fleet. Train's naval commands have also included the U.S. Sixth Fleet.

Robert F. Trimble is Vice-President, Contracts, Martin Marietta Aerospace. He retired from the U.S. Air Force in 1975 with the ránk of Major General. His last military position was that of Director of Procurement Policy for the U.S. Air Force. He has also served as acting deputy under secretary of defense for acquisition management.

Edward L. Warner is a senior defense analyst at The RAND Corporation office in Washington, D.C. He has written widely on Soviet defense and contemporary arms control issues. A former air force officer, Warner's 20 years of service included working as assistant to General Lew Allen, U.S. Air Force Chief of Staff.

Jasper A. Welch retired from the U.S. Air Force in 1983 with the rank of major general. Presently, he is a private consultant to government and industry. He is the author of *Atomic Theory of Gas Dynamics*.

Robert H. Wertheim served in the U.S. Navy for 35 years retiring with the rank of rear admiral. Prior to his retirement in 1980, he was director of strategic systems projects, responsible for research, development, and production of the Navy's fleet ballistic weapon systems. Admiral Wertheim is currently senior Vice-President, Science and Engineering with the Lockheed Corporation.

Togo D. West, Jr. is a partner in the New York and Washington, D.C. law firm of Patterson, Belknap, Webb and Tyler. He was general counsel to the Department of Defense from 1977 to 1981.

John P. White is chairman of the board and chief executive officer of the INTERACTIVE Systems Corporation. He served as deputy director of the Office of Management and Budget and assistant secretary of defense for manpower, reserve affairs and logistics during the late 1970s.

R. James Woolsey is a partner in the law firm of Shea & Gardner and general counsel of CSIS. Among other positions in the U.S. Government, he has served as under secretary of the navy, a member of the START delegation, and general counsel to the Senate Armed Services Committee.

ABOUT THE EDITORS

Barry M. Blechman is president of Defense Forecasts, Inc. and a senior fellow at Georgetown's Center for Strategic and International Studies. He served in the government as assistant director of the Arms Control and Disarmament Agency. He has published extensively on issues of foreign and defense policies.

William J. Lynn is an analyst with the Institute for Defense Analyses and an adjunct fellow at Georgetown's Center for Strategic and International Studies. He served as executive director of the CSIS Defense Organization Project. An attorney, Lynn has worked previously at the U.S. Mission to NATO in Brussels.